A Cognitive Theory of Magic

COGNITIVE SCIENCE OF RELIGION SERIES

Series Editors: **HARVEY WHITEHOUSE**
and **LUTHER H. MARTIN**

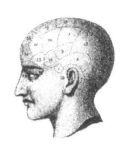

The Cognitive Science of Religion Series publishes research into the cognitive foundations of religious thinking and behavior and their consequences for social morphology. The emphasis of the series is on scientific approaches to the study of religion within the framework of the cognitive sciences, including experimental, clinical, or laboratory studies, but works drawing upon ethnographic, linguistic, archaeological, or historical research are welcome, as are critical appraisals of research in these areas. In addition to providing a forum for presenting new empirical evidence and major theoretical innovations, the series publishes concise overviews of issues in the field suitable for students and general readers. This series is published in cooperation with the Institute for Cognition and Culture at Queen's University Belfast.

TITLES IN THE SERIES

Modes of Religiosity: A Cognitive Theory of Religious Transmission
By Harvey Whitehouse

Magic, Miracles, and Religion: A Scientist's Perspective
By Ilkka Pyysiäinen

Why Would Anyone Believe in God?
By Justin L. Barrett

Ritual and Memory: Toward a Comparative Anthropology of Religion
Edited by Harvey Whitehouse and James Laidlaw

Theorizing Religions Past: Archaeology, History, and Cognition
Edited by Harvey Whitehouse and Luther H. Martin

How the Bible Works: An Anthropological Study of Evangelical Biblicism
By Brian E. Malley

Mind and Religion: Psychological and Cognitive Foundations of Religion
Edited by Harvey Whitehouse and Robert N. McCauley

God from the Machine
By William Sims Bainbridge

FORTHCOMING TITLES

The Evolution of Religion
By Harvey Whitehouse

A Cognitive Theory of Magic

Jesper Sørensen

PRESS

A division of
ROWMAN & LITTLEFIELD PUBLISHERS, INC.
Lanham • New York • Toronto • Plymouth, UK

ALTAMIRA PRESS
A division of Rowman & Littlefield Publishers, Inc.
A wholly owned subsidiary of The Rowman & Littlefield Publishing Group, Inc.
4501 Forbes Boulevard, Suite 200, Lanham, MD 20706
www.altamirapress.com

Estover Road, Plymouth PL6 7PY, United Kingdom

Copyright © 2007 by AltaMira Press

All rights reserved. No part of this publication may be reproduced, stored in a retrieval system, or transmitted in any form or by any means, electronic, mechanical, photocopying, recording, or otherwise, without the prior permission of the publisher.

British Library Cataloguing in Publication Information Available

Library of Congress Cataloging-in-Publication Data
Sørensen, Jesper, 1968–
  A cognitive theory of magic / Jesper Sorensen.
    p. cm. — (Cognitive science of religion series)
  Includes bibliographical references and index.
  ISBN-13: 978-0-7591-1037-3 (cloth : alk. paper)
  ISBN-10: 0-7591-1037-9 (cloth : alk. paper)
  ISBN-13: 978-0-7591-1040-3 (pbk. : alk. paper)
  ISBN-10: 0-7591-1040-9 (pbk. : alk. paper)
 1. Magic. 2. Magic--Religious aspects. 3. Cognition and culture. 4. Psychology, Religious. I. Title.

BF1621.S673 2006
133.4'301—dc22

2006028454

Printed in the United States of America

Contents

Figures		vii
1	Introduction	1
2	Magic in the History of the Social Sciences	9
3	The Cognitive Foundation of Magical Action	31
4	Magical Rituals and Conceptual Blending	63
5	Transformation and Manipulation: A Typology of Magical Actions	95
6	Frames of Ritual Action: Causation, Diagnosis and Prognosis	141
7	Ritual Purpose and the Relation Between Magic, Culture and Religion	171
References		193
Index		209

Figures

Figure 4.1: The genetic blend	75
Figure 4.2: Trobriand genetic blend	79
Figure 4.3: Azande genetic blend	83
Figure 4.4: Catholic genetic blend	86
Figure 4.5: The linguistic blend	88
Figure 5.1: Sanctification of bread and wine	99
Figure 5.2: Essence transfer and essence-link	103
Figure 5.3: Forward contagion in Holy Communion	104
Figure 5.4: Backward contagion	114
Figure 5.5: Trobriand mapping between women and garden	118
Figure 5.6: "The belly of my garden"	119
Figure 5.7: Zande spell delaying sunset	121
Figure 5.8: Trobriand garden exorcism I	124
Figure 5.9: Trobriand garden exorcism II	126
Figure 5.10: Mapping between the domain of kin relations and the garden domain	127
Figure 6.1: Non-ritual event-frame	149

Figure 6.2: Ritual event-frame   152

Figure 6.3: Network of factual and counterfactual event-frames   156

Figure 6.4: Dynamic interaction between ritual and
            classificatory event-frame   162

Figure 6.5: Interaction between CONTAINER- and
            TRAJECTORY-schemata   167

Figure 7.1: Schematic model of parameters involved in
            representations of ritual purpose and meaning   172

Figure 7.2: Loop between symbolic interpretation, ritualisation
            and agent-based magical agency   184

1
Introduction

In the ritual service celebrating the Median of the Great Lent in an Armenian Church in Istanbul a number of relics take centre stage. The silver-cast forearm of a saint plays a special role and, during the service, it is brought into contact with numerous objects, there among water. After the service is completed, a number of people gather in front of the altar where the relics are put on display. They not only touch the relics, a ritual action found in many Christian churches, but the water, once in contact with the silver-cast forearm of the saint, is brought into contact with inflicted parts of the body, such as limbs and eyes, in order to alleviate or cure the affliction.[1]

According to a Coptic papyrus from the ninth Century C.E., saying the following words upon a piece of fruit will evoke the desires of a particular woman when she eats it: "I adjure you by your name and your powers and your amulets and the glorious places where you dwell, that you come down upon these pieces of fruit that are in my right hand, so that when she eats them, you may give her desire for me, and she may desire me with endless desire and come to me in the place where I am, and I may lay my breast upon her and satisfy all my desires with her, and she may satisfy all my desire right now, right now, at once, at once" (Meyer & Smith 1994: 160-61).

In a recent Danish television show, "The Power of the Spirit", a man claimed to be possessed by the Devil was exorcised by a Danish Lutheran priest. During the exorcism it was established that the possession could be traced back to the victim wearing a sweatshirt carrying the image of a goat. It was concluded that this image was responsible for establishing a link to the devil, and the man was allegedly cured after disposing of the shirt.

Events such as these obviously call for a scientific explanation. Are there any principles that unite these apparently different actions? Can we find common psychological or sociological structures that can explain their occurrence and form? The reader of this book will of course be primed to look for instances of magic, and the examples do in fact contain a number of 'classical' instances of magical behaviour. Essence is transferred by means of physical contact, a saying produces what is said, and relations of pictorial similarity can transfer an essence.

Often we meet such instances of magic in descriptions of exotic places and distant times. People, living deep in the tropical rainforest, are represented as 'still' believing in the power of the magic that has been expelled from the enlightened Western societies and their predominantly Christian religion a long time ago. A more thorough examination, however, reveals that this is far from the case and that magic still dwells among people living in Western societies. Magic is not something found in our own 'primitive' past or in equally 'primitive' societies far away. It can be found everywhere, in all historical periods and in all cultural settings. The universality of magical practices has been used as an argument for abolishing the term altogether. It is argued that its embeddedness in colonial history and ideologies of primitivism make it unsuitable for modern research, and that examples of magical ritual found in Western societies point to what was the case all along: that magic is not a 'belief' of so-called primitive people but a derogatory category used to describe others peoples ritual actions and expressive behaviour.

Faced with this criticism scholars have attempted to abolish the concept, but they have faced the problem that even if undesirable, they find it difficult if not impossible to avoid using the concept of magic as it seems to cover a recurrent and persistent type of observed human behaviour. A regrettable result of the reluctance to produce a universal definition, the concept is instead typically defined in an *ad hoc* manner, used to describe observable traits of behaviour in particular cultural settings but without being embedded in a more comprehensive theoretical framework. Both abandoning the concept and relying on *ad hoc* definitions are problematic. First of all it is difficult to see what is gained by exorcising such broad synthetic terms as magic (or 'religion' for that matter). The whole idea seems to rest on a dubious reminiscence from logical positivism where concepts, and especially scientific concepts, are thought of as neutral reflections of real things found out there in the world. Of course, 'magic' is not a natural category found in the world, but neither are 'religion', 'society', and 'elephant'. Concepts refer to models of the world and what distinguishes scientific concepts from colloquial concepts is not this model-dependency, but rather the reflective and epistemological status of the underlying models. Whereas everyday language is characterised by an almost endless amount of models more or less invisible to the speakers, scientific models are (or should be) subject to a much more explicit scrutiny and a grounding in more comprehensive theories.

Second, concepts such as magic and religion are not explanatory concepts, but rather descriptive concepts that subsume a particular range of observable phenomena, in this case human behaviour, under a common heading. Such observable behaviour is not explained by reference to the concept but can only be explained by recourse to theories explaining the observable behaviour. Concepts like magic cannot be subject to explanatory theories as they are too comprehensive and complex to be circumscribed by a simple explanation. In the phrasing of anthropologist Pascal Boyer magic is an impure object that must be analysed into its constitutive parts that subsequently can be subject to explanatory theories (Boyer 1996). If it turns out that having the broad descriptive category is detrimental to explaining the underlying parts, then, of course, it should be abandoned, but so far this has not been shown to be the case. Instead, magic shall be seen as a synthetic concept that covers a broad range of cognitive, cultural and social phenomena. This approach has the obvious disadvantage that it will not be subject to any single explanatory theory, but calls for several types of theoretical models addressing different descriptive levels. The challenge for the scholar, then, is to construct a comprehensive model that links these different explanatory levels. The solution lies not in terminological cleansing but rather in better theoretical models.

This book attempts to provide such a theoretical framework, by means of the following four steps:

(a) Discussing and re-evaluating older theories of magic in order to differentiate valuable ideas from obsolete ones. The purpose is to embed the ensuing discussion in a framework that most readers will recognise, and also to systematise the different approaches into four groups, each with their specific types of associated questions.

(b) Re-addressing fundamental questions within the framework of cognitive science. The systematisation of older approaches makes it possible to restate the fundamental questions concerning the intellectual, symbolic, performative and emotional aspects of magic in a cognitive framework. As cognitive science is an ever-expanding field of inquiry with competing theories, different approaches will be discussed in order to construct a single theoretical framework for the study of magic. This framework has repercussions for the more general cognitive study of culture, as it reconciles theoretical trends in cognitive science in order to explain the complex phenomena underlying 'magic'. Thus the book is not restricted to problems in the cognitive science of religion, but also addresses matters of concern under research of cognition and culture in general.

(c) Developing a theory of magical actions. Based on this theoretical framework, taxonomic distinctions are made between different types of magical actions based on three dimensions: First, *who* is the 'agent' responsible for the action's efficacy? Second, *how* is the action represented as being accomplished? Third, *what purpose* does the magical action fulfil in a larger structure of other actions? These taxonomies are not *ad hoc* but based on the different cognitive processes involved, and so the framework provides a basis for cross-cultural comparison of magical actions.

(d) Identifying possible developmental trajectories of institutionalised religion. This addresses the old question of the relation between magic and religion based on the findings of the previous discussion and analysis. Several novel approaches to this problem will be presented, arguing that magic plays a pivotal

role in the development of all religious institutions and traditions. The book thus addresses a classic debate in both anthropology and the study of religion, but from a new angle based on cognitive science.

Having established the reasons for treating magic from a cognitive perspective, a short outline of the book and its central hypotheses is in place.

In chapter 2, four anthropological approaches to the problem of magic are discussed: Rationalist, Symbolist, Pragmatic, and Emotionalist. The scholarship discussed dates mostly from the 1970s and back—this is for two reasons. First, the topic of magic underwent a declining interest from the early seventies as it became subject to the same type of terminological exorcism as concepts like 'mana' and 'totemism'. This was a result of the widespread scepticism towards universal categories in general and explanatory ones in particular following the poststructural, relativist and postmodernist turn in scholarship. From being a central question in anthropology, 'magic' receded into the background as topics and agendas more in line with these recent theoretical developments proliferated. Within one of these, post-colonialism, the concept itself is seen as a part of the ideology of primitivism and therefore has to be discarded. Second, prior to the seventies, anthropologists still discussed a number of 'grand theories' in which the problem of magic was of central concern. It was pivotal in attempts to distinguish 'modern' from 'traditional' mentalities and directly related to explicitly defended, theoretical, positions. In addition, most of the positions in these 'old schools' are self-proclaimed, rather than attributed by others. The chapter is, therefore, not a comprehensive discussion of all relevant approaches to the problem for the last 150 years. Rather, the aim is provide key examples of how scholars have theorised about magic in order to elicit strengths and weaknesses of existing literature as a point of departure for the cognitive hypotheses defended in this book.

While this discussion of former approaches highlights some of the basic problems that must be addressed in a study of magic, chapter 3 presents and discusses the cognitive theorising used to address these problems in the remainder of the book. The chapter combines cognitive theories often seen as opposed. One approach is based primarily on cognitive psychology and focuses on *domain-specific* inference and cognitive constraints on human categorisation and points to universal patterns of culture. The other approach, primarily based on cognitive linguistics and cognitive semantics, is more focused on *domain-general* aspects of human categorisation and on how human beings construct meaning. It thus addresses the cognitive mechanisms underlying cultural diversity. By combining the two approaches it becomes possible to describe the limitations presented by human cognition on cultural formations, i.e. its universal foundation, and how this universal layer can give rise to a high degree of cultural diversity through common mechanisms of meaning construction. This 'eclectic' approach is motivated by an attempt to construct a model of human cognition capable of explaining the phenomena synthesised under the concept of magic. The synthetic character of the concept, however, requires another type of eclecticism or plurality of methods. Due to the different explanatory levels involved in giving an account of magic, different theories are called for. The account of how 'conceptual blending' is used within rituals is complemented by an account of how ritual actions differ from other types of actions, how rituals contribute to large representations of related actions, as well as an account of how ritual actions relate to symbolic interpretations. None of these levels can be reduced to each other and therefore no single theoretical approach will suffice to explain them all.

Chapters 4 to 6 all address two fundamental questions in the study of religion in general that are of particular importance in a theory of magic: why do people represent ritual actions as efficacious? And how does this representation come about? Chapter 4 argues that an important element in building representations of ritual effect is ritual participants' representations of one or more ritual element as having a special quality. This element is referred to as 'magical agency' and is the necessary condition for the ritual to be construed as potentially effective. Thus, the Priest must be correctly ordained and the correct words must be pronounced in order for the Catholic Mass to have effect, whereas specific material substance is represented as sufficient among the Azande of southern Sudan. Magical agency is a necessary condition for the ritual to have effect but other ritual elements can be altered as they are of no importance in this respect. Therefore rituals can be modelled as a blend of necessary and contingent elements, but the particular blend will differ among types of ritual and across cultural settings. In addition, chapter 4 addresses the classical problem of why ritual actions have a propensity for employing strange, exotic or downright nonsense language (e.g. 'abracadrabra'). It is argued that through the employment of strange linguistic forms, ritual actions are represented as referring to and communicating with possibly powerful agents. Strange linguistic forms are thus one of the important (but not the only) means to construct rituals believed to have effect—a fact that can help to explain the widespread resistance to liturgical reforms involving modernisation of language.

People do not represent rituals as having just any type of effect. They represent magical rituals as having specific effects and they often perform ritual actions with very particular goals in mind. In chapter 5 it is argued that the represented effects of ritual actions are related directly to—but not determined by—the perceptual features present in the ritual action, notably by relations of similarity and contagion. Similarity and contagion enable representations of a 'causal' connection between otherwise distinct domains of reality. Magical rituals thus utilise specific means to produce their effect. Further, rituals can be distinguished by their purpose. A typology will be presented based on the basic distinction between rituals aimed to *transform* and rituals aimed to *manipulate*. In Transformative Ritual Actions essential qualities are transferred by means of such actions as touching and eating, i.e. by more or less direct physical contact (e.g. when grace is received through ingestion of sanctified bread). In Manipulative Ritual Actions ritual elements are used to manipulate an inaccessible domain by means of an accessible domain (e.g. when a doll is used to harm a person not present). It is shown that this distinction rests upon a cognitive distinction between the essential and the schematic aspects of things and this gives rise to a number of specific principles of magical ritual actions.

Rituals are not performed in a contextual void but are related to other events and actions, both prior to and following the performance of the ritual. In chapter 6 the relation between ritual actions and the pragmatic context is discussed, as the context has profound influence on both how and why magical actions are represented as having effect. The chapter starts with a cognitive explanation of how ritual actions are distinct from other types of actions, and why they play a special role in unfolding strings of events and actions. This explanation is then related to a distinction between *prospective* and *retrospective* rituals. Whereas prospective rituals aim to produce a new state of affairs (e.g. getting X to love you), retrospective rituals aim to amend a disrupted state of affairs (e.g. getting cured from a disease). This distinction has important consequences for how ritual actions are related directly to other actions and events, and more generally how ritual actions are related to explanatory models of events and actions. It is argued that rituals do not result from strong notions of events in the world being caused by superhuman agents like gods, spirits or ancestors. Rather, the performance of ritual actions involving superhuman agents is a prerequisite for explanations of non-ritual events (such as disease) as caused by such agents. This argument is supported using evidence from experimental psychology.

In chapter 7 the arguments of the preceding chapters are drawn together in a model that depicts the broad parameters involved in representations of magical rituals, providing a condensed summary of the most important findings and hypotheses of the preceding chapters. This leads to a discussion of the intricate relations between magical rituals on the one hand, and cultural conceptual systems, institutionalised rituals and religion on the other. The discussion is a general attempt to relate cognitive hypotheses concerning magical rituals to wider conceptual and institutional contexts. It will be argued that magical rituals function primarily as an innovative factor in relation to cultural conceptual systems, and only secondarily as the conservative force often ascribed to them. This is so because magical rituals focus almost exclusively on ritual effect, which in turn prompts the construction or borrowing of new ritual forms interpreted subsequently. Not only does magic facilitate such import, however, it is also one of the driving forces in the emergence of new religions. As magical agency can be invested in living persons (e.g. gurus and prophets), such persons can institute new ritual structures themselves or, if they fail to do so, their followers will construct ritual actions that facilitate the transfer of magical agency, once the founding person has gone. Ritualisation is a means to solidify new religious groupings in an orthopraxy and at the same time to control representations of magical agency in order to abolish competing ritual structures. This solidification, however, leads to a growing body of symbolic interpretations of the ritual action that risks diminishing representations of ritual efficacy, thereby provoking a search for magical agency elsewhere. Thus it will be argued that we find a dynamic tension between a tendency to ascribe ritual efficacy to enigmatic rituals, and a countervailing tendency to evoke new symbolic interpretations that diminish representations of ritual efficacy. This dynamic tension is a major driving force in the historical development of religious traditions.

This book is based on my Ph.D. thesis submitted at the Faculty of Theology, University of Aarhus, August 2000, and defended publicly in February 2001. A special thank is therefore extended to my supervisor, professor Jeppe Sinding Jensen, for support, encouragement, and inspiration throughout this process. The evaluation committee, Professor Armin Geertz, Professor Harvey Whitehouse and Professor Frederik Stjernfelt made an extensive evaluation and their critical comments have been an invaluable guideline in rewriting the thesis into this book. Special thanks shall also be extended to the editors of the AltaMira bookseries on the Cognitive Science of Religion, Luther Martin and Harvey Whitehouse; to Don Wiebe for reading through the whole manuscript adding valuable comments; to Kevin De Ornellas for a thorough language revision; and to Søren Ebbesen for redrawing the graphics. Throughout the process, numerous people, both colleagues and friends, have commented on my ideas and provided crucial input for their development. Special thanks to Michael Aktor, Lars Albinus, Vagn Andersen, Veikko Anttonen, Justin Barrett, Per Bilde, Tom Bolwig, Anine Boisen, Pascal Boyer, Per Aage Brandt, Peer Bundgaard, Dorthe Refslund Christensen, Henning Lind Eriksen, Gilles Fauconnier, Kæv Gliemann, Christian K. Højbjerg, Edwin Hutchins, Tim Jensen, Signe Krogh, Hans-Jørgen Lundager Jensen, Bodil Klausen, George Lakoff, Tom Lawson, Anita Leopold, Terkel Leth, Anders Lisdorf, Bo Madsen, Bob McCauley, Joel Mort, Anders Klostergaard Petersen, Ilkka Pyysiäinen, Jens Peter Schjødt, Michael Støvring, Eve Sweetser, Leonard Talmy, Mark Turner, David Alan Warburton, Alison Warner, Peter Westh and Svend Østergaard. Last, but not least, a deep thank to my parents for support and encouragement and to my family, Marianne, Klara and Frode for being there and reminding me where the magic of life is really found.

Note

1. Personal experience, Istanbul 2001.

2
Magic in the History of the Social Sciences

As mentioned in the introduction, magic is a classic topic in both anthropology and the study of religion. In this chapter, I will discuss how magic is presented in the "grand theories" of these and related fields, but I do *not* attempt to make a thorough presentation of all the theories of magic presented during the last 150 years. That would be an immense task that would sidetrack us from the more important question of how recent developments in the cognitive sciences can inform a contemporary theory of magical actions. I restrict myself to a discussion of the questions raised by representatives of four different approaches to theorising about magic: a Rationalist, a Symbolist, a Pragmatic and an Emotionalist approach. All have their specific answers to questions posed by observations of specific types of ritual behaviour, and in my opinion, all contribute to a more comprehensive understanding of the phenomena referred to by the concept 'magic.' At the same time, these approaches all have serious fallacies that need to be criticised in order to extract the valuable ideas.

When the social sciences crystallised in the latter part of the nineteenth century, magic was already an established concept used for more than two thousand years in the European languages. *Magos* and related *mageia* came into the Greek language in the sixth century BCE as cognates of the Persian *magus*, which referred to a member of the priestly caste of Persia. *Magus* is a suffixed form of the Indo-European root *magh* meaning "to be able, to have power."[1] Shortly thereafter, it began its long career as a polemical concept in opposition to both established religion (Graf 1995: 31; Meyer & Smith 1994: 2) and to the emerging Greek science (Lloyd 1993: 15, 56). Thus, it became entangled in what historian of religion J. Z. Smith has labelled "the reduplicated duality," entailing that magic becomes negatively defined in relation to both poles in another opposition, that between 'science' and 'religion' (J. Z. Smith 1995: 13). This polemical aspect of the concept was emphasised in early Christianity as designating all other religions including their ritual practice. During and after the Reformation the concept became an important derogatory term in Protestant polemics against the Catholic Church. The meaning of the concept changed from denoting everything connected with non-Christian religions to a special type of ritual practice based on beliefs in automatic efficacy also found inside Christianity, notably in the Catholic sacraments (Thomas 1991: 88).

It was this last sense of the concept that dominated its appearance in the emerging social sciences. Even though 'primitive people' were more prone to magic, it was still understood by most early writers as an altogether different type of activity from religion, and the conceptual distinction between magic and religion were rigorously upheld in most early theories of magic.

2.1 Modes of Thinking: Rationalist Explanations of Magic

Inspired by rationalist and empiricist philosophy, early anthropological works were focussed on two related questions. The first concerns the mental procedures believed to underlie magical actions. Is there a special type of thinking involved? And how can it be distinguished from the modes of thinking believed to underlie religion and science? The second question concerns the beliefs purported to underlie magical actions as their rationale. What types of practical and theoretical propositions underlie magical actions? Together these two aspects are central to the rationalist or intellectualist approach. Rationalist explanations of magic claim that rational processes underlie magical actions, and these provide sufficient grounds for their explanation. According to R. Shweder, rationalist approaches form part of an enlightenment tradition based on the premises

> that the mind of man is intendedly rational and scientific, that the dictates of reason are equally binding for all regardless of time, place, culture, race, personal desire, or individual endowment, and that in reason can be found a universally applicable standard for judging validity and worth (Shweder 1984: 27).

An important legacy of the enlightenment rationalism is the doctrine of the psychic unity of humanity and the claim that actions can be explained by reference to underlying mental processes ultimately consisting of more or less conscious beliefs. What follows is that it is possible to judge these beliefs on a universal standard based on their correspondence to (theories about) the real world. This view of the relation between public actions and underlying mental beliefs has had important implications for theories of magic.

From the middle of the nineteenth century, anthropologists, sociologists, and scholars of religion were looking for patterns of thought believed to underlie magic. The Victorian anthropologists Edward Burnett Tylor and James George Frazer worked within an evolutionist framework that formed the intellectual zeitgeist of their time. Both saw it as their job to explain the relation between magic, religion and science as a progression intimately connected to levels of cultural evolution. In short, cultural evolution is described as the evolution of rational thought leading from simplicity to complexity, from the concrete to the abstract. The evolutionary theories of Tylor and Frazer are easily criticised and should not concern us in the present context. Of more importance is their insistence on describing the mode of thought believed to underlie magical actions by the principles of associative psychology prevalent in their time. In *Primitive Culture* (1871) Tylor points to the importance of analogical reasoning in understanding magical actions. Inspired by the empiricist philosophers Hume, Locke and Mill, Tylor claims that primitive people replace cause and effect with association of ideas based on similarity, contagion and contiguity. The savage is not only a primitive philosopher contemplating the mysteries of life and giving crude but intelligible answers to them. He is a primitive empiricist who seeks to explain and subsequently control his environment through understandable but erroneous reasoning based on ideal associations. Having observed regularities in nature that by analogy lead to similar regularities in thought, our primitive philosopher makes his decisive mistake and, by means of yet another analogy, believes regularities of thought are able to create regularities in nature (Tylor 1866, 1871, 1881, 1883).

In *The Golden Bough* Frazer elaborated on Tylor's ideas of magic into the famous typology of sympathetic magic (Frazer 1911). According to Frazer, two laws of associations of ideas are found in the thinking underlying magical actions. The first is the Law of Similarity, based on the principle that like attracts like, and the second is the Law of Contact or Contagion, built on the principle that entities once in contact will retain a connection even when spatially divided. When applied in magical actions, these universal principles of thought yield two types of magic. Homeopathic magic is expressed in such practices as manipulation of an effigy in order to harm an enemy, and Contagious magic is expressed in such practices as manipulation of the hair or nails of a person in order to harm its former owner (Frazer 1911: 52ff). Both types are subsumed under the general heading of Sympathetic magic, "since both assume that things act on each other at a distance through a secret sympathy" (54). It is evident that Frazer is interested in the mental processes and abstract beliefs underlying magical actions. The magician works under the more or less unconscious belief that things can act upon each other at a distance, but in fact this belief is an unintended result of specific universal mental procedures, namely the association of ideas. In this respect it is important to notice that both Tylor and Frazer claim that magical actions are based on ordinary cognitive principles employed to explain and manipulate the social and physical world. They are rational and explicable as they are the products of universal mental faculties, but they are erroneous as they are based on a misapplication in futile and ineffective actions. Unfortunately neither Tylor or Frazer give a convincing explanation of why these principles are misused in some but not in other cases, and they both attempt to circumvent the problem by placing them onto different steps on a ladder of cultural evolution. That magic persists in more 'evolved' societies is thus difficult to explain except by recourse to a notion of evolutionary survivals of certain types of actions due to 'habit'—a most unsatisfactory explanation of the profound diffusion of magical practices in all societies. However, this should not lead to the abandonment of the important insight that magical procedures seem to be based on specific cognitive principles. This aspect of the rationalist approach is retained in a somewhat different unfolding and theoretical underpinning in the present work.

More recently, the intellectualist and rationalist approaches have been rejuvenated by writers who took part in the so-called rationality-debate in the late nineteen sixties and early seventies. Discarding evolutionary presumptions, these writers argue that both magic and religion should be understood as types of explanation not fundamentally different than those produced in science. Horton (1970) expresses the basic tenets of neo-intellectualism. He argues that religion, magic, and science should be understood as being based on similar intellectual processes and as directed towards the same intellectual purpose, and that they are only distinguishable by the constraints on their idiomatic expression imposed by the local context. Both science and religion (in which Horton includes magic) are products of "the quest for explanatory theory" as an attempt to impose order on a chaotic universe, and in both cases this is attained by explaining a diversity of events as an expression of a few kinds of forces. "Like atoms, molecules, and waves, then, the gods serve to introduce unity into diversity, simplicity into complexity, order into disorder, regularity into anomaly" (Horton 1970: 134). This implies that both religion and science, *qua* explanatory theories, are utilised in cases where common-sense knowledge is insufficient (142-3). The apparently fundamental difference between the personalised forces of religion and the impersonal forces of science are no more than "a difference in the *idiom* of the explanatory quest" (152, emphasis added), a feature explained by reference to differences between Western and African societies (146-7). Thus, a fundamental dichotomy between 'traditional' and 'modern' societies replaces that between religion (including magic) and science. Traditional societies are characterised by their "closed" predicaments, in contrast to the "open" predicaments of modern societies. People living in traditional societies have no awareness of alternatives to the established explanatory theory found in their tradition in contrast to the almost built-in criticism of theoretical tenets and awareness of possible alternatives found in scientifically oriented or modern societies (153). The difference between scientific and religious explanations is, therefore, a product of the idiomatic and discursive styles imposed by society, and this difference tends to hide a more fundamental likeness both in mental procedures and aim.

Jarvie and Agassi expressed a similar line of reasoning in two articles levelling an aggressive attack on the 'symbolist' approach to magic and religion, exemplified by anthropologist John Beattie's *Other Culture* (Jarvie & Agassi 1967; Agassi & Jarvie 1973). Jarvie and Agassi question the prevalent symbolic distinction between rational practical acts (such as planting) and symbolic ritual acts (such as chanting), as both are performed in order to make crops grow. The authors argue that both should be classified as rational actions because participants consider them a united instrumental activity performed in order to achieve a given goal. As such they are equally intentional and rational actions motivated by certain beliefs (Jarvie & Agassi 1967: 66). Jarvie and Agassi distinguish between three types of rationality: (1) *weak* rationality pertaining to actions explained by reference to goal-directed actions; (2) *relatively strong* rationality where the standard of rationality evoked is that of one's own community; (3) *very strong* rationality, where the standard of rationality is the highest known, especially that of critical thinking (Agassi & Jarvie 1973: 243). Analysed through this distinction, they claim that the rationality of magic is based in the first two types. Magic is a goal-directed mode of action based on an internal standard of rationality. In short, "magic is false theory, no more no less", which makes it "science *par excellence*" (245). The echo of Frazer can hardly be much clearer.

The rationalist approaches are correct in their insistence that the instrumentality of magical actions cannot be ignored or explained away without seriously misrepresenting the agents' motivations and representations of these actions. But there are serious problems in other parts of the rationalist account of magical actions. The first major problem is the lack of an adequate theory of ritual.[2] In the attempt to explain magic as actions that are rational by reference to underlying mental procedures and beliefs, they disregard the very special status of these actions—that they are exactly *ritual* actions—and thereby almost explain the phenomena away. That practical and magical actions (planting and chanting) alike are deemed necessary in order to reach the desired result does not imply that there is no fundamental difference between the two types of actions, and that participants cannot tell the difference. As we shall see in the following chapters this is a very serious flaw, because one thereby misses one of the primary mechanisms for understanding how ordinary cognitive procedures are utilised to produce what is observed as magical actions, and how participants can represent magical actions as instrumental.

The second major problem with the rationalist account is its emphasis on explanation as the major purpose or function of religion. It poses the obvious problem why people who have access to more correct explanatory theories, continue to be religious and to practice magical actions.[3] An important consequence of the claim that religion and magic are explanatory theories is that these explanations are seen as the *mental* causes of ritual actions. Actions are explained by reference to underlying motivating beliefs that can be translated into propositional statements. This gives rise to two further problems. (a) The question whether religion and magic should be understood as explicit and coherent explanatory systems or whether this is a result of the theologising tendency of the anthropologist or scholar of religion (cf. Boyer 1994). Throughout this book I will argue that it makes no sense to understand magic as a consistent or even coherent explanatory system. Magic is a type of action and a mode of understanding action, not a system of thought. (b) Even if we grant magic and religion explanatory power, it is not at all certain that relations found between representations on a cultural and symbolic level are equivalent to the underlying cognitive processes. That certain ritual actions are explained explicitly by reference to certain beliefs does not necessarily mean that there is a direct causal connection from beliefs to actions, and that beliefs are not subsequent interpretations rather than the ultimate cause of the actions. The conflation between the logic of explicit representations and cognitive procedures is a general problem in the rationalist account and, as I will argue extensively later, what we need is the applications of cognitive theories in order to explain the relation between explicit cultural models and individual's representations. Taken together, the insistence on the explanatory character of magic and religion, and the conflation between explicit representations and individual mental representations, leads to a kind of *transparent social determinism* in which all individual actions can be explained by reference to socially determined and explicitly expressed structures of belief.

To summarise the account given above, I believe the rationalist approach rightly emphasises two aspects: (a) that mental or cognitive mechanisms underlying magical action and thinking are both universal and general principles not restricted to magic and religion; (b) that magic has an instrumental character answering a human need of explanation, control and manipulation. But the rationalist approach has two fundamental problems as well: (a) it equates individual human cognition with external conceptual and cosmological systems. This implies that ritual actions are based in explicit structures of belief that can be expressed in a propositional form. (b) It fails to recognise ritual as a mode of behaviour that differentiates magical action from practical action among participants themselves.

2.2 Modes of Living: Symbolist Explanations of Magic

The problems inherent in the rationalist account are addressed in what can be labelled the symbolist approach to magic. In this context, 'symbolist' covers a far broader range of approaches to the study of magic, than the 'rationalist' approach. Since the beginning of the century, different scholars have proposed many different symbolic explanations of magic. A common thread in these, and the reason for uniting these otherwise miscellaneous proposals, is the notion that what meets the eyes as magical behaviour must be understood as an external and therefore symbolic expression of some hidden cause. Anthropologist John Beattie's work is a telling example of this approach when he argues that "although magic *is* magic because it is essentially expressive and symbolic, the people who use it think it is instrumental" (Beattie 1964: 212). Magic is not, as it is agreed upon by the users and the rationalist described above, an attempt to manipulate the world by a basically instrumental technique. Rather it is a symbolic expression of something else and therefore the anthropologist must decipher the symbols in order to reach the real significance. Of course, there are substantial scholarly divergences as to the nature of this hidden reality, and a substantial number of anthropological debates have concerned themselves with what kind of symbolic interpretation is correct, rather than the appropriateness of the symbolic approach to begin with.[4]

The symbolic approach has certain advantages compared to the rationalist account. First, by rejecting the literal interpretation of magical rituals as manipulative actions, symbolic explanations avoid the embarrassing question of why people, who in most respects master their environments by perfectly rational technologies, suddenly turn to magical rituals in interacting with certain aspects of the same environment. As expressive symbols, magical rituals are totally different sorts of actions not subject to the same type of rational judgement as ordinary instrumental actions, but rather akin to expressive or symbolic behaviour in modern Western cultures. 'Planting' is a fundamentally different activity from 'chanting.' This is recognised by Durkheim, who rejects the intellectualist notion that religion and magic had their origin in mental mistakes and misapplied cognitive principles. Instead he argues that widespread institutions such as religion have to be expressions of some part of reality, that they must be true in some sense (Durkheim 1965: 14, 87, 465).

The French sociological school proposed to see religion as a symbolic expression of society, as society's sanctification of itself and, being derived from religion, this applies to magic as well. However, this does not mean that the distinction between magic and religion is abandoned. Neither Durkheim or Marcel Mauss and Henri Hubert question the dichotomy between religion and magic inherited from the Victorian rationalists and from the European conceptual structure. They merely reverse the evolutionary sequence. As religion is intimately related to the very foundation and emergence of society, religion must necessarily precede magic, and magic is understood as a later and immoral exploitation of the socially generated sacred domain containing *mana*. A central problem addressed by Mauss and Hubert in their outline of a theory of magic (Mauss 1972), is how the alleged anti-social character of magic can be reconciled with the definition of magic as a social phenomenon in need of a sociological explanation. If religion and magic are opposed, and religion is understood as the social *par excellence*, in what sense is magic a social phenomenon? To answer this question Mauss and Hubert turn to the classificatory system and social representations utilised by and surrounding magic. Magic can be recognised by its application of the margins of both the classificatory and the social system. The agents, actions and social representations appearing in magical rituals all share a common characteristic of marginality and classificatory ambivalence. The magicians are for instance recognised by their strange deformed physical appearance, their liminal position, or their tendency to enter into ecstatic states (Mauss 1972: 27-9). Magical actions are recognisable by their ritual structure containing non-causal relations between action and reaction based on an iterative sequence of conventionally specified actions. Further, due to their abnormality, magical rituals tend to multiply the ritually efficacious elements in the ritual, thereby providing a strong defence against falsification of the ritual (the more complex the ritual, the more things can have gone wrong). Finally, Mauss and Hubert acknowledge the sympathetic aspects of magic described by Frazer, but contrary to Frazer they insist that these are social representations, i.e. that relations of similarity and contagion are conventional and pre-specified by the social classificatory system and not by abstract mental laws (Mauss 1972: 77). They argue that mere abstract laws cannot account for the specific choice of sympathetic relations out of the countless possible connections between all objects. Thus, the elements used in magical rituals are not part of a conscious reasoning:

> In magic and religion the individual does not reason, or if he does his reasoning is unconscious. Just as he has no need to reflect on the structure of his rite in order to practice it, or to understand the nature of his prayers and sacrifice, so he has no need to justify his ritual logically, nor does he worry about the whys and wherefores of the properties he employs, caring very little to justify in a rational manner the choice and use of his materials. (Mauss 1972: 75)

Rituals, both religious and magical, are not defined by the logical relations they contain, but rather by the pre-specified symbolic relations and their ability to express fundamental values, orientations and representations of society through this symbolic system.

Besides their common external characteristics, magic can be distinguished from religion by the immoral, antisocial and individual purpose of magical rituals. Therefore Mauss and Hubert end up defining magic as consisting in what the local community classifies as magical, that is, being in opposition to the openly performed, legitimate rituals conducted with socially approved purposes by socially respectable agents. As religion reflects the positive values of society, magic is its negative symbolic reflection. However, this *emic* definition runs into serious problems as individual purposes can easily be reconciled with religion and need not be immoral, and what is condemned as magic is often merely competing ritual practices. From this perspective one man's religion is another man's magic. Even more seriously, this definition reduces magic to a purely polemical concept used locally to condemn certain types of ritual actions, and thereby empties the concept of any positive characteristics. One cannot compare magical practices cross-culturally but only the polemical use of the concept or concepts like it in local discourse. Actually there are no such things as magical practices, only rituals condemned as such by persons with locally contingent motivations.

I think that this approach is flawed. The phenomena described by the analytical concept of magic do not disappear with the concept. People still conduct rituals involving dolls getting pierced by needles, and reducing magic to a concept employed in local polemics does not bring us any nearer an explanation of such actions. Mauss and Hubert do, however, point to the important fact that institutionalised religions in general are hostile towards competing ritual practices, and that the conflict generally centres on who can define the agency responsible for ritual efficacy, or what I will refer to as 'magical agency.' This will be treated further in chapters 4 and 7.

Most writers using a symbolic approach are aware of the barrenness of defining magic as actions locally condemned as 'magical.' The problem originates in an excessively strict insistence on the dichotomy between magic and religion, and once this dichotomy is relaxed, one can view magical actions as they interact with other types of symbolic behaviour—one can discern its symbolic function. Evans-Pritchard's Zande study is a good example of this approach (Evans-Pritchard 1937). According to Evans-Pritchard, central ideas in a culture are mutually reinforcing and constitute a system of belief and practices, "each part making sense only in relations to the others, and the system itself making sense only in relation to other institutional systems, as part of a wider set of relations" (Evans-Pritchard 1971: 112). Evans-Pritchard refuses to give a general definition of magic, and instead situates it as one side of an interacting triangle consisting of witchcraft causing misfortune, oracles used to find the culprit responsible, and magic used to alleviate the effect of the witchcraft. Instead of proposing general theories of magic as a universal category, one should use the concept to define certain practices in systematic relationship to other practices found in a specific culture. Thus, definitions can only be made *ad hoc* as they fit the symbolic system under investigation. Evans-Pritchard's concern is one of *translation* rather than one of universal theories and definition.

This approach has been followed in a substantial amount of anthropological research aimed at describing specific cultures through the analysis of culture-specific symbolic systems. If one nevertheless looks for some defining aspects of the concept of magic as it is used in this symbolic approach, two aspects emerge. The first one is the alleged instrumentality of magical rituals. In contrast to religious rituals, magical rituals seem to have clearly defined goals and the performance of certain rituals is understood as instrumental in achieving these goals. This approach seems to be a heritage from Malinowski (1992). The second defining characteristic of magic is its coercive nature and the related beliefs in the automatic efficacy of the rite. This again points to the instrumental aspects and practical aspect of magical rituals. But as we saw in the beginning of this section the symbolists actually disregard these defining aspects, and judge them as kinds of epiphenomena hiding the real and more important symbolic meaning of the actions. The real cause underlying the performance of magical rituals is not their ascribed instrumentality, but rather the symbolic content, and the true meaning of the ritual can therefore be found by placing the symbols in the proper position in the culture-specific symbolic system. This entails that rituals can be understood as a kind of language expressing the central values of a society in a similar manner as natural languages are used to express propositions. As one must learn to encode and decode a foreign natural language, so one must learn to decode the underlying symbolic system in order to understand ritual actions. Magic is not about *doing* but about *expressing* the central values of the culture one belongs to. Therefore one needs to make a division between practical and symbolic action, the latter being defined as not *really* working.

The problem, of course, is who makes the distinction between practical and expressive actions and on what grounds it is made. Is it really legitimate for the observer to claim that 'planting' is instrumental and 'chanting' is expressive, *despite* the explicit statement of the opposite by the participants themselves? I believe not. In trying to save 'primitive man' from being wrong, i.e. basing some of his technology on magic, the symbolist ends up making a much graver allegation, namely that 'primitive man' does not even know why he is doing what he does, but needs the observer to tell him.

To summarise, the symbolists tend to replace the dichotomy between magic and religion with one between practical and symbolic action, the latter confining both magic and religion. Magic should not be understood as based on intellectual mistakes or wrong theories about the world, but rather as symbolic expressions that one must place in their proper symbolic environment in order to interpret. Systems of classification are a major concern as they are understood as a fundamental constituent of the symbolic system, and language is understood as its most direct expression. Other types of actions, notably ritual, are also described as symbolic expressions, even if their reference to the symbolic system is less direct. The symbolists therefore agree with the intellectualists that individuals are deeply socialised and they subscribe to a degree of *social determinism*. Contrary to the intellectualist, however, the symbolists all but disregard the explicit explanations and intentions given by the agents performing ritual actions, and instead understand these actions as an *opaque* communication or expression of a symbolic system unconsciously internalised, revitalised and made manifest by participants through ritual action. The symbolists make a strict dichotomy between symbolic and practical action and these two types of action must be kept apart in order to understand behaviour even if they are confounded in a particular situation.

I believe the symbolist are on the right track on the following points: (a) that expressions in magical rituals in no simple manner refer directly to the beliefs and intentions of agents, and that magic needs to be addressed precisely as ritual in order to be explained; (b) that magic is woven into the social fabric and exploits the symbolic system and cultural models present in any culture. The main problems in the symbolic approach are: (a) the analytical division between symbolic/expressive and practical action. It is the observer, and not the participant, who decides which actions are practical and which are symbolic. This disregards explicit beliefs and intentions of the participant, who is therefore understood as not *really* believing that rituals are as instrumentally important as other types of actions. (b) The disregard or explaining away of the obvious instrumental aspect of magical rituals actually makes the concept superfluous.[5] The symbolists' recognition that ritual is a special type of action, and that symbolic structures and cultural models are used in magic must be combined with the recognition that magical actions are represented as instrumentally efficacious and that they are based on general cognitive processes. In order to combine these aspects, we must direct our attention to the pragmatic and performative aspects of magical actions.

2.3 Modes of Acting: Pragmatic and Performative Explanations of Magic

The primary question raised by the pragmatic and performative approach to magic is, in what way knowledge about pragmatic situations and performative repertoires can help explain what goes on in magical actions? How do people actually behave while performing magical rituals, and in what way are these actions related to the purported goal of the whole ritual: that is, how does the ritual action relate to the context of the ritual? The question is built on the simple, but pertinent, observation that magic primarily is a specific type of action employed in specific pragmatic situations with specific goals in view. Contrary to the symbolist approach, the pragmatic approach thus acknowledges the instrumental character of magical actions but relates this instrumentality to certain performative aspect of the actions in each specific case.

One of the firsts to recognise this important aspect of magic was the Polish-British anthropologist Bronislaw Malinowski who directed a large part of his work to the question of magic. Often, and for good reasons, Malinowski is categorised as defending an emotionalist approach to magic and religion (e.g. Evans-Pritchard 1971; Cunningham 1999). Malinowski does indeed place a strong emphasis on the function of emotions in prompting magical actions, but this emotionalist aspect is, as we shall see below, very common in most theories of magic. Another aspect of Malinowski's thinking about magic is more important in this context. He attaches a 'psycho-functional' explanation, emphasising the psychological functions of magic and religion, to a radical pragmatism, according to which the meaning of both linguistic expressions and actions are found *only* through reference to their immediate pragmatic context. This immediate context consists in both the specific practical situation in which the words are used and are as such part of human behaviour, and the situation's embedding in a broader cultural frame of knowledge relating to specified domains of action. In his general theory of meaning, Malinowski focuses on the pragmatic effects of language[6] and thereby anticipates the later performative turn in ritual studies inspired by Austin's and Searle's work on speech acts and performative utterances. "Words in their primary and essential sense *do, act, produce, and achieve*" (Malinowski 1935b: 52).

This is of great importance for his theory of magic. First, Malinowski believes language plays a major part as a means to distinguish magic from practical endeavours. In magical rituals a "sacred language" is easily distinguished from ordinary language by its strange linguistic forms. It has an effect, not on the superhuman agents invoked, but on participants' motivation and belief in the future, and this effect does not depend on the semantic meaning of the words used but rather on the immediate ritual context, a context created partly by the strangeness of the linguistic forms utilised. Magical words contain their own efficacy as they, due to their origin in mythic time, have a "direct hold over reality [and] need not conform to the rules of grammar and word formation of ordinary language" (Malinowski 1935b: 224).[7]

Second, such a pragmatic optic precludes that magic is understood as a general "mode of thinking" characteristic of "primitive", "undeveloped", or "traditional" societies. Instead magic is a specific type of *action*, performed in specified pragmatic situations and employing certain linguistic devices, and acknowledged by participants and observer alike as distinct from mere practical action. According to Malinowski, the function of magic is to relieve anxiety by filling the gap left by technological or scientific insufficiency and its practical aim makes it distinct from religion as well. One could say that magic is the employment of sacred language and actions in mundane pursuits at present beyond the technological control of a given society—it is a "substitute activity" that takes over where technology and practical activity end (Malinowski 1935b: 79-80). This position has been attacked as empirically false, as magic does not cease to exist with advances in technology, and as it does not always fill out all the gaps left by technology (Tambiah 1990: 73; Thomas 1991: 785-9).

Even though this beyond doubt is true, lack of control in the unfolding of events is an important generator of magic rituals, as humans will attempt to control temporal processes by ritual means and seek solutions to undesirable situations, either inside or outside established explanatory systems. Thus it will be argued in chapter 6 that the ritualisation of action is a universally recognised mode of interacting with agencies believed to influence aspects of life beyond the control of the individual or the group. The great contribution of Malinowski (besides his groundbreaking new standards of fieldwork) is his insistence on the importance of the pragmatic context for meaning in general, and the importance of the ritual context in the analysis of magic in particular. Words and actions must be understood in their pragmatic setting, and this contextualisation gives a new picture of magic, as neither a faulty science made by an always rational, but primitive, empiricist, nor as an expression of primitive mentality deeply embedded in emotional relations. Rather it is a repertoire of meaningful actions performed in a special pragmatic setting, involving certain authorised agents, a special attitude to actions and objects involved, and based on observance of tradition and adherence to form. One need not agree with Malinowski's utilitarian and behaviourist theories of religion and magic in order to appreciate this basic insight.

About thirty years after Malinowski published *Coral Gardens and Their Magic*, and following the renewed philosophical interest of the pragmatic function of language epitomised by Austin's *How To Do Things With Words* (1962), pragmatic aspects once again came to the foreground in the performative approach to ritual action. One of the foremost proponents of a performative approach to the study of magical rituals is anthropologist Stanley J. Tambiah (1968, 1979, 1985, 1990, 1996). Tambiah's extensive work on the performative aspects of magic and ritual can be somewhat crudely summarised in two perspectives. The first lies in direct prolongation of Malinowski's focus on the magical word, that is, the special role played by words and language in ritual performance, and in particular why certain words are believed to contain efficacy. The second perspective concerns his attempt to fit a theory of performativity into a conception of humanity as possessing two complementary modes of thought, one based on causal and eventually scientific thinking, and another based on performative and participatory experience.

As we saw in the discussion of Malinowski, several interesting problems are related to the use of words and language in most magical rituals. Two aspects concern Tambiah in particular: the apparently strange form of the words employed and their alleged magical power or direct efficacy. The question is how we can explain that people employ words they might not understand themselves but still believe contain not only meaning but also practical efficacy in both the social and physical environment? Tambiah argues that we must distinguish between several types of ritual language used inside a particular ritual. He exemplifies this with a Sinhalese rite of exorcism that contains a whole hierarchy of languages, iconically reproducing the cosmological hierarchy, and used in order to address different gods, demons and powers in their own particular languages (Tambiah 1968: 177-8). Different parts of the ritual having different types and styles of language will serve different communicative purposes. The fact that participants and even the exorcist in the ritual do not understand the languages involved is beside the point, as the words are still experienced as an act of communication. The exorcist can address demons through a demon language he does not understand but whose effect is conventionally established.

Tambiah therefore rejects theories explaining the power of words based in beliefs of the real identity between words and things, or the so-called "denotative fallacy". Proponents of such theories are based on a prior and flawed assumption that primitive people do in fact have a magical attitude to words in the first place, and Tambiah argues that the answer to the question instead must be found, first in a detailed analysis of the "interconnexion between words and actions" in magical ritual (Tambiah 1968: 184), and second in how ritual action relates to the non-ritual activities prompting it. Concerning the ritual action itself, Tambiah points to the importance of metaphor and metonymy in spells and incantations. Metaphors, as a trope used in everyday language, enable "reflection and ... abstract thought on the basis of analogical predication" (189). In magical rituals, the spell "exploits the metaphorical use of language, which verbally and in thought makes the transfer" of attributes between entities (189). Thus, sacred and magical language should not be understood as a special type of language but rather as an exploitation of ordinary linguistic properties in a special performative or pragmatic context. The same goes for metonymy. In ordinary language metonymy functions as a kind of referential device by which one can refer to a thing through a part (*pars pro toto*) and it is therefore a "complement" of a thing based on either contiguity or context. In magic the use of metonymy has implications "for lending realism to the rite, for transmitting a message through redundancy [e.g. by enumerating all the parts of an object], for storing vital technological knowledge in an oral culture, and for the construction of the spell itself as a lengthy verbal form" (190). Taken together, the intensive use of metaphor and metonymy in magical rituals expose an active use of "the expressive properties of language" that, when combined with perceptual properties of objects employed and the instrumental properties of physical actions performed, constitute the magical ritual (190).

Tambiah thereby restates the distinction between expressive and instrumental action claimed by Beattie and other symbolists (see above). The words are not *really* believed to have any efficacy in themselves, but have to be combined with material actions and infused in material objects in order to be represented as changing external states of affairs. Representations of efficacy observed in magical rituals thus originate in the material substances used in the ritual to materialise otherwise purely expressive metaphors and metonymies. A magical "technique gains its realism by clothing a metaphorical procedure in the operational or manipulative mode of practical action; it unites both concepts and actions, word and deed" (194).

The understanding of ritual as an act of expressive communication points to Tambiah's second perspective, namely the hypothesis of two coexisting and complementary modes of thought. Inspired by Lévy-Bruhl's notion of a primitive mentality, Tambiah argues that all humans posses two modes of approaching the world. One based on causality, clearly expressed in distanced scientific reasoning, the other based on performativity, a mode of thinking clearly expressed in ritual action filled as it is with performative utterances. Based on Austin, Tambiah argues that magical rituals should be analysed as performative actions that obtain their objective due to their very enactment (Tambiah 1985). This distinction has important consequences for the study of magic. As ritual actions are performed in the second, performative mode, they cannot be verified or falsified due to their relation to the real world. Magic should be understood as based on "conventional intersubjective understanding" and "the performative efficacy of communicative acts", rather than the "instrumental action" and "fragmentation of phenomena" belonging to the casual mode of thinking (Tambiah 1990: 109).

As we shall see in the coming chapters, there are fundamental problems with this distinction between two modes of thinking, especially in relation to notions of causality. In general, cognitive theorising cannot support such a crude dichotomising of human thinking, especially without any theoretical notion of how they interact or why they should be universal aspects of human cognition. Rather than being based on observations and theories of human cognitive functioning, they seem to be a transformation of the old symbolist distinction between expressive and communicative behaviour on the one hand and practical action on the other criticised above.

Tambiah's focus on the importance of metaphor and metonymy in magical rituals is more promising especially in connection to the use of material substances. But his explanation is stained by his insistence that magic is not really about manipulation but about *persuasion*, and that it is not directed at the surrounding world but at the human participants. This functionalist hypothesis depends on the view of ritual as a special type of communication. However, it is not always clear who is understood as communicating with whom. Is it between participants and gods, as when the "weirdness" of sacred language is explained by reference to the peculiar properties of the recipients (gods, spirits and demons)? Or is it a covert social communication in which society, by means of ritual, communicates to itself abstract meaning to do with "interpersonal orchestration and with social integration and continuity" (1979: 133)? There is, of course, no doubt that ritual contains and reflects social relations, but it does not always propagate social integration and continuity, and as an explanation of *magical* ritual it misses the important instrumental dimension for the participants. The hypothesis that magic is always antisocial *is* an exaggeration but it points to the importance of ritual efficacy inherent in magical rituals, even in cases where this is against what some define as common social interests.

Despite the many interesting and relevant observations, the understanding of magical rituals as persuasive and communicative and belonging to a special mode of thinking actually moves Tambiah away from an explanation of the magical or efficacious word. This can be exemplified by his explanation of the role of metonymic redundancy in magical ritual. Tambiah argues that the purpose of the often-reported extreme redundancy in magical rituals is "to transmit its message" and "store information" (1968: 192-3). Elsewhere he unfolds this information-theoretical perspective in an understanding of redundancy as a method to overcome "noise" in the transmission of the "meaning" (rather than "information") inherent in rituals (1979: 130-4). I will argue in the following chapters that the redundancy found in magical ritual often has the exact opposite effect. It effectively removes all symbolic, or referential, meaning from the utterance by repetition and thereby transforms the word from a symbol with reference to a kind of object believed to have direct efficacy. Tambiah is on the right track with his focus on the role of metaphor and metonymy in magical rituals, but is wrong when he interprets magical ritual as a kind of expressive communication.[8] Thereby belief in real efficacy of words and ritual actions is explained away rather than tackled.

In general the merit of the pragmatic and performative approach is the attention given to the immediate pragmatic context of the ritual action and to the importance of understanding ritual as a special pragmatic repertoire with certain performative characteristics. Performative and pragmatic theories have directed our attention to the fact that ritual is a specialised type of action and therefore one should not equate it with scientific and practical activity, nor understand actions and beliefs expressed in rituals as an expression of general beliefs hold at all times and in all situations. This, however, should not lead us to understand magical rituals as a kind of expressive or aesthetic genre with no representations of instrumental intentions involved. Similarly, the positive input from speech-act theory should not make us understand all magical actions as a kind of speech-acts. In ritual actions it is often unclear who the agent really is, and magical rituals contain a substantial amount of incomprehensible utterances whose performative aspects, in the linguistic sense of the term, are at least obscure. As I have argued elsewhere, it is more likely that certain types of speech-act contain magical actions than magic can be explained by reference to theories of speech-acts (Sørensen 2005).

2.4 Modes of Being: Emotionalist Explanations of Magic

After considering the role of thinking, symbols and pragmatic repertoires in magical action, we need to address theories that focus on the obvious emotional aspects of magic. Emotionalist approaches all bear a certain resemblance to the symbolic approach, as both claim that magical actions must be explained by reference to something other than the explanation given by the ritualists themselves. But where the symbolist approach points to symbolic systems expressing basic values of a given society, emotionalist accounts all turn to basic human conditions, some emotional situation or disposition, in order to explain magical actions. The emotionalist approach focuses on whether emotions, affections, or feelings can be found as the origin of magical actions and on how magical actions function in this regard. By focussing on emotions there is a tendency to turn to the individualistic aspect, most akin to the intellectualists, the main difference being that emotional approaches focus on irrational, unconscious and affective aspects of the individual psyche. However, emotions are not created in a void. People live in groups, and social conditions will to a large extend determine the form and content of magical actions thereby relating the emotional aspects to the symbolic forms in a given society. Finally, emotions are shaped by and expressed in pragmatic situations thereby relating the emotionalist approach to pragmatic descriptions.

One of the very first to propose a decisively emotionalist theory of magic was R. R. Marett. Working in the shadow of Frazer's intellectualist account, Marett argues that the intellectualist account misses the proper origin and function of magical actions by focussing on the rational basis (Marett 1930, 1979). According to Marett magic has its origin in emotional outbursts such as love, anger, and hate. In want of its proper object, feelings are directed towards the object's "shadow" instead, such as the glove or picture of the loved one. This rudimentary magic based on emotions is later developed into magic proper, in which the participant is conscious about the symbolic character of the shadow, and its relation to the object is now based on "make-believe" instead of "naive beliefs" (Marett 1979: 41). By recognising this symbolism, the shadow is transformed into an instrument that is imbued with the willpower of the magical agent, described by Marett as *mana*. Later on this *mana* obtains an independent existence, and hence the gods are born as a projection of a human proclivity to spontaneously and emotionally address the shadow of an object. The function of magic is basically cathartic as it relieves the subject of his or her emotional tension through a symbolic action, and this cathartic function actually produce the make-believe, as the subject gets a positive emotional feedback and therefore makes inferences supporting the make-believe.

The importance of this theory lies not in its evolutionary implications, the development from magic to religion and from spell to prayer, all of which are very speculative. It lies in Marett's insistence that magic is based on a universal human psychology, and that the cool rationality of Frazer's associative principles need to be complemented by an emotional force functioning as the impetus for its development. Marett's explanation is still basically individualistic, as the basis of magic proper, *mana*, is regarded as a projection of individual willpower. He supplements Tylor's and Frazer's rationalist accounts with an emotional aspect, but like them he disregards the social and the ritual aspects of magical actions.

This deficiency is to a large extend filled by Lucien Lévy-Bruhl who became (in)famous for his theory of 'prelogical mentality.' Belonging to the fringes of the French Sociological School, he adopted Durkheim's notion of social facts and collective representations implying that social phenomena, such as magic and religion, cannot be reduced to psychological or intellectual phenomena. Society is a *sui generis* descriptive level, and it produces and determines individuals' conception of all basic categories. However, Lévy-Bruhl radicalises the social determinism of Durkheim by distinguishing two radically different types of societies, and subsequently two radically different mentalities determining the conception of the world. This is the basis of the theory of "primitive mentality"—a distinct way of understanding the world allegedly possessed by "primitive people" due to the primitive stage of their society. I will not enter into the lively debate following the proposals of Lévy-Bruhl (see Littleton 1985), and I will not dwell at the obvious misconceptions or even misreading of his works (e.g. Hill 1987).[9] Instead I will discuss how Lévy-Bruhl's thinking affects his view upon magic, and in this respect, the central theoretical concept is that of "participation", the main explanatory principle in his analysis of magical practices.

Having stated that the object of study is collective representations, Lévy-Bruhl explains how the collective representations of "primitive people" can be distinguished from those of modern man. He argues that primitive representations are "more complex states in which emotional or motor elements are *integral parts* of the representation" (Lévy-Bruhl 1985: 36). As they are acquired in a ritual context whenever the primitive encounter the representation "[a] wave of emotion will immediately surge over him ... strong enough for its cognitive aspects to be almost lost sight of in the emotions which surrounds it" (37). These 'non-logical' properties led Lévy-Bruhl to propose that primitive representations are governed by a "law of participation," according to which representations are intimately connected to other representations, forming a network or grid of participatory connections.

This view has a profound impact on the notion of magic. Where Frazer argues that magic is based on the more or less conscious association of distinct categories, Lévy-Bruhl argues that these connections are pre-established and rest on participatory connections. It is the very constitution of concepts, their "polysynthetic" nature, that ensures that all representations participate in each other, thereby facilitating connections employed in magical rituals (44-45). Mystical or magical powers simply permeate all collective representations. Lévy-Bruhl exemplifies this by the elaborate magical procedures involved in such activities and social institutions as hunting and fishing (228ff).[10] Ritual activities are not distinct or segregated parts of representations involved in the activity, but are intimately intertwined with the practical activity itself. "[H]unting is an essentially magical operation, and in it everything depends, not on the skill or strength of the hunter, but on the mystic power which will place the animal at his mercy" (236). Collective representations involved in hunting, fishing, warfare, etc. contain a mystic dimension fuelled by the emotions this provokes in the individual, and interacted with through numerous socially prescribed rituals.[11]

Lévy-Bruhl points to the intricate and reciprocal connection between emotional and affective aspects of representations on the one hand and cultural conceptual systems on the other. Even though people are born into their culture and appropriate an already existing conceptual system, this system is confirmed by people's *emotional* experience of participatory connections. So, where Marett relates the emotional aspects of magical actions to an individual and intellectualist approach, Lévy-Bruhl emphasises the collective *and* emotional aspects of a cultural conceptual systems, thus explaining magic by reference to emotional aspects of the social symbolic system.

A central problem in Lévy-Bruhl's account is, as mentioned, his insistence on two distinct mentalities. This is grounded in his failure to recognise the importance of rituals. Instead of appreciating how rituals function as a prerequisite for the employment of participatory connections, he maintains that primitive people always move around in a mystical haze. This position is convincingly countered by Malinowski, who strongly favours a pragmatic and performative approach to ritual actions. He therefore rejects the idea that primitive people do not distinguish between ritual and practical actions (Malinowski 1992: 25ff). Instead, emotions are triggered in specific situations and magical actions are means to control socially disruptive emotions.

Another writer pointing to the intricate relation between emotion, magic and ritual action is of course Sigmund Freud. In his essay "Obsessive Actions and Religious Practices" (Freud 1995a), Freud compares the symptoms of people suffering from "obsessional neurosis" (known today as Obsessive Compulsory

Disorder, or OCD) to that of religious ritual practice. Both the private rituals of neurotics and the social rituals of religions are really symbolic actions that by the means of displacement actions express fundamental but repressed psychological desires. In the case of neurosis these are of a purely sexual origin, whereas religious rituals express more broadly displaced and repressed egoistic feelings that are unacceptable to society. In both cases the job of the analyst is to unearth the real psychological motives underlying the displaced ritual action in the first place, and ritual actions can as such be understood as a substitute action relieving the anxiety produced by the repression of unwanted psychological desires or instincts.

Inspired by the early anthropologists, in particular Robertson Smith and Frazer, Freud distinguishes magic from religion by its evolutionary emergence. In his essay "Animism, Magic, and the Omnipotence of Thought" published as a part of *Totem and Taboo* (Freud 1995b) Freud claims that magical practices in primitive societies are based on the belief in the omnipotence of thought—a narcissistic belief also found among neurotic patients. As in the case of neurotics, magic has the psychological function of relieving the anxiety, stress, and guilt produced by above all the primeval killing of the father by the sons prompted by their incestuous sexual desire towards their mother and sisters. This drama of origin, more a psychological foundation myth than a scientific theory, underlies the development of totemism and magical rituals and taboos related hereto. Through this highly speculative description of the genesis of culture, Freud not only relegates magic to an early period of human cultural evolution, as did Tylor and Frazer, but he equates these cultural stages with those found in the psychosexual development in early childhood (Freud 1995b: 90). Like Marett, he rejects the cool rationalism of Tylor and Frazer in favour of an emotional explanation of magic. Magical rituals are based in emotional distress that produces a narcissistic withdrawal of the Ego, which ultimately leads to the representations of omnipotence characterising magical actions. As children satisfy their unrealisable wishes in a hallucinatory manner through autoeroticism, the wishes of primitive man are accompanied by a motor impulse, giving rise to a hallucinatory experience of satisfaction. "As time goes on, the psychological accent shifts from the *motives* for the magical act on to the *measures* by which it is carried out—that is, on to the act itself" (Freud 1995b: 84, original emphasis). Thus, magical actions are displaced behaviour functioning as a substitute action aimed to satisfy unrealisable desires or wishes, just as we find substitute ritual actions relieving sexual desires and anxieties in the case of obsessional neurosis. Obsessional neurosis is actually a re-emergence of primitive magical thinking in people that belong to more developed cultures. "It is in obsessional neurosis that the *survival* of the omnipotence of thought is most clearly visible and that the consequences of this primitive mode of thinking come closest to consciousness" (Freud 1995b: 86, emphasis added).

Even though both Freud's evolutionary scheme and his Lamarckian notion of future generations' inheritance of the guilt caused by the primeval parricide have proven wrong, Freud's comparison of magical rituals and obsessional behaviour is not without substance. There are a number of similarities between magical rituals and Obsessive Compulsory Disorder, but rather than arguing that these are expressions of the same kind of mentality or emotional anxieties, one should look at the cognitive processes involved. As it will be argued extensively in the following chapter, magical rituals entail a radical de-emphasis of conventional symbolic meaning and a transformation of the intentionality of the agent performing the action, provoking the employment of alternative hermeneutic strategies based on fundamental cognitive mechanisms. The same might be true in cases in OCD. Thus, magical rituals and OCD may not have the same psychological origin, but rather both 'utilise' ritualised actions that eventually provoke similar cognitive processes.

Emotions definitely play an important role in magical actions even if Freud's myth of its origin in narcissistic delusion must be rejected. Malinowski also emphasises the emotional foundation of magical actions, but rejects Freud's explanation in favour of an account of emotions as the result of humans' pragmatic impotence in specific endeavours leading to another pragmatic activity, namely magic. As mentioned above, Malinowski argues that magic is a substitute activity, not prompted by some unconscious desire getting a displaced expression in magical ritual, but rather it substitutes real actions with pseudoactions that vent anxieties about some pragmatic outcome. So, instead of a general psychological mechanism or disposition as argued by Freud, Malinowski argues that we shall look for how emotions prompt magical actions in relation to concrete pragmatic situations that for some reason give rise to emotional anxiety.

At a more general level, the emotionalist approach cautions the student of magic to be aware that magical actions are not performed in an emotional void. Magical actions are often prompted by states of affair with strong emotional content, they themselves are able to produce certain emotions in participants, and cultural symbolic systems employed in magical rituals are emotionally valued. Emotions, however, cannot by themselves explain the more or less universal existence of magical actions, or the specific cognitive processes involved. How emotions relate to magical actions in general must await more results from the ongoing attempt to integrate emotions and affections into cognitive theories. Lévy-Bruhl argues correctly that concepts are emotionally valued and that conceptual relations can be emotionally grounded. The contribution of the present work is the very modest emphasis on the role of emotions in establishing and strengthening conceptual connections found in magical rituals.

Notes

1. "Appendix of Indo-European Roots", in *The American Heritage Dictionary*, 3rd edition, Delta Books, 1992: 945.
2. An exception to this is philosopher John Skorupski's attempt to incorporate a theory of ritual in the intellectualist program found in his book *Symbol and Theory* (1976). However, Skorupski's theory of magic is strangely disjoined from his intellectualist program. He applies an "identificationist" approach according to which magical actions rest on a believed identity between symbol and the symbolised prevalent in traditional societies, and ends up in an unfruitful and resigned statement. "We cannot make such a pattern of thought fully clear, since it is intrinsically incoherent: to make it clear in this sense would be to falsify it" (144).
3. The problem of intellectualist explanations of religion has been brilliantly captured by Lawson and McCauley: "On the intellectualist view the real primitives in far off lands think straight but are wrong, whereas the most civilised religious people in their own culture do not even think straight!" (Lawson & McCauley 1990: 36)
4. Sperber (1975) is a noteworthy exception to this.
5. A consequence that is taken by Pocock (1972) in his introduction to the English translation of Mauss and Hubert (1950).
6. Malinowski's pragmatic theory of meaning is found in his essay, "Magic, Science, and Religion" from 1925 (1992) and elaborated in great detail in the second volume of *Coral Gardens and Their Magic* (1935b).
7. Malinowski believed the origin of beliefs in the efficacy of magical words was to be found in infantile language where children's inarticulate sounds have a direct impact on their surroundings. This theory is refuted in recent developmental studies (Tomasello 1999; Avis & Harris 1991).
8. In the 1979, article Tambiah actually points to the de-symbolising function of ritual behaviour. Due to its conventional nature, ritual behaviour distances the individual from the actions performed, and thereby removes intentional meaning from the particular action in the ritual. This aspect will be treated in depth in chapter 6 in the discussion of the work of Humphrey and Laidlaw (1994).
9. For a recent discussion and evaluation of the work of Lévy-Bruhl, see Littleton 1985; Shweder 1986; Wiebe 1987; and Saler 1997.
10. Lévy-Bruhl acknowledges that he might as well have used to word "magical" instead of "mystical". He refrains from using "magic", as he agrees with Mauss and Hubert that the meaning of "magic" varies depending on the social type studied (Lévy-Bruhl 1985: 293).
11. This description of primitive representations exposes a certain affinity with recent results in cognitive semantics. The notion that representations combine emotive, affective, motor interactive and cultural aspects is very close to the notion of "Idealised Cognitive Models" found in Lakoff (1987), the main difference being that cognitive semantics rejects the difference between primitive and civilised mentality. In fact, Lévy-Bruhl's makes an asymmetric juxtaposition as the logical aspects of representations ascribed to so-called developed or civilised people are normative ideals of very formalised

languages in science, whereas the emotional and affective aspects ascribed "primitives'" representations seems to be an inherent part of representations among all people.

3
The Cognitive Foundation of Magical Action

Having addressed four different approaches to magic, and found both positive and negative aspects in each, we will now turn to how a cognitive approach can provide answers to some of the questions left unanswered by former approaches and how the advances already made can be integrated in a cognitive approach. As a point of departure, all four positions can be reformulated as asking specific types of questions in relation to a cognitive explanation of magic. The rationalist approach concerns the cognitive mechanisms responsible for the performance of magical actions. Of particular interest is the explicit use of relations of similarity and contagion, or metaphor and metonymy, and how perception, categorisation and conceptualisation constrain magical performance. The symbolist approach concerns the interface between the symbolic or conceptual structures and human cognition. How does human cognition constrain, appropriate and reformulate the pre-established systems of signs that precede all individuals? What cognitive principles will help explain the formation of such semiotic structures? And how do these structures influence individual cognitive development? The pragmatic and performative approach concerns how different pragmatic repertoires such as magical rituals influence perception and cognitive processing. An important question is how specific pragmatic frames influence epistemic evaluation; that is, whether structures of externalised beliefs are restricted to certain pragmatic events, and how these beliefs relate to intuitive assumptions. Finally, the emotionalist approach concerns the relation between cognitive processes and emotion, for instance the emotional or affective valuation of different parts of the conceptual system, in this case especially religious concepts. The emotional or affective value plays an important part in facilitating belief in ritual efficacy to elements used in magical rituals and in motivating the performance of numerous magical rituals, whether for hate, love or fear.

Many of these questions will be addressed in the rest of this book. Of central importance, however, is the treatment of the cognitive principles underlying magical actions, and the influence of representations of events constrained by pragmatic and performative repertoires or frames. This is for two reasons: (a) general cognitive theorising has been much concerned with principles of thought (as a cognitive phenomena) and of representations of pragmatic repertoires, and the whole range of emotions have only more recently been related to cognition; (b) the comparative approach naturally entails an emphasis on universal aspects, wherefore I cannot adequately address the complex question of the interaction between specific cultural system and individual cognition, that would necessitate thorough studies in the field. The aim of this book is another. It addresses what cognitive theories can tell us about the *cross-cultural* aspects of magic, and in that case questions concerning general processes of human cognition and pragmatic and performative frames are of central concern.

In order to ease the following—rather technical—discussion of the importance of cognitive findings in the study of magic, it is perhaps appropriate to give a preliminary definition of magic. Magic is about *changing the state or essence of persons, objects, acts and events through certain special and non-trivial kinds of actions with opaque causal mediation.* This manipulative and transformative aspect of magical action will place a substantial part of the analysis of magic in the realm of psychological or cognitive theories and explanations. Therefore an analysis of the cognitive mechanism underlying human categorisation and conceptualisation is necessary in order to explicate what makes magical action special and to expose the systematic character of the actions described.

A more general remark is necessary at this preliminary stage. It is not necessary or even profitable to claim the existence of any special cognitive centres or mechanisms in order to explain the mental representations underlying magic and magical behaviour. Instead, the combination of several ordinary or everyday cognitive mechanisms and the special relationship of magical actions to both semiotic systems and performative pragmatic repertoires constitute what can be described as a special class of action called 'magic.' Magic is an impure or synthetic object constituted by several independent structures and mechanisms each explicable on separate descriptive levels.[1] These structures and mechanisms can only be explained on their own level of analysis even while they interact with the other levels to produce observable phenomena that *we* classify as magic. This entails that it is impossible to make an explanatory theory of magic as such, as only the underlying mechanisms and structures constituting the phenomena can be the objects of causal explanations. Therefore, usage of the synthetic term 'magic' to describe observable phenomena will not necessarily entail that all of the structures described in this analysis are found in each case. I subscribe to sociologist Daniel O'Keefe's description of the category of magic as based on 'family-resemblance' (O'Keefe 1982), depending on which other structures the observable phenomena are related to. Thus, there is no such a thing as a *magical system* according to which singular magical actions can be evaluated. A theory of magic as an impure object uniting several distinct levels of analysis might shed light on the effect these procedures and actions have on more established meaning systems notably religions. This book will present several hypotheses in that regard.

This chapter is concerned with how findings in cognitive science can be of assistance in the analysis of magic, magical action, and magical ritual. The discussion will be kept at a general level, as several strands in cognitive science will be combined in order to give a comprehensive picture of human categorisation, conceptualisation and meaning construction that underlie the performance of magic in its diverse forms. Three broad headlines will structure the discussion. First, the importance of basic-level categorisation will be discussed. Recent studies in cognitive science give a whole new picture of human categorisation that is of great importance in the formation of religious and magical representations. Second, we shall see how the construction of conceptual domains and cultural models form an essential constituent in the performance of magic, both in its directly semantic and in its temporal aspects. It will be argued that conceptualisation forms a bridge between externalised or cultural symbolic or semiotic systems on the one hand and cognitive constraints on categorisation on the other. Third, conceptual structures are combined into more complex structures in conceptual blending. Magical rituals employ all sorts of conceptual structures in order to achieve a pre-specified instrumental goal and, as we saw in the discussion of Frazer, metaphorical and metonymic projections have long ago been recognised as an essential aspect of magical rituals.

3.1 Basic-level Categorisation

Why are rituals in general and magic in particular so attention-demanding? Why do participants, observers and scholars agree that these actions are special, that they need special preparations and conditions from the perspective of the participants, and special interpretations and explanations from the perspective of the scholar? In the last chapter, we saw how anthropology and the study of religions have used several approaches in order to explain and interpret this particular phenomenon. Here I will show how cognitive science can shed light on the role of human categorisation in magical action.

3.1.1 Domain-specific Aspects of Human Categorisation

One of the basic hypotheses concerning human categorisation argues that human cognition should not be seen as a unified system using general procedures to deal with its environment but rather as several such systems applied to specific domains of interaction. According to this view, humans universally categorise the world in relation to distinct cognitive domains that guide expectations of such things as causal behaviour and essential properties. This is called the domain-specificity hypothesis. The basic assumption is that human beings have certain innate or early-acquired principles guiding the extraction of information first of all from their perceptual field and secondarily from other cognitive domains (Karmiloff-Smith 1995). A basic observation pointing to some degree of domain-specificity is the fact that during development children seem to extract the most relevant information out of the almost infinite amount of information supplied by perception—this is called the *problem of induction*. In order to explain how the child distinguishes relevant from irrelevant perceptual information one must postulate the existence of either innate modules (such as for face-recognition), domains, or at least dispositions that constrain what kind of information will be processed by the mind of the developing child. These constraints ensure that only the right information is processed and facilitate learning by removing unwanted 'noise'. In the words of developmental psychologist Annette Karmiloff-Smith:

> Domain-specific constraints *potentiate* learning by limiting the hypothesis space entertained. They enable the infant to accept as input only those data which it is initially able to compute in specific ways. The domain specificity of processing provides the infant with a limited yet organised (nonchaotic) system from the outset, and not solely at the tail end of the Piagetian sensorimotor period (Karmiloff-Smith 1995: 11-12).

Thus, the domain specific approach entails that different areas of human learning and cognition might be constrained be different principles, not only in the organisation of knowledge, but also in the mechanism selecting and processing information. Of special importance in this context is that these domains are universal and not constrained by explicit cultural representations about the ontology of objects represented. They therefore form an excellent background for performing cross-cultural and comparative studies.

Before describing the domain-specific constraints relevant in the study of magic, a short critical remark on the notion of 'domain' is in place. There seems to be a tendency within cognitive science to create domains *ad hoc*. All sorts of phenomena are given their own cognitive domain, from mathematics and language, to naive physics and chess. I propose a basic analytic distinction into four distinct types of cognitive domains. The first type is *ontological domains* concerned with the human proclivity to categorise the perception of the world in relation to ontological assumptions related to distinct domains with strict constraints on possible properties. The second type is *perceptual domains* based on perceptually salient structures such as face-recognition and colour-perception. Partly overlapping this second type is the third type, *functional domains*, such as language and mathematics, which eventually form perceptually independent domains but are based upon a distinct function rather than a distinct perceptual modality. The fourth type is *conceptual* or *epistemic domains* making an at least relatively integrated whole out of perceptual data originating in disparate domains, thus integrating ontological, perceptual, functional, and conceptual knowledge into one structure. It is evident that the different types of domains will be built in different ways and at different times in human development.

At this point in the argument, I am primarily concerned with the ontological domains as these impose important constraints on both basic categories and subsequent complex concepts. Among cognitive psychologists, there is a lively debate concerning the number, extent and structure of innate and early acquired ontological assumptions (for a summary see Hirschfeld & Gelman 1994; Cosmides & Tooby 1994; Sperber 2001). There seems to be a broad consensus about a distinction into at least four ontological domains with distinct causal assumptions.

1. *The physical domain*: A substantial number of developmental studies show that already as early as three months of age, infants have expectations concerning the behaviour of physical, inanimate objects as opposed to animate objects (Spelke et al 1995; Baillargeon 1994; Baillargeon et al 1995). Spelke et al list three basic ontological assumption about solid physical objects, namely *cohesion*, *continuity* and *contact*: "Young infants appear to know that inanimate objects move cohesively, exist and move continuously, and act upon each other on contact." (1995: 51). Besides these characteristics, Leslie shows how recognition and categorisation of physical objects are connected to assumptions about mechanics and agency (Leslie 1994, 1995). He argues that physical objects are defined by not having any internal source of energy, which entails that they have to be influenced by an external source of power in order to move, and that already initiated movement can only be affected by external factors. This has consequences for representations of agency, as physical objects, lacking an internal source of energy, most likely will be understood as non-agents, and that actions in which physical objects are perceived as the mechanical cause, will have possible agents automatically ascribed. The type of causality expected in this domain is a *mechanical causality*, having a billiard-ball launching event as an ideal type in which one ball transfers movement to another ball by contact (Leslie 1994). In a similar strain Keil defines actions in the physical domain as "non-teleological", as children seem to ascribe far less purpose to perceptual characteristics of physical objects (non-tools) than to animate objects (1994, 1995). A difficult problem is whether physical objects and materials are mentally represented as possessing a defining 'essences' (Medin & Ortony 1989). As we shall see in the treatment of the biological or animate domain, the automatic ascription of essence entails that objects are categorised on the basis of the assumption that they posses an inner essence that will remain unchanged even if perceptible properties are changed to a substantial degree. Seemingly, ascribing essential qualities to physical objects, such as stones or mud, is superfluous, as these will be lost if the object is worked into something else. But anthropological studies, discussed in the following chapters, indicate that ascriptions of essence to material objects are found, even if it is more vague than in the animate domain.

2. *The biological or animate domain*: Evidence for a special domain structuring categories of animate entities comes from three different lines of

research. The first argument is the overwhelming evidence of cross-culturally similar categorisation of living kinds on the folk generic level, for example of 'cats', 'dogs' and 'lemon trees' (Atran 1995). This, however, is not in itself a strong argument for the domain-specificity of biological classification, but only for the cognitive foundation of *all* basic-level categorisation. The second argument is from developmental psychology. Experiments indicate that, even in infants, the self-propelled movement of any object will be represented as an animate agent with an internal source of energy (Mandler 1992). But movement will not do it alone. Self-propelled movement is related to assumptions about kinds of goals and functions responsible for the motion (R. Gelman et al 1995). The basic causal principle guiding expectations of actions in this domain is therefore *instrumental* or *teleological causality*. Animate movement is judged to be the result of an agent with a goal exerting force on a physical object (Keil 1994). The third argument for the domain-specific nature of living kind categorisation is the 'essence' ascribed to such 'natural kinds'. Gestaltic surface properties of animate objects are simply not sufficient for the construction of stable categories of living kinds. According to Medin and Ortony (1989) people represent things in general as having an inner essence ("psychological essentialism"), and this seems to be more so in categorisations of animals. Changes of perceptual features do not imply a similar change of category membership, as the essence remains stable. Together, cross-culturally similar categorisation, ascription of animacy on the basis of movement and essentialist assumptions, give evidence for the plausibility of a biological or animate ontological domain.

3. *Mental or psychological domain*. This domain organises and processes information of representations of other people's mental states. It is also referred to as "naive psychology", "folk psychology" or "theory of mind" (ToM). It is an unanswered question to what extend Theory of Mind is influenced by the conceptual system prevalent in a given culture (D'Andrade 1987). There are, however, certain universal elements that must be explained by domain-specific principles unfolding in specific developmental stages (Gopnik & Wellman 1994). A central assumption is that other humans are represented as entertaining beliefs about affairs in the world that lead to goal-directed actions. This is also known as "belief-desire reasoning" whereby human actions are inscribed in a causal chain leading from perception, over belief and intention, to action. The causal principle guiding expectations in the mental domain is thus *intentional causality*, as it automatically ascribes intentional states as the driving force behind actions, and thereby explains actions by reference to beliefs. The actions of human beings, based on beliefs and goals, are seen the typical examples of agents in the fully expanded version of the term (Leslie 1994). Belief-desire reasoning plays a central role in the notion of agency ascribing these attributes of a causal-intentional chain to events in the world as a default-mechanism. There is good evidence that belief-desire reasoning is a cross-cultural phenomenon, both in content and in developmental unfolding, despite huge differences in explicit cultural theories about the mind and its mechanisms (Avis & Harris 1991). This

points to the general fact that explicit cultural theories about 'minds' are extensions of very basic and implicit core assumptions. Another important feature of the mental domain is connected to belief-desire reasoning. Agents are ascribed attitudes towards the truth of their own and other people's propositions (Leslie 1994). People can lie, be uncertain about the truth of a proposition, or relay information in which they do or do not believe themselves, but that others will hold to be true. All these features give rise to a host of possible inferences about the psychological motives of people's actions or lack of actions: whether they are truthful or not, what goal they are trying to reach, and what their intentions are for seeking that goal. This is an important example of how basic categorisation interacts with conceptual structures. The ascription of attitudes is properly spontaneous and universal, but the content of this ascription is conceptual and, to a certain extent, culture dependent.

4. *The social domain.* The existence of a separate social domain is as disputed as the existence of a special biological domain. Anthropologist Lawrence A. Hirschfeld (1988, 1994, 1995) is the most outspoken proponent of a theory of domain-specificity including a separate social domain. He distinguishes between two types of social categories. The first type is explicitly human in origin and based on collective pressure and individual choice of friendship, occupation etc. and will often be based on more or less formal criteria of membership. The second type consists in 'natural-like' social categories like race, gender, ethnicity, kinship, age, clans, castes and privileged occupational positions. Hirschfeld's central thesis is that individuals' acquisition of this second type of social categories cannot be explained by reference to explicit tuition (from parents or peers) or external perceptual qualities alone (like skin colour, uniform etc.). Social categories are, according to Hirschfeld, dependent on the ascription of "an underlying natural similitude" (1988) or a "psychological essentialism" (1994, 1995) like the one found most explicit in the biological domain. Humans have an inborn proclivity to classify groups of human beings by reference to a common essence, even before they can adequately place individuals in the correct categories. Essentialism applied in the social domain differs from the natural kind essentialism in two respects: (1) it is a relational and not an individual property, meaning that one is a member of a given social category by reference to a special connection to other members; and (2) it can be possessed to a greater or lesser degree. It is not convincing that the division between purely formal and essence-based social categories can be upheld in all cases. Individual members of social categories where membership is explicitly expressed as determined by formal criteria alone, will often be judged upon the extent to which they are believed to posses the right individual essence to fill these social positions. A "*real* priest" does not necessarily differ from a priest "who was never *really* a priest" according to formal criteria, but by reference to external perceptual features understood as indices of the possession or non-possession of a specific essence of "priesthood." The concept of an occupational vocation has this essentialist flavour. Most religious social categories consist in a combination of formal, per-

ceptual and essential criteria, according to which individual members are judged by abductive reasoning, understanding external behaviour simultaneously as *expressions* of a given essence, and as *indices* of the possession of this essence (see Boyer 1993, 1994). Thus, essentialised social categories are important in the analysis of magical actions, as they are the basis of the classification of privileged agents that, by virtue of a special essence, can perform special kinds of actions, e.g. magical rituals.

Theories of cognitive constraints on categorisation in general and the hypothesis of domain-specific constraints in particular have had an important influence on the study of religion (Boyer 1990, 1994, 2001; Lawson and McCauley 1990; McCauley and Lawson 2002; Sperber 1975, 1996). Anthropologist Pascal Boyer, for example, has worked on how cognitive constraints influence the structure, transmission and memorability of religious ideas. Boyer argues that religious ideas and concepts are based on a specific balance between counterintuitive properties that enhance memorability, and intuitive properties that ensure inferential potential. Whereas the intuitive principles are based on domain-specific categorisation leading to strong causal expectations, the counterintuitive aspects violate these expectations in a salient and attention-demanding manner. And where all individuals, thanks to domain-specificity, infer the intuitive principles, the counterintuitive properties are explicitly taught in a cultural environment. Thus, in the religious representation of a ghost, only the attention-demanding counterintuitive aspects need to be explicitly expressed (a dead body moving, ability to move through solid objects etc.), whereas other intuitive aspects are automatically inferred by participants (e.g. that the ghost is governed by belief-desire psychology and as such interacts with the living based on beliefs and desires and possibly in order to achieve something). Boyer argues for a division between a schematic core of the concept consisting of domain-specific expectations giving rise to inferences, and a fringe of non-schematic assumptions necessary for successful transmission in a given cultural environment but without inferential potential. One part of the concept is used to think with; the rest is used to remember by.

Boyer's theory addresses a whole range of fundamental problems in the anthropology of religion, including the general tendency to over-represent the 'mysterious' and 'mystical' aspects of other people's religious representations, as these are the explicitly taught part of a more complex concept. He also addresses the problem of transmission and memorability in a convincing manner that places emphasis on the role of category structure for the survival of ideas in a selective process—an approach strengthened in his latest work (Boyer 2001). However, Boyer's claim that the non-schematic aspects of religious concepts carry no inferential potential goes counter to results from cognitive semantics pointing to the importance of conceptual integration or blending in which schematic aspects from several domains are integrated in order to create complex concepts (Fauconnier & Turner 1998, 2002). We need to refine this aspect of the theory by explaining how inferential potential from two or more domains can be integrated to form more complex concepts.

3.1.2 Domain-general Aspects of Human Categorisation

In order to get that far, it must be determined how domain-general features of human categorisation enable the interaction of different domains. In short we need to find the cognitive format that enables different domains to interact in the construction of complex concepts, as domain-specific accounts of human categorisation give rise to a basic problem. If one postulates a very high degree of domain-specificity or modularity, a lesser degree of cognitive flexibility follows as a logical entailment: the processing of information will be automatic and therefore less receptive to domain-external information. On the contrary, if one postulates a low degree of domain-specificity the problem of induction arises once again, the very problem domain-specific theories set out to answer in the first place (Karmiloff-Smith 1995: 9). As humans possess both a very high degree of cognitive flexibility and seem to avoid the problem of induction we need to combine theories of domain-specificity with a description of how domain-general cognition enables human cognitive flexibility or fluidity (Mithen 1996). Humans everywhere seem to be able to connect different domains, treat physical objects as animate and intentional, animals as humans and social groups as intentional agents. The question is what fundamental domain-general principles underlie the human ability to unite aspects of different ontological domains into complex concepts?

Linguist George Lakoff and philosopher Mark Johnson made a serious impact on the cognitive study of language in their 1980 book *Metaphors We Live By*. It is important to emphasise that the metaphor theory does not entail that *all* cognition is based on metaphorical mappings. Two important theoretical concepts are seen as underlying the widespread mechanism of metaphorical mappings: *basic-level categorisation* and *image-schemata*. Both are understood as pre-conceptual and non-propositional structures that arise in the interaction between the individual cognitive and physiological systems on the one hand, and the world on the other. As this interaction is pre-conceptual and embodied, these structures are directly meaningful and not based on relations in the conceptual system—hence their non-propositional status (Lakoff 1987: 268, 443).

The theory of basic-level categorisation argues that, contrary to philosophical speculations, the most fundamental level of human categorisation is the middle or the generic level, in which we find categories such as 'dogs', 'chairs', 'oaks' and 'flowers.' Thus a 'cup' is the highest level on which it is possible to form a mental picture—you cannot form a picture of 'tableware' except as a collection of basic-level entities. You form a gestalt picture of 'cup' with the relevant part-whole structure as 'inside-outside' and 'handle', which is connected to a general motor program controlling your interaction with the 'cup'.

'Cup' is a shorter word than words at both superordinate (tableware) and underlying levels (teacup), and the word is neutral and widely distributed in a linguistic community. It is important to notice that basic-level categories get their prominence from human interaction with and perception of the world, and not from disembodied logical properties of category relationships. Basic-level categorisation is in this respect strongly constrained by human physiology, perception and neural systems giving rise to gestalt perception and general motor programs guiding interaction with objects in the world. This is an embodied view of human cognition, arguing that categorisation arises in our motivated interaction with a physical world (Lakoff 1987: 265-68).

Directly related to the notion of basic-level categorisation is the theory of prototypes, proposed by Rosch (1977). Even though most scholars working in this area acknowledge prototype-effects, there is disagreement about how these effects arise. These differences aside, prototype-effects point to the fact that basic-level categories have an internal structure: not all cups are judged as good examples of the category 'cup' as it would be postulated by a classical view of the definition of categories based on necessary and sufficient conditions. What specific cup is judged as the best example, however, will differ substantially depending on situation and context.

The second important feature of pre-conceptual categorisation is image-schemata, analysed most thoroughly by Mark Johnson in his 1987 book *The Body in the Mind*.[2] As image-schematic structures will be crucial in the analytic models of magical action presented below, this theoretical concept must be treated in some depth. The basic function of image-schemata is that they structure human organisation of spatial relations among objects in relation to a viewpoint, all at a pre-conceptual level. Johnson defines image-schemata as midway between abstract propositions and rich mental images. They are not propositional in the traditional sense of the word, as they are based on experiential interaction with the world resulting in embodied figurative structures that, although they have an internal structure, cannot be broken up in parts without destroying their cognitive function. At the same time, they are much more abstract than the rich mental pictures connected to particular things, events, or pictures, as they can conform to all kinds of specific instances and can be mentally manipulated.

> A schema consists of a small number of parts and relations, by virtue of which it can structure indefinitely many perceptions, images, and events. In sum, image-schemata operate at a level of mental organization that falls between abstract propositional structures, on the one side, and particular concrete images, on the other. ... [I]n order for us to have meaningful, connected experiences that we can comprehend and reason about, there must be pattern and order to our actions, perceptions, and conceptions. *A schema is a recurrent pattern, shape, and regularity in, or of, these ongoing activities.* ... I conceive of them [image-schemata] as *structures for organizing* our experience and comprehension (Johnson 1987: 29).

Image-schemata are one of the most basic cognitive tools used in creating order and organisation in human experience and for connecting different experiences through recurrent patterns. At this point an example can illustrate what an image-schema might consist of. Take the image-schema of CONTAINMENT, and think of all the physical experiences involving CONTAINMENT. A person being *in* a room, the apple being *in* the bowl, the farmer being *in* the field, the man being *in* love etc. Despite their differences, all these instances have a common schematic structure. This simple structure consists of an inside, where the entity in question is now located, an outside, and a boundary between the two. As the example illustrates, it might be understood as both two-dimensional (a field), as three-dimensional (a room) or as a state (love). This might initially seem like a very scant structure by which to organise such diverse types of experience. Often, however, image-schemata are combined to form richer structures and they impose important inferential potentials and constraints when implemented. In order to *get into* a container you have to *cross* the *boundary*; you can be *close* to the boundary both from *outside* and from *inside*; if you are *in* A, and A is *in* B, you are *in* B.[3]

Johnson summarises the most important features of image-schemata in four points (Johnson 1987: 25-26):

1. They are cross-modal. The same image-schemata appear in different perceptual and expressive modalities. This explains the possible interaction of both similar and different image-schemata expressed in different perceptual domains in magical actions (e.g. in visual, phonetic and linguistic expression). Image-schemata are among the formats enabling conceptual mapping and conceptual blending.

2. Image-schemata are easily manipulated. Imagine a circle and a triangle interconnected with a line. When mentally rotating the two structures they can uphold their internal relation.

3. Image-schemata can be transformed. An example of such transformations is the relation between focus on a path ("he walked over the hill") and focus on the endpoint of a path ("he lives over the hill"). This shows that different image-schemata or different aspects of the same schema expressed by the same prepositional term often are in a systematic relationship to each other.

4. Image-schemata are influenced by general knowledge. Evidence of this comes from experiments in which linguistic cues for recall affects subjects' drawings of recalled visual stimuli, an effect not seen in recall of rich mental pictures or images. This, however, entails an intimate connection between non-propositional image-schemata and propositional structures of categories of objects appearing in experience. I will return to this problem as it is strongly related to the notion of force.

The structure of image-schemata is thus rich enough to impose order on experience and constrain inference but at the same time flexible enough to apply to different sorts of experience, in different modalities and, through manipulation and transformations, to adapt to difference in focus and viewpoint. Image-schemata can unite aspects of otherwise disparate conceptual domains and cultural models.[4]

We still miss a crucial factor in the construction of image-schematic gestalts. As all image-schemata are grounded in the embodied physical interaction with the world, they must be connected to notions of physical force in order for the schemata to have any dynamic unfolding. All movement in the physical world is constrained by two dynamic factors: *force* and *resistance*. This has been studied in depth by linguist Leonard Talmy in his theory of "force-dynamics in language and cognition" (Talmy 2000). A basic notion is that all objects are understood as possessing or lacking force: "The [force dynamic] interpretation is that an object has a natural force tendency and will manifest it unless overcome by either steady or onset impingement with a more forceful object from outside" (8). This does not mean that objects in the physical world actually have such tendencies, but only that human categorisation of the physical world naturally ascribes such tendencies to objects. Like image-schemata, force-dynamics are applied to different cognitive and conceptual domains. The movement of humans, and possibly of animals as well, is understood as driven by psychological forces (forces driving the otherwise inert body in a given direction). The notions of both *agency* and *intentionality* are unthinkable without a force-dynamic schema connecting psychological force with physical objects. Animate action is understood as a result of psychological force, but even in the purely psychological domain, notions like "wills can clash" or "I must restrain myself" yield an understanding of the interaction of psychological force taken from naive physics (16ff). This also applies to the social domain according to which "governments can exert pressure on labour unions" or "a carnival will ease the popular pressure". In these cases we have force-dynamic relations mapped from the physical domain, via the psychological or mental domain (making social entities sentient actors), to the social domain, yielding an understanding of relations of power in terms of physical force to name but one example (21ff). Further, Eve Sweetser (1995) has shown that this even applies to the epistemic domain. Knowledge is seen as an exerting force, as in "these results *force* us to revise our theory" or "I feel *attracted* to a realistic philosophy".

In bodily experience, image-schemata and force-dynamics are interwoven. All schemata involve notions of relations of forces (thus a CONTAINER will have a border that one must exert some force to overcome), and all exertion of force will have a schematic quality organising the spatial relation among the parts. Further, force-dynamics are an essential part of all causal scenarios used to distinguish important from unimportant parts of a given scenario. Elements exerting or resisting force will be judged as more important than elements that do not, and primary among these are the exertion of psychological force, i.e. intention. This allows what Talmy has referred to as the "windowing of attention", by which humans parse event-structures into their most relevant dynamic aspects and leave out the rest, affecting both memory and linguistic encoding (Talmy 2000).

The intimate connection between force-dynamics and image-schematic structures raises a fundamental question about the representational format of these very basic structures. As mentioned above, image-schemata are understood as non-propositional, analogue representations of spatial relations, cross-modal in nature and extended to other cognitive domains. Representations of force, however, seem to be both directly experienced in physical and perceptual interaction with the world and are intimately connected to our categorisation of objects in the world. Further, representations of force are directly constrained by the ontological categorisation of objects possessing the force. Not all objects are understood to be able to exert force by themselves, and different ontological domains have specific force-dynamic properties.

Thus, the domain-general approach must be supplemented by the domain-specific approach. The question is, how we reconcile these two lines of cognitive research? I propose to understand the two perspectives as describing two general 'cognitive strategies' interacting in basic-level categorisation:

Domain-general features:
- Basic-level categorisation, based on the bodily interaction with the world and the formation of perceptual gestalts; taking place on the generic level of categorisation, and strongly related to motor interaction structures.
- Image-schemata, structuring spatial relations between and movements of entities by dynamic schematism, allowing schematic manipulation and transformations, and imposing inferential constraints and potential; non-propositional and analogue in format.
- Force-dynamics, embedding the image-schematic structures in a field of force and resistance, and placing agency in chains of action.
- Psychological essentialism, ascribing hidden properties to entities as a defining character.

Domain-specific features:
- Instantiations of image-schemata, force-dynamics and psychological essentialism in pre-specified ontological domains, making specific forms apply to each ontological domain in a prototypical fashion.
- Domain-specific types of causality determining causal expectations to entities in relations to specific ontological domains.
- Domain-specific types of agency based on implicit assumptions about the possibility and form of agency in each ontological domain.
- Predicate structure entailing implicit judgements of possible properties of entities belonging to the separate domains, and giving rise to propositional models or schemata.

How this double structure, combining domain-general and domain-specific features in categorisation, can be modelled in a realistic description of the brain, and whether any of the two is primary, is both beyond the scope of this book and the competence of its author.[5] Both approaches to categorisation, however, are necessary in order to explain higher-level cognitive mechanisms such as conceptualisation and conceptual mapping. Domain-specific cognitive mechanisms create highly structured expectations to and knowledge about entities in the world, and potentiate learning by informational constraints. Thereby the problem of induction is avoided by the application of pre-specified constraints on the relevance of different parts of the perceptual and conceptual input. But without domain-general structures, the human cognitive system would be extremely inflexible. Some domain-general features (image-schemata, force-dynamics, and psychological essentialism) have domain-specific instantiations and this entails that a similar representational format is present between different ontological domains, enabling conceptual mapping. This gives the cognitive system the flexibility not present in a purely domain-specific account, by facilitating transfer of inferential structures between both ontological and conceptual domains.

There is, however, a second line dividing both domain-general and domain-specific accounts of categorisation. It separates theories of categorisation based on external features and perceptual similarity (Mandler 1992), and categorisation based on intrinsic properties represented by the mechanism of psychological essentialism and theory-driven categorisation (Medin & Ortony 1989; McCauley 1987). Again, both mechanisms are necessary in forming a complete picture of human categorisation. Combining external perceptual similarity and internal theory-driven essentialism is a perfect combined strategy when categorising the world. Categorisation by perceptual similarity ensures an embodied dimension of categories by its reliance on the human perceptual system and the physical interaction with the world. Thus, categorisation will retain a situated and motivated character. Such categorisation, however, runs the risks of being extremely unstable in changing perceptual environments and by changing motivated interaction. Psychological essentialism and theory-driven categorisation ensures a stability of basic categories by ascribing essential qualities to its members thereby facilitating propositional reasoning.[6] Besides, as we saw in the treatment of the social domain, there is a complex interaction between external appearance on the one side, and judgements of internal essence, on the other—a balance properly determined by the ontological domain in question. In the biological domain, psychological essentialism is very strong, and judgements based on similarity relative weaker. In the physical domain, artefacts, especially tools, are predominantly judged on external qualities, such as function and look, with only a very weak essence ascribed. Using the terminology of C. S. Peirce (1931) this can be described as an alternation between iconic and indexical interpretations of objects as signs. Where iconic interpretations are based primarily on the recognition of perceptual similarity and identity, indexical interpretations use the same perceptual features as indices of underlying essences or traits. For example, a specific coughing can be an indicator leading to the general diagnosis of a sore throat. The importance in this context lies in the intimate relation between the two types of reasoning. Indexical signs incorporate iconic aspects by the automatic ascription of a causal connection between perceptual features and inner essence. Iconic representations, on the other hand, often entail the ascription of common essence or even identity between objects with the same perceptual features. As we will see later on, both structures are crucial in the study of magic. External perceptual qualities (similarity) and internal essence (a prerequisite for contagion) alike are actively used in magical actions. All this will be developed in depth below, but first we must look at the integration of both domain-specific and domain-general properties in concepts and conceptual domains.

3.2. Conceptual Structures, Cultural Models and Event-frames

As mentioned above, human experience and conceptualisation are never domain-specific in the ontological sense. When individuals move around, solve problems, interact with each other or attend works of imagination, like stories, paintings and music, different domain-specific and domain-general properties of cognition interact, without the individuals doing any conscious mental work or even noticing it. Many experiences and experience-based conceptual domains might involve strong emphasis on knowledge from one particular ontological domain (e.g. physical, when playing pool), but emphasis might shift and knowledge from other domains take over or influence actions at any time (e.g. loosing deliberately in order to gain other goals). Similarly, most of our concepts, both basic-level, more complex and abstract, are used in all kinds of different situations and are seldom tied to specific ontological domains, but defined relative to cognitive models applied to pragmatic situations. Therefore, conceptual structures are complex and dependent on several formative mechanisms building on and extending properties of both domain-specific and domain-general categorisation on the one hand, and pragmatic situations and cultural definitions on the other. They have a double nature, as they are constrained by cognitive mechanisms, and at the same time are informed by cultural pragmatics and semantic configurations. Three types of conceptual structures are relevant in the analysis of magic. First, concepts are formed by a selective process based on motivated usage and interaction. Second, conceptual structures give rise to and are dependent on entrenched cultural models. Third, concepts are related to event-frames that organise the temporal aspects of given concepts.

3.2.1 Idealised Cognitive Models

In *Women, Fire, and Dangerous Things*, George Lakoff argues that concepts are best understood as part of more encompassing Idealised Cognitive Models (ICM). An ICM consists of at least four structuring elements: (1) Propositional structures specifying properties, elements and relations between them in a specific domain. (2) Image-schematic structures that specify the schematic properties of the elements involved. (3) Metaphoric structures, which consist in mappings of propositional or image-schematic models from another domain. (4) Metonymic structures connecting one part of the models to another. To exemplify this we can take the Trobriand Islanders model of "gardening" (Malinowski 1935a, 1935b; Hutchins 1980). As we shall see in the coming chapters, the Trobrianders not only have propositional models defining garden instruments by their function, but also image-schematic models relating these functions to a wider set of schematic properties, metaphoric models relating the garden to several other domains (e.g. the sea), and metonymic models using one element in the garden to represent the whole domain (e.g. the axe used in rituals). The concept of "garden" cannot be defined by necessary and sufficient conditions but must instead be described as consisting of several models and structures delineating the domain in an experientially relevant way. ICMs are thus motivated models that employ both metaphoric and metonymic extensions in order to structure the concept as it is utilised in interacting with the social and physical world. This has great importance for the study of magical ritual, as the ritual framing ensures that metaphoric and metonymic aspects are highlighted in order to promote the representation of basic schematic structures.

3.2.2 Cultural Models

The Trobriand example of "garden" also illustrates that many, if not most, ICMs are not individual constructs, but are shared models, more or less widely distributed within a given cultural environment. Such widely shared cognitive models are known as cultural models. In order to avoid misunderstandings I need to discuss this notion in some detail. The notion was most precisely elaborated in the volume *Cultural Models in Language and Thought* edited by D. Holland and N. Quinn. The basic theory is that cultural presuppositions and other kinds of cultural knowledge have the form of idealised models and that they have a great impact on human understanding in all domains of experience. Cultural models will spread out on a continuum between accessibility and inaccessibility to people entertaining them, and their relation to behaviour is complex, both on a purely cognitive level (from external model to mental representation) and on a cognitive-cultural level. They relate to types of authority representing the models, different types of discourse and different pragmatic or performative repertoires (Quinn & Holland 1987). In his 1996 book *Culture in Mind* anthropologist Bradd Shore distinguish between types of cultural models: instituted and mental.

> Instituted models are the public life of culture, empirically observable social institutions that are available as resources for a community. Mental models, by contrast, are cognitive representations of these instituted models but are not

simply direct mental mappings of social institutions. The complex relationship between mental and instituted models defines what I have termed the "twice-born character" of cultural forms (Shore 1996: 68).

Shore's notion of the "twice born character" of cultural forms equals the relationship between material crystallisations and pre-established configurations of meaning on the one hand, and the motivated use and appropriation of such external models by individuals, on the other. It also implies a distributed view of human cognition according to which cultural artefacts are seen as extensions of human cognitive capacities often related to shifts in modality of interaction (Hutchins 1994).

Theories of cultural models have been criticised by several scholars. Pascal Boyer finds two basic problems. First, theories of cultural models do not account for how an ideal or non-material construct—the cultural model—gets a material instantiation in the brains of members of a given culture (Boyer 1994: 87). This argument relates to Boyer's more general criticism of (the lack of) anthropological theories of transmission of knowledge. Second, cultural models, if understood as deductive models determining the behaviour of individual members of a given culture, do not fit anthropological findings (198ff). Concerning the first argument, cultural models should not be understood as free-floating idealistic constructs. They are physically instantiated in materials influencing various perceptual modalities, such as vision (pictures) and hearing (language), and in the neural and chemico-electrical states of the brains belonging to individual members of the society in question. Certainly, theories of cultural models propose no explicit theory of the exact ways materials get transformed into neural (material) activity. Rather, they postulate that structures of meaning are preserved through this transformation to a certain degree, and that cultures differ as to the style, pragmatic setting and conventional mappings used to create different conceptual models. In fact, without this notion of a higher or lower degree of meaning preservation through material transformations the whole idea of writing down scientific results, in order for other people to understand them, would be futile. The impact on individuals' conceptual structure by the recurrence of similar external meaning configurations (by a significant number of other people communicating or in several material crystallisations), and the usage of culturally constructed systems of conventional symbols (like written language), can be used as an argument for a notion of *cultural* as opposed to purely cognitive or mental models. This, of course, does not imply that these models are not constrained by deep-level cognitive structures as described by Boyer. It merely questions whether cognitive constraints in the individual are enough to explain the recurrence of specific conceptual structures, or whether they must be supplemented with a theory of cultural models as culturally preconfigured structures of meaning.

Boyer's second argument concerning the deductive character of cultural models is obviously true, and ought to convince anybody actually holding the position that cultural models are deductive frameworks. Given the line of reasoning above, I subscribe to the idea of abductive reasoning supported elsewhere by Boyer, according to which cultural models are *possible* frameworks for action, interpretation and production of meaning applied in each situation as an available and manipulable model. An example could be the prevalence of vulgarised Freudian concepts in cultures in the Western Hemisphere. I could use such Freudian concepts as the 'id' or the 'unconscious' to explain actions by a friend (A). I might act in specific ways accordingly and produce utterances informed by these concepts. However, another friend (B) might disagree in a fundamental way to my Freudian interpretation of the actions of A, even though he *understands* what the model is about. Instead he might explain A's actions by reference to another, say a Christian model of the temptation of the flesh. Thus competing cultural models can be used to refer to the same situation. The abductive character of the models implies that a specific situation will be interpreted by means of a given model *as if* the model would yield the situation in a deductive manner. In my constructed example, both the Freudian and the Christian model deductively predict the actions of my friend (A), even though the actual reasoning goes in the opposite direction, from a single situation seen as a sign of a more global model. This illustrates how abductive reasoning combines induction (from instance to hypothesis) and deduction (from hypothesis to instance) thereby creating a qualified guess. The hypothetical character of instantiations of cultural models entails that new information about the situation can alter the appropriateness of a given model, creating a new search for a culturally appropriate model.

Closely related to the notion of cultural models is 'symbol' as a conventional and habitual structure of signs (Peirce 1931).[7] Thus, internal structure and relations between ontological and conceptual domains are not constructed only by icons, based on similarity, and by indices, based on the causal relation between perceptual features and inner essence, but also by symbolic connections based on pre-established cultural models. The mappings explicit in Trobriand gardening are symbolic by reference to culturally specified conceptual connections. It is crucial to recognise that symbolic connections always contain both iconic and indexical connections that specify the exact mappings between two domains. But icons and indices cannot by themselves explain the appearance of some and not other conceptual mappings, as they express an almost infinite number of possible connections. All things can in theory resemble or be like any other. The constraining factor needed is symbolic, based on conventional reference, and determined by cultural habit and tradition.

3.2.3 Event-frames

The last aspect of conceptual domains that I want to treat in this context is the temporal aspect. Conceptual domains are not just structured by the internal relation of its concepts and possible metaphoric and metonymic connections. A very important aspect of a wide range of conceptual domains is that they have a more or less schematised structure guiding the expectations of a real-world, temporal unfolding of events within the domain. This resembles concepts of "scripts" proposed by Schank and Abelson (1977), "frame semantics" proposed by Fillmore (1982) and the notion of ICMs (Lakoff 1987). All argue that individual concepts must be understood relative to a model structuring the relations between several concepts. Concepts like 'Buyer' cannot be understood except by reference to what Fillmore calls a "commercial event scene" structuring the relations between concepts like 'Seller', 'Goods', 'Money', 'Spend' and 'Cost' in an event structure (Fillmore 1982). The conceptual elements, however, are not just related by the structure of the frame, but also by a temporal and dynamic unfolding of this structure. The Seller starts out with the Goods and end up with Money, and the Buyer start out with the Money and ends up with the Goods. Thus, mental representations of an Exchange are structured by a spatio-temporal schema that organises the relative positions of the Goods exchanged.

A very important component in such structures, besides the propositional models of single entities, is the image-schemata applied to the frame. This is evident in dramatic and narrative examples of exchanges with high stakes, as in drug-dealing, in hostage exchange or in sacrificial exchange with the gods. In all cases the relative spatial position of both goods and actors and the temporal unfolding of the exchange plays a significant role. Other kinds of frames are less dramatic but nonetheless structured by image-schemata. In this light, I believe that frames can be seen as miniature narratives governing expectations to real-world events, and they are structured in a prototypical way by image-schemata, by models determining relevant roles and by propositional models describing the content or value of these roles. Such *event-frames* are the conceptual level counterparts to the causal expectations implicit in the categorisation of entities as belonging to specific ontological domains. Event-frames will, of course, normally be dependent on the causal properties ascribed entities of the distinct domains, and will order and integrate the relations and connections between different causal principles. Typical actions include both agents, intentions and purposes, objects, forces, path-schemata and instruments including the implicit assumption connected to each of these, and all this is co-ordinated into one frame representing an event as a coherent temporal unfolding. This seems like a very complex representation. One of the prime candidates for a mechanism limiting the complexity of event structures is the windowing of attention described by Leonard Talmy (2000). According to Talmy, linguistic expression (and probably memory) will 'window' attention to the important parts of the event-frame, and ignore the rest. This might explain the universal human tendency to ascribe causal responsibility to a (super-)human agent for serious events and more or less ignore the exact nature of the causal link between the agent and the result. The existence of cultural models creating an idealised link between certain agents and certain events (e.g. between 'witches' and 'diseases') facilitates this windowing of attention. It also implies the implicit underdetermination of exact causal relations connecting a specific witch to a specific patient, leaving only the causal properties of the constituent entities ('witches' having belief-desire psychology and 'diseases' having mechanical causality). As we shall see in chapter 6, rituals are represented as a special type of event-frame, marked off from ordinary actions, and related to a whole network of other event-frames in which the ritual action takes place.

Cultural structures
cultural models
language & conceptual systems
pre-established configurations of meaning
pragmatic situations
conventional metaphors
symbolic structures
material crystallisations

Conceptualisation
concepts and conceptual domains
idealised cognitive models
frames and temporal unfolding
metaphoric and metonymic extensions
constructions of meaning

Categorisation

Domain-general properties	*Domain-specific properties*
gestalt perception	ontological domains
basic-level categorisation	domain-specific categorisation
image-schemata	image-schema instantiation
force-dynamics	essence instantiation
psychological essentialism	causal structure
iconic and indexical structures	types of agency

Table 3.1: Categorisation, Conceptualisation and Culture

To summarise, concepts and conceptual domains have a complex structure combining elements from many sources. At a basic level, conceptual domains incorporate *synchronic* representation, specifying the elements in the domain and their internal relations, and *diachronic* representations, specifying both temporal unfolding actions and participants' procedural knowledge of these actions. At a more general level, conceptualisation is understood as a convergence zone between universal cognitive mechanisms of categorisation on the one hand, and culturally pre-specified configurations of meaning on the other. This entails a notion of 'inheritance' according to which a conceptual domain will inherit cognitive constraints of both domain-specific and domain-general character, giving the domain a very rich structure. At the same time, however, cultural properties will influence conceptual domains to a substantial degree by their embedding in culturally specified systems of conventional symbols, material crystallisation, and pre-established configurations of meaning. Table 3.1 depicts conceptualisation as a zone of convergence between cognitive constraints and cultural influence. The lines dividing the conceptual level from both categorisation and cultural structure should not be understood as too rigid. There is probably no exact point at which conceptualisation takes over from categorisation but rather a continuum depending on several factors, notably cognitive development and contextual demand. Similarly, there is no absolute distinction between culture and conceptualisation as culture can only be understood as a conglomerate of internalised cultural models and externalised cognition. Therefore, the cultural level predominantly represents the individually experienced 'transcendence' of cultural forms, such as language and material culture but also pre-established conceptual structures.

We still miss a crucial description of how new conceptual domains arise in an interactive process that combines both conceptual and ontological domains and results in the creation of new meaning and new conceptual domains. Whereas most of the cognitive processes described above are concerned with cognitive constraints on categorisation and conceptualisation, we must now turn our attention to the cognitive mechanism underlying semantic and conceptual expansion and creativity.

3.3 Mapping, Mental Spaces and Conceptual Blending

Metaphorical projection is one of the basic mechanisms guiding the construction of complex concepts. Several theories seek to explain this phenomenon, whether it is called "analogy" (Gentner 1983; Holyoak & Thagard 1996; Shelley & Thagard 1996), or "metaphor" (Lakoff & Johnson 1980; Lakoff 1987; Johnson 1987). Common to these otherwise different or even contrasting approaches, is the recognition of the important role in cognition played by the projection of structures and elements between different domains of knowledge. One can understand cancer treatment in terms of an attack on a well-defended fort (Holyoak & Thagard 1996) or conceptualise an argument as a war including strategies, attacks and counterattacks (Lakoff & Johnson 1980). Lakoff and Johnson argue that metaphors are not mere stylistic functions of language, but point to a much more fundamental level of cognition in which metaphorical mapping is used to construct and structure conceptual domain and to project structures between domains. We construe arguments as war, love as a journey and theories as buildings, not to make superfluous stylistic expressions, but in order to understand a less ordered and more abstract domain by means of structures from a more ordered and more experientially concrete domain. Mappings are produced in order to create or extend meaning in a target domain by mobilising inferential structures from a source domain. This can be done in several ways, for instance by mapping a concrete domain onto a more abstract domain, or by mapping a dynamic onto a static domain. A couple in a "dead-end-relationship" (LOVE IS A JOURNEY) either have to "split up" ("leave the vehicle") or "go back" in order to find the "right track." These examples illustrate that the theory of conceptual mapping expressed in metaphor theory needs refinement. In a "dead-end-relationship," elements from both target domain ("relationship") and source domain ("a dead end") are blended in the linguistic expression that connects elements from both domains. This is not an exceptional example but an instance of a general tendency to mix aspects from two or more conceptual domains.

In order to tackle this and related problems linguist Gilles Fauconnier and literary scholar Mark Turner have proposed the theory of "conceptual blending". This cognitive theory solves some of the problems left over by conceptual theory of metaphor, specifically the existence of poly-directional mappings between domains, the common linguistic finding of integration of elements stemming from two conceptual domains into one mental scenario, and the problem posed by partial mapping between domains. As this theory is extensively utilised in the cognitive theory of magic presented in the following chapters, it must be discussed in some detail.

Conceptual blending is a more general theory supposed to encompass cases of metaphoric projection in a more comprehensive framework explaining all sorts of conceptual mappings. Forming a background to the theory of conceptual blending is the theory of "mental spaces" developed by Gilles Fauconnier (1994). The basic idea is that meaning is constructed and manipulated inside mental spaces and in mappings between such spaces:

> Mental spaces are small conceptual packets constructed as we think and talk, for purposes of local understanding and action. Mental spaces are very partial assemblies containing elements, and structured by frames and cognitive models (Fauconnier & Turner 1998: 137).

Mental spaces are distinguished from conceptual domains and cognitive models by their partial nature. They are not equal to specific conceptual domains, but activate elements and structures from these that are necessary for pragmatic and inferential reasons. Activation of elements, frames, or models of a given conceptual domain, facilitates the retrieval of additional elements from that particular domain should it prove necessary or convenient in a pragmatic situation. Mental spaces are thus primarily defined by their pragmatic or inferential utility and based on a degree of cognitive opportunism. In conceptual blending, elements and structures from two or more mental spaces are projected into a new space, a blended space, in which a new emergent structure can arise. The conceptual blending approach allows multiple mappings and projections into one blended space. At least four spaces are used in the model: (1) two input spaces with all relevant elements, frames and models, with some of these mapped from one input space onto a counterpart in the other input space; (2) a generic space accounting for the mappings between the two input spaces at a very abstract or fundamental level; and (3) the blended space, consisting of elements and structures projected from both input, and containing an emergent structure not present in any of the input spaces (Fauconnier 1997: Ch. 6; Fauconnier & Turner 1996, 1998: 136-42; Sweetser & Fauconnier 1996).

Usually, conceptual blending goes on unnoticed. It is part of our everyday cognitive apparatus, working on an unconscious level, and revealing itself only through explicit analysis or in extreme or non-conventional cases. There are different kinds of blending. In some cases, the structure found in the blend is projected from one domain, and only elements from the other (one-side topology network). This is the case in LOVE IS A JOURNEY where the blend is structured by the domain of journeys, and most of the elements come from the domain of love. Most conventional metaphors are one-sided topology networks as they are characterised by elements of a source-domain structuring the meaning of a target. In other cases structures are taken from both input domains, as in the case of the desktop interface of a computer, where some structures come from the physical desktop (folders, files, trashcans etc.) whereas others come from the domain of computer-interaction (buttons, marker, command-curtains) (Fauconnier & Turner 1998: 166-7). Yet others are based on a shared topology, in which the same frame structures all inputs, as when to temporal distant instances of the same type of event are directly matched (e.g. in attempts to break records in athletics). As we shall see in the following chapters, magical rituals exploits all kinds of topology networks in order to make different structural principles and frames interact in the ritual blend, even though one-sided topology networks are very prevalent.

The importance of blending does not lie in the fact that it combines structures and elements from several domains of experience, but that it facilitates the emergence of a new structure and new meaning not found in any of the domains and mental spaces. Fauconnier and Turner describe three principles that govern the creation of emergent structure in the blended space:

1. *Composition*. When elements from two different domains are projected into a blended conceptual space, new relations will emerge. We can bring together elements from domains that ordinarily never interact. Composition also facilitates the fusion of elements from two different spaces in a blended space. Thus an (mental) image of a centaur combines elements from the domain of horse and the domain of man and fuses them into one being with an emergent structure.

2. *Completion* is the recruitment of a structure not present in any of the input spaces. As we shall see in the analysis of magical rituals, the *structure* of ritual action cannot be described by reference to conceptual blending. The ritual structure (described in chapter 6) will be recruited in order to structure relations between elements in the blend.

3. *Elaboration* is the development of the blend through "imaginative mental simulation" (Fauconnier & Turner 1998). We can elaborate on our centaur blend by imagining greater details, and we can even imagine how the centaur will combine behavioural traits from the horse and man domain respectively. This points to the important fact that in "running the blend" we can recruit further elements from each of the input domains in questions in order to elaborate on the blend.

The emergent structure arising in the blend by virtue of these principles can result in the solidification of the blend into a new conceptual domain structured by its own frame and with specified elements and logical property. Therefore, blending plays a significant role in the formation of conceptual models, both in the form of metaphors, as described above, but also in non-metaphorical cases. New scientific disciplines, theories or areas of interest are excellent examples of such solidification. Thus, the finding of a new effect or new domain calls for explanation and models and structures from a known domain are mapped to elements in the new domain and both are projected into the blend creating an emergent structure that eventually can be experimentally tested (Fauconnier, 1997; for examples see Hesse, 1966). Such solidifying blends will have to withstand a very thorough elaboration in the process of constituting themselves as a separate domain of knowledge.

Besides such inferential qualities, blending can be used as a purely heuristic device, evident in teaching by analogies, as when the atom is equated with the solar system. Again, it is only a partial mapping of structure from the solar systems domain and entities from the atom domain. Planets are not (directly) influenced by quantum mechanics and electrons are not inhabited. The projections are partial and constrained by a heuristic motivation, and the blend will only survive as long as it serves its restricted heuristic purpose as its inferential potential is limited by unwanted feedback to any of the input spaces.

This heuristic principle points to one of the principles of blended spaces, namely that the elements in the blend are connected to their respective input spaces (Fauconnier & Turner 1998: 162-3). Blending is prototypically used to convey or create knowledge and information by transferring inferential structure between domains. All people with experience from teaching will know the importance of giving relevant examples and analogies in order to explain new areas (from the students' point of view). But as a dark side to this default understanding, blends can be deliberately obscure. As we shall see this is often the case in magical rituals that build on esoteric knowledge, in which access to one input domain will be restricted to certain individuals, thus leaving the whole blend opaque. Blends can be used to express relations of power and knowledge, and deliberate hindrance of access from the blended space to one of the input spaces might be a very important pragmatic strategy, not just in the context of religion and magic, but in all sorts of social contexts. Just think of scholars making farfetched or obscure blends, combining a domain most people know about with a deeply 'esoteric' domain, in an attempt to gain intellectual prestige by revealing the 'ignorance' of listeners. Thus, access from blended to input spaces might differ between participants according to pre-specified or emerging social positions. Blending as a cognitive strategy, however, is neutral to these matters. It can be used both as a heuristic device to enhance understanding and as a device to enhance personal power and prestige. The negative usage is to a certain extent parasitic on the positive usage because the blending procedure will not work but for the implicit understanding that there is something to be known—in principle the blend can be unfolded and reveal the secrets of the opaque input space.

Attention should also be drawn to the feedback of inferential structures from the blend back to the input spaces. Without this feedback effect the whole mechanism of blending would have limited cognitive advantage and merely fit the old view of metaphor as a purely stylistic procedure reserved for poets, and avoided in rational conversation and reasoning. Guided by its emergent structure, blends are generally constructed with the purpose to produce new inferential structures subsequently exported back to an input space (Fauconnier 1997). This is clearly evident in magical rituals in which blends are not only used to create new domains but to manipulate one domain by means of structures and elements of another. Elsewhere I have argued that the evolutionary origin of conceptual blending was most likely to be instrumental and practical (Sørensen 2005), a fact highlighting the importance of inferential feedback.

But how are input spaces connected in the first place? What cognitive mechanisms are responsible for relating aspects of two different conceptual domains to each other? Earlier in this chapter, I discussed how domain-general aspects, such as basic-level categorisation, image schematic structures, force-dynamics, and psychological essentialism, are important aspects of human cognition facilitating a common format or interface between different cognitive domains. These structures are all active in forming a generic space present as a cognitive background enabling the establishment of counterpart connections relating elements from different domains. Here I will draw the attention to three types of counterpart connections all of central importance to the study of conceptual blending of magical rituals and they will be discussed, both in relation to basic cognitive constraints found in the generic space, and to their semiotic aspects as different interpretations of signs.

1. Identity, Metonymy and Index.
This very important class of counterpart connectors facilitates the preservation of relations of identity and part-whole metonymy between different input spaces. If I claim that "the committee kept me in the dark in these matters" (Grady, Oakley, and Coulson 1999), there is a relation of identity connecting the 'I' belonging to the space of the committee, and the 'I' being kept in the dark (based on the SEEING IS KNOWING metaphor).

Often, however, the same person, object or event, will not appear in both input spaces, but instead be related to other entities by metonymic counterpart connectors. For instance, a flag can be a metonymic representation of a nation, in which case 'flag-burning' can be understood as a direct attack on a nation, because the nation and the flag is fused in the blend. If the flag's conventional, symbolic and arbitrary nature is emphasised thereby creating a conventional link such a fusion is precluded. As the example illustrates, understanding by metonymic links are dependent on background knowledge and beliefs linking the salient feature that is chosen as metonymy to the thing referred to as a whole.

Underlying connections of identity and metonymy we find the basic cognitive principle of psychological essentialism (Medin & Ortony 1989). Psychological essentialism ensures that persons and other elements 'remain the same' even if their outer perceptual features change considerably (e.g. with age). It also ensures that elements can partake in a common essence uniting elements across mental spaces. Thus ascription of essence ensures the permanence of elements across time and space guided and constrained by ontological assumption and causal expectations. As described in the section on domain-specific categorisation, essentialism is one of the methods used to retain consistency of both categories and individual elements. Two related features are of importance in relation to magic: (1) the connection between essentialist assumptions and *pars pro toto*-based metonymy, and (2) the possibility of transferring essence between elements or changing the essence of certain elements by metonymic connectors. Psychological studies indicate that metonymic relations, responsible for the transfer of essence between two elements, are extremely powerful cognitive principles at work in all cultural settings and responsible for the widespread belief in contagion (Rozin & Nemeroff 1990; Rozin et. al. 1992; Nemeroff & Rozin 1989, 2000). Metonymic relations and psychological essentialism are basic ingredients in beliefs in contagion—beliefs that are further strengthened by concrete physical contact. The relationship between nation and flag illustrates this point. The metonymic connection relating flag and nation is often developed through repetitive and ritualised actions of physical interaction between individuals and the flag as a representation of the nation, creating a motivated link between the two (e.g. in such acts as pledging). A strong metonymic link is established, as these actions would otherwise be meaningless. Directly presupposed in essentialist representations are two image-schemata: The CONTAINER schema implies that all elements ascribed some essence is understood as elements with an outside of perceptual features and an inside containing the essence. The LINK implies that some sort of connection exists between elements with common essence. These schematic implications of essentialist representations are important in explaining magical actions, as they inform how and to what extend essences can be transferred and manipulated.

In a semiotic perspective the metonymic counterpart connectors give rise to indexical interpretations because of the motivated character of the link between the part and the whole or the sign and the object of the sign. Peirce defines an index as a sign "which refers to an Object that it denotes by virtue of being really affected by that Object" (Peirce, 1931, II: 143). Several kinds of motivations allow metonymic extension to be interpreted as indices: Pragmatic, contextual, conventional, episodic and causal relations, can all motivate metonymic extensions. What happens in the example with the national flag is the transformation of a conventional symbolic sign, by which the flag refers to the nation by habit alone, into a motivated indexical sign, in which the flag is understood as an outward manifestation of the inner essence of the nation. As all symbolic signs contain both iconic and indexical elements, this transformation comes about quite easily by *de-emphasising* the symbolic and conventional aspects of the sign, where meaning is created through relations to other conventional symbols. Instead the direct perceptual and essentialist aspects are emphasised and the sign is understood as a (super-)natural and essential extension of the object. As we will see below, the transformation from symbolic into indexical and iconic interpretations of a sign will prove to be an important aspect of magical rituals as it facilitates ritual manipulation and transformation of persons, objects and actions.

2. Metaphor, Similarity and Icon.

This type of counterpart connector is based on the ability to categorise by motivated perceptual resemblance and entrenched experiential and conceptual association. Metaphor is the most common denominator of these similarity-based relations. Even though we find obvious cases of metaphors not based on any immediate similarity, *motivated* (in contrast to *natural*) resemblance still place a fundamental role in many metaphorical connections, especially as they are elaborated. In LOVE IS A JOURNEY the metaphor itself is not based on experiential correlation or direct perceptual similarity between the two domains. Still, single counterpart connections will often be constrained by either perceptual similarity or common category membership. Thus, 'lovers' maps onto 'travellers' and not 'road' or 'vehicle', by virtue of both roles matching self-propelled human agents driven by belief-desire psychology. Other metaphors describing the same target domain will make altogether different mappings. In the metaphor LOVE IS A PHYSICAL FORCE (Lakoff & Johnson 1980:49) (e.g. "I was drawn towards her") the counterpart mappings are based on the (image-schematic) similarity between human attraction, on the one hand, and mechanical force on the other. In this case, the human agent is mapped onto a physical object governed by mechanical causality and force-dynamic relations, and is therefore deprived of its role as an intentional agent. So, whereas LOVE IS A JOURNEY leaves the human agent in control and with inferential potentials based on the schemata of a journey, LOVE IS PHYSICAL ATTRACTION deprives the subject of intentionality and leaves it as object of physical force. The point of these examples is that even in conventional metaphors at least one counterpart connection will be based on either common category membership or perceptual similarity, ensuring a common standpoint or perspective on the subsequent unfolding of transferred inferential structure and related mappings. Thus, direct perceptual similarity plays a very important role as cross-space counterparts and examples are numerous. Similarity is important in all counterpart mappings constructed on-line without any conceptual entrenchment, and perceptual similarity is one of the major strategies for creating new counterpart connections.

It is important to notice that metaphors, besides their experiential, conceptual or perceptual entrenchment and motivation, will also be pragmatically motivated and constrained by communicative relevance. Calling an athlete "a real cheetah" will imply the mapping of speed from the feline to the human domain, whereas the same metaphor used about a woman at a nightclub will have somewhat different mappings and therefore a different meaning. In the generic space, the abstract features ensuring the counterpart mappings can be divided into two groups. The first group consists of deeply entrenched primary connections based on *experiential correlation*. Such primary metaphors are probably neurologically hardwired, or at least stored in long-term memory as stable connections (Grady 1997), and some conventional metaphors will be deeply entrenched in the cultural conceptual system as preconfigured relations between domains, transparent to members of that culture. The second group consists in *image-schemata*, *force-dynamics* and *basic-level categorisation*. Image-schematism and force-dynamics, as described in the first section of this chapter (6.1), are both cross-modal and domain-general mechanism facilitating connections between different domains and mental spaces. Mappings grounded in image-schemata connect otherwise disparate cognitive and conceptual domains, that could never be connected through metonymic extension. Image-schemata can model both the purely morphological features constituting elements in a general way as bounded objects in space with, for instance, UP-DOWN and CONTAINMENT structures, and the relation between elements in space, for instance in a PATH or REJECTION schema.

A problem is the precise delineation between metaphoric and metonymic connections. As described above, perceptual similarity is one of the important indications of essential identity used in human categorisation, which entails that metaphoric connections can transform into metonymic extensions. This is of great importance in the analysis of magic, as it is a common procedure to create metonymic links, able to transport essential qualities, through the establishment of similarity-based connections. Thus, similarity will be understood as an index of underlying essential identity, enabling manipulation of one object through a similar object. This is not a mysterious as it might sound, considering the double strategy of basic categorisation, using perceptual features, ontological assumptions and ascription of essence.

This leads us to the semiotic features of metaphoric counterpart connections. Understood as signs, the metaphoric connection between sign and referent leads to *iconic* interpretation by virtue of its reference to the object by some sort of similarity or by its functions as motivated images of what it describe. One could argue that primary and conventional metaphors cannot be understood as iconic as their construction are not based on similarity, and that they would more correctly be described as *symbols* defined by conventional reference to other symbols. But, as described above, most conventional metaphors contain at least one similarity-based counterpart connector, and even in cases with deeply entrenched primary metaphors, these will function as schemata structuring their target, and thereby construct an *experience* of similarity. So even if they are most precisely described as experiential or conventional symbols, they contain or construct iconic counterpart connections. Peirce defines an icon as "a sign which refers to the Object that it denotes merely by virtue of characters of its own, and which it possesses, just the same, whether any such Object actually exists or not." (Peirce 1931, II: 143). This may sound like a deterministic relation, but Peirce emphasises the motivated and relevance-based character of most icons: "Anything whatever, be it quality, existent Individual, or law, is an Icon of anything, in so far as it is like that thing and used as a sign of it (143)." Thus, no objective similarity defines iconic relations. It is the motivated interpretation of some element as similar to some other element that constitutes the icon.

The motivated character of similarity makes it quite easy to find iconic relations even in the most conventional symbols. In magic the purely symbolic or conventional part of metaphors used are *de-emphasised* or, in order to emphasise the iconic and indexical aspects, are primarily based on image-schemata, force-dynamics and psychological essentialism. This has important consequences for the relation of magical actions to religion understood as more or less coherent symbolic systems, a problem that will be treated in later chapters.

3. Role-Value:
The third type of counterpart connection is based on the existence of culturally defined frames specifying the relation among elements as functional *roles*. A specific person fulfilling the role of the priest is called a *value* of the role (Fauconnier 1997: 103, 106). We can distinguish three types of criteria determining the connection between role and person filling the role: formal, functional and essentialist criteria.

Formal criteria define the relation between role and value, as when the President of the United States is elected following precise formal criteria such as eligibility (US-born citizen), proceedings of voting, etc. One can say that this is a purely symbolic connection, as it depends on other symbolic constructions, such as the American Constitution, and the symbolic acceptance from a majority of the people that the formal criteria have been respected. But the example shows that formal criteria often are insufficient to describe the role-value connection. Even with roles as formally defined as President of the United States, the connection is judged by non-formal criteria as well, such as the ability to fulfil certain expectations related to the position.

This points to the *functional* criteria of role-value connections, which are based on external and perceptual factors such as appearance, actions and results. The impeachment case against President Clinton was an example of how formal and functional criteria might conflict. The case was rejected because of insufficient *formal* grounds for terminating the connection between role and value, but the case could be prolonged because of violations of the *functional* connection between role and value, according to which Clinton's actions were regarded as "unworthy of his position". The functional connection between role and value is iconic, as role and value is related through similarity of appearance, actions and results.

The third type of connector between role and value is based on the ascription of inner, *essential* qualities as a prerequisite for or result of filling out a role. This is a common characteristic of many positions in the religious domain, where individuals are understood as having a special essence that entitles them to a specific social position. All notions of occupational vocation, however, carry aspects of this essentialist understanding, according to which people are connected to certain social positions by virtue of an ascribed inner quality. In such cases the essence ascribed to the single individual must be the same as the one defining the role. In other cases, there is a "flow of essence" from the role to the value, as when the role of the presidency affects people's reactions to Clinton as a private person. This flow of essence is very strong in religion and magic, as positions usually will be judged as possessing some "sacred essence" (see Boyer 1994). In the following analysis of magical action, this feature is evident in some rituals believed to contain efficacy by reference to the special quality of the agent. All three types of role-value connectors are to a greater or lesser degree present in any specific linkage between a role and a value, no matter whether the external and public definition is strictly formal. The formal interpretation based on a symbolic network will seldom be sufficient in the judgement of a role-value connection, and both functional (iconic) and essential (indexical) criteria will be applied as well.

Besides the elements generated by the character of the role-value link, such as image-schemata and psychological essence, the elements in the generic space common for both role and value will be highly general and abstract representations of common category membership, such as Agency, Action, and Object. These will be constrained by the categorisation of the role as belonging to a certain ontological domain, leading to assumptions about types of agency and causal expectations.

I will end this chapter with a summary of the elements of conceptual blending described above:

*Input Space*s are temporary mental and discursive constructs that consist of elements, persons, objects, actions and events, constrained by presuppositions and assumptions from basic categorisation (including both domain-general and domain-specific assumptions), and structured in idealised cognitive models. Counterpart connectors map single elements, frames and models in the respective spaces. Some elements, frames and models of the input spaces will be projected into the blended space. Thus a partial projection from the input spaces creates a new, blended space.

A *Blended Space* is a temporary mental and discursive construct, in which elements and structures projected from each input space can be combined in a novel way resulting in an emergent structure. Three principles are responsible for the construction of this emergent structure: Composition, Completion and Elaboration. The selected projection of elements and frames from the input spaces results in a topological structure that determines the relation between the blend and the input spaces, and constrains potential inferential feed-back from the blend to the input spaces. A blended space may solidify and become a conventional mapping or even a conceptual domain.

A *Generic Space* is a temporary mental construct, in which the abstract properties enabling the construction of counterpart connections between elements in the input spaces are represented. The most important elements are psychological essentialism, image-schemata, force-dynamics, experiential correlation and common abstract categories, such as Agency, Action and Object, constrained by both domain-specific and domain-general features. Thus the elements of the generic space all originate in deep level cognitive processing active in human categorisation.

Counterpart Connectors are, contrary to the generic space, constrained by pragmatic and conceptual features such as motivation, relevance and convention. The connectors relevant for the analysis of magical rituals can be broadly distinguished into three types. (a) The first contains connectors based on identity and metonymic extension, enabled by psychological essentialism in the generic space, and having a semiotic expression in indexical signs. (b) The second type is connectors based on metaphoric, analogical and similarity-based mapping, enabled by generic space image-schemata, force-dynamics, basic-level categorisation, and experiential correlation, and expressed in iconic signs. (c) The third type is role-value connections, based on formal symbolic, functional iconic, and essential indexical relations.

Notes

1. See Boyer (1996) for the notion of religion as an impure object. The review article is a part of an illuminating debate between Boyer and Malley concerning the possibility of systems level explanation of order in religious systems (Malley 1995, 1997).

2. See also Brugman (1988) and Kreitzer (1997).

3. An important feature of the CONTAINMENT schema in this context is its potential to delineate time as a bounded space, by virtue of the very basic metaphorical mapping from space to time. This is crucial in the performance of rituals, where both space and time as understood as bounded areas or objects containing special qualities, and where the transgression of these borders are marked by elaborate rituals (see van Gennep 1909, Turner, 1969, Leach 1976).

4. An excellent example is the construction of domestic, agricultural, ritual, and cosmological space by common schematic structures, as demonstrated by anthropologist William Hanks in his work on the relation between language and conception of space among the Maya Indians of Yucatan (1984, 1990).

5. Recent development in connectionist modelling looks promising in this regard in two ways. First, inborn proclivities to categorise in a specific way can be build into the system as weighted biases constraining the development of the connectionist system. Second, connectionist modelling might also explain the emergence of encapsulated domain-specific processing by the specialisation of neural network during learning. This is what Karmiloff-Smith refers to as "modularization" (Karmiloff-Smith, 1995: Ch. 8).

6. Keil (1987) has proposed a developmental shift in types of categorisation from "characteristic-to-defining" in children. This indicates a developmental change in the weight played by the two cognitive approaches to basic categorisation.

7. The concept of 'symbol' should here be understood opposite the understanding of Sperber (1975). Whereas Sperber understands symbols and symbolicity as an independent and partly irrational cognitive mechanism attaching meaning to otherwise meaningless signs, 'symbol' used in this book follows C. S. Peirce (1931) in referring to the conventional, lawful and habitual application of signs to entities in the world, by reference to cognitive models and conceptual structure. It is in this last sense that the word will be used in this book.

4
Magical Rituals and Conceptual Blending

The rather technical discussion of cognitive theories in the previous chapter has supplied the necessary building blocks to develop a cognitive theory of magic. A basic claim in this book is that ritual in general and magical rituals in particular involve conceptual blending, but blending theory must be expanded and supplemented by other cognitive theories in order to explain magic.[1] In this chapter I will expand the model to cover a very broad range of perceptual modalities united in a solidified domain of 'ritual'. I agree with Lawson and McCauley that participants represent religious rituals as an independent type of action, forming a special domain involving certain expectations and formal constraints (Lawson & McCauley 1990). At a general level, religious and magical rituals involve a blended space consisting of elements projected from input spaces themselves created by elements from two general domains—'sacred' and 'profane'—and structured by a ritual frame.

As the concepts of sacred and profane have a long history in both the study of religion and anthropology (Anttonen 1992, 2002), I find it necessary to explain what I mean by these terms. 'Sacred domain' refers to a conceptual domain containing concepts, frames, idealised cognitive models, and knowledge that *by participants* are given a special status as: (1) containing a breach of ordinary ontologies, properties and/or abilities, (2) being connected to fundamental myths and narratives explaining the creation and/or the nature of the world and its relations, and (3) being interpreted as belonging to a distinct part of reality that one must perform special kinds of actions in order to interact with. The sacred domain thus involves special beings violating ordinary ontological assumptions, special and privileged discursive repertoires, and special modes of interaction. This notion of a sacred domain is closely related to how religious categories are constructed. Following Boyer (1994, 2001), religious concepts are based on a combination of intuitive and counter-intuitive properties that enhance memorability and transmission, and sets them apart form other concepts.

At this point it is crucial to recognise that the sacred domain is not a logically consistent system of representations, but rather a formation of coherent structures around pragmatic styles, like narratives and rituals, pre-established conceptual clusters and modes of behavioural interaction, such as ritual actions. Theologians around the world attempt the construction of consistent theological systems, but, in general, people's religious representations are not systematised and will often contain contradictory ideas.

The 'profane domain', on the other hand, contains concepts, frames, and idealised cognitive models that structure our knowledge of the everyday world we live in. As it should be clear from the analysis in the preceding chapter, such knowledge includes both culture-independent, universal assumptions and schemata taken from basic-level categorisations of the world, as well as culture-specific cultural models extending this basic categorisation by metaphor and metonymy, creating conceptual structures specific for every cultural system.

What is important in this context is the fact that religious concepts are used in rituals in order to create notions of ritual efficacy by connecting them to elements from the profane, everyday world. In magical rituals, elements of the sacred and the profane domain can interact and thereby facilitate ritual manipulation of aspects of reality otherwise beyond reach. Therefore, the division between the sacred and the profane domains should not be seen as too rigid. Some concepts, models and frames contain elements belonging to both domains and thus form conceptually entrenched connections between the two. Further, ritual participants do not move into or directly manipulate a sacred space as such, but rather interact with a locally constructed blended space consisting of a mixture of sacred and profane elements giving rise to an emergent structure. This might happen any time and place prompted by any kind of object, person or event. It will only be limited (but not determined) by (1) acceptable pragmatic and behavioural repertoires present in a given cultural and historical setting that organise and authorise ritual blends, and (2) the cultural conceptual system with its pre-established links between the profane and the sacred domain. This entails the hypothesis that ritual is a universally recognised behavioural modality structured by certain principles and that religious and magical rituals are recognised by the interaction between the profane and the sacred domain. One of these principles is the presence of *action* in all rituals, which entails a mental representation, such as the "action representation schema" of Lawson and McCauley (1990), and the necessary involvement of certain functional roles such as Agent and Action and, possibly, Objects, Patient and Participants. Other less crucial candidates as principles of ritual structure will be things like *formality*, *invariance* (Rappaport 1999) and *recursion*. How rituals deviate from ordinary modes of actions will be analysed in chapter 6. Here it suffices to state that such ritual principles are used to construct the frame subsequently used to structure the conceptual blend of elements from the sacred and the profane domain. Thus, the ritual frame itself should not be understood as stemming from either of the input domains, but as a frame applied to the blend structuring a specific interaction between the sacred and the profane domain as a ritual interaction.

4.1. Magical Agency and the *Genetic* Blend

Even though magical rituals can be understood as a particular kind of instrumental action aimed to have an effect on the surrounding world, it is obvious for everyone, both performer and observer, that it obtains this efficacy in a special way. As we shall see in chapter 6, the process of ritualisation produces a displacement of agency and intentionality, and this provokes a search for another source of agency in the ritual. The ritual must contain specific elements and, most notably, certain objects, actions or person(s) must be present in order for the ritual to work. This might be said of all types of action, but in rituals it is not obvious how these stipulated elements are related to the purported effects, and why specific elements are represented as crucial to this effect. Why a Catholic priest must be ordained and perform a specific performative utterance in order for the Eucharist to have an effect is not obvious in the same way as an agent, a stone and a window are all causally and intentionally related in the action of breaking a window. In magical rituals, at least one element will be invested with the *magical agency* necessary for the ritual to have any effect, and this agency is constructed by a mapping between the sacred and the profane domain.

By far the most important elements in the ascription of magical agency in rituals are Agent, Action and Object. These elements are basic to all sorts of actions, including actions performed in magical rituals. Combined, they constitute a schematic "action representation system" structuring the representation of an action as an experiential gestalt in the blend. This experiential gestalt is a necessary part of the ritual frame (Lawson & McCauley, 1990). What is of interest at this point, however, is the origin of each single element. This will give us a precise indication of the ascription of magical agency and efficacy, that is, the important element responsible for the transfer of power from the sacred to the blended space necessary in order to attain the change of state implied in the magical action.

4.1.1 Agent-based Agency

In this theoretical framework, *Agent* refers to the actual agent performing a magical ritual action. The actual agent must be distinguished from *magical agency* that refers to the active source of efficacy present in the ritual. This need not be invested in the agent performing the action and in some cases action or objects are represented to contain the magical agency necessary for the ritual to have effect, no matter who acts as the agent. Personalised magical agency, however, plays an important role, as persons are the prototypical wielders of agency in ordinary actions. In these cases the agent is the prime wielder of ritual efficacy, facilitating a transfer of essence between the sacred and the profane space, either through a role-value counterpart connection or through an identity connector.

If we take shamanistic practices as an example, a particular shaman is typically understood as a value filling the role of the general social category of 'shaman', as this is modelled in mythical narratives or other types of authoritative discourse. As described in the section on role-value connectors, a person can be said to fulfil a role on purely formal or symbolic ground (e.g. having performed a specific initiation ritual). As argued by Pascal Boyer, however, religious categories are often ascribed essential qualities so the person functioning as a value of a particular religious role will be understood as containing a special essence (Boyer 1993). This entails that both metaphoric and metonymic connections are established between the sacred and the profane space. The metaphoric or iconic connections relate the value to the role through interpreting specific external and functional features of this value (like appearance or external action) as reproductions of similar external features of mythical, ideal type shamans. Such iconic role-value connections are found in such things as ritual uniforms and pre-specified actions connecting the specific value with the general role. Appearance and action will not only connect the value to the role, but also to other individual instantiations of the role forming a class of instantiations. However, metaphoric connections are not sufficient. Anyone can dress up and act like a shaman without really being one and the *real* shaman can omit such outer paraphernalia. The genuine shaman is related by metonymic connections based upon the ascription of essential qualities relating the actual shaman to the sacred space role. This essence-based counterpart connection is evident in the numerous cases in which the possible agent of a magical ritual is constrained by hereditary rights. A genealogical line connects an individual to a specific social role by reference to an essence shared by people of a certain family or a hereditary clan. In the case of hereditary authority, the essence is seen as being shared by blood and sexual relations. But also in cases involving no such genealogical connections will there often be highly indexical signs, specifying the ascription and origin of ritual efficacy. Touching and similar direct or indirect physical interaction establishes metonymic links between an actual and a potential value (e.g. between a shaman and an apprentice), links that facilitate a flow of essential qualities. In this manner, the new value of a role is connected to former values of the role, creating a line of descent, possibly all the way back to the mythic times in which the first ritual specialists were given or acquired a connection to the sacred domain. Such 'pseudo-genealogical' lines of descent point to the intricate nature of indexical networks delegating ritual efficacy and flow of essence through numerous metonymic connectors.

As described in chapter 3, symbols, icons and indices all play a role in connecting a value with a role. Formal, functional and essential features are combined in instancing and confirming a given individual as a value of a social role.

In other cases, the relation between the agents of the two input spaces takes the form, not as a role-value connector, but as an *identity connector*. This is the case in temporary examples of possession, in which an agent belonging to the sacred space simply takes over the agent of the profane space. When performed inside the boundaries of the ritual, it is an example of institutionalised identity connectors. However, notions of possession and identity, connecting agents in the two spaces, are not restricted to such controlled conditions. Possession by gods, demons or other 'sacred' agents may be a prolonged affair and can exist outside (authorised) ritual structures. Eventually, humans or other possible agents can be understood as genuine incarnations of gods, demons or spirits. In relation to magical rituals, such non-institutionalised identity connections between the sacred and the profane space have two interconnected entailments. (1) It places a heavy emphasis on the belief in the ritual agent, that is, on the credibility of the identity connector. Such credibility can be established through the performance of magical or miraculous actions that function as indices to the sacred identity of the agent. This gives the whole thing a circular appearance as the identity and power of the agent guarantees the efficacy of the magical performance, and at the same time these performances are seen as indices of the identity connector. The magician can work miracles because he is a magician and he is a magician because he can work miracles. This points to the abductive character of the reasoning involved, combining perceptual features and ascribed essence in categorisation. (2) Given credibility, the identity connector can give rise to new ritual forms, thereby forming new ritual traditions. This has great importance in the dynamic relation between representations of ritual efficacy and social and institutional morphology. This will be further treated in chapter 7.

In all cases involving ascription of magical agency to the actual agent of the ritual action, psychological essentialism is the primary generic space category underlying the connection. Formal (symbolic) or functional (iconic) connections, established through entrenched conceptual connections or image schemata, might strengthen the connection, but the main characteristics of representations of efficacy of ritual agents derive from their sharing of a common essential quality relating the profane to the sacred domain. They must be made of 'the right stuff'. Iconic and symbolic connections will eventually be interpreted as indices of a metonymic connection based on common essence, all pointing to the special qualities of the ritual agent.

4.1.2 Action-based Agency

In other cases *Action* is the primary element containing magical agency. By Action, I mean a pre-specified sequence of motor behaviour believed to create a specific result by virtue of being a reproduction of a similar sequence of action ascribed to the sacred space. This sacred space paragon is expressed in places like mythic narratives or dogmatic treatises, giving rise to ritual frames specifying the content of specific ritual actions. Thus, in an ideal scenario, it does not matter who the agents, objects and participants are. As long as the ritual action is correctly performed, the desired result will follow. The efficacious sequence of action is often not the same as the ritual structure taken as a whole. It might only be a subsection of the ritual action believed to contain the actual efficacy, whereas other parts will have other ritual functions. Embedding the action in a larger ritual structure indicates the procedural character of both the ritual frame as a whole and of the specific part containing the ritual agency. The procedural character of ritual actions insures that they can be acquired without any specified semantic interpretation (cf. Humphrey & Laidlaw 1994). An important feature of action-based agency confirms this: the efficacy of the actions does not lie in their instrumental or direct perceptual effect, but in the similarity to actions ascribed to the sacred space. This similarity ensures the connection between the ritual action performed and the desired effect of the action, despite their lack of perceptual or causal connections. In fact, the procedural character of such actions, devoid of direct ascription of both symbolic meaning and direct instrumental causality, is an important part of the general tendency in magical rituals to de-emphasise symbolic interpretations. These are replaced with connections transferring ritual efficacy through iconic and indexical relations.

Strengthening this tendency, a very important aspect of action-based ritual agency lies in the use of spells and formulas in magical rituals. The more general use of various linguistic effects and mechanisms in the creation and performance of magical rituals will be further treated in the end of this chapter. In this context, it is important to recognise that spells and formulas are a special kind of speech-acts, believed to establish or create a desired state of affairs by their performative power alone, or by coercing supernatural powers to produce it (Austin 1967, Tambiah 1979, 1985). Besides ordinary illocutionary speech-acts working by combining semantic and contextual features, many magical spells deliberately exploit non-sensical or archaic word-forms, almost totally devoid of any semantic or direct referential function for the individuals participating in the ritual (Tambiah 1968, 1985). There is, of course, a significant difference in the perception and understanding of such ritualised language depending on the role in the ritual filled by an individual. Some individuals will know the meaning, others will not. In some cases, however, even ritual specialists do not understand, or have only superficial understanding, of the meaning of words used in ritual sequences. By de-emphasising the possibility of symbolic interpretation, the words are stripped down to an identity or similarity connection to the sacred space, ensuring the transfer of magical agency. This is marked by diverse iconic elements in the utterance itself, such as prosody, intonation, and iteration—all elements prolific in ritual language in general.[2]

What these special kinds of speech-acts have in common with ritual action is their use of elements with neither direct communicative effect nor symbolic content. The relation between 'non-semantic' or de-symbolised usage of words and ordinary, profane usage of words corresponds directly to the relation between efficacious ritual action and ordinary instrumental action. In both cases the possibility of symbolic or direct instrumental (causal) interpretations of the action is de-emphasised, and there seems to be no direct semantic or instrumental connection between the action and the desired state of affairs they are believed to cause. Instead, through imitative reproduction, they are connected to a similar action or utterance in the sacred space, facilitating the transfer of efficacy through an iconic link. So, whereas the agent-based agency results in an indexical interpretation of all iconic and symbolic signs confirming a common essence, the action-based agency results in an iconic interpretation of all symbolic and indexical signs confirming the resemblance or identity between the profane space performance and its sacred space counterpart. This does not mean that these rituals are devoid of metonymic and conventional reference. It only means that in the cognitive processing of the transfer of action-based agency, e.g. in a discussion as to whether a given ritual was correctly performed, all symbolic and indexical signs are evaluated on the basis of their similarity to the sacred space model. The instrumental efficacy of this type of magical ritual is based on interpreting perceptual indexes of single ritual actions as iconic reproductions of a similar action in the sacred space. Iconic connections subsequently authorise an indexical interpretation of the ritual as a whole, according to which the ritual has a causal connection to its overall result (i.e. the ritual produces a certain state of affairs). This can explain why the failure of a ritual to produce the desired result (an indexical relation) can be interpreted as the result of a failure to reproduce the ritual sequence correctly (an iconic relation).

4.1.3 Object-based Agency

Representations of object-based agency are widely spread in popular culture in notions of magical portion, swords and stones. Contrary to Agent-based agency, based on metonymic links and generic space essentialism, and to Action-based agency, based on perceptual similarity and generic space image-schemata, Object-based agency is based on both metonymic and metaphoric counterpart connections. There are several types of object-based agency, but common to them all is the notion that by virtue of a particular object, performing an action involving this object can create a given state of affairs.

The first kind of object-based agency involves objects containing ritual efficacy by virtue of origin. Being a part of or having touched an agent from the sacred space all enables the establishment of metonymic counterpart connections between the profane and the sacred space. This is the case in examples of religious relics believed to contain magical powers, for instance to heal. One could argue that this kind of object-based agency is parasitic to the agent-based agency, because the power ascribed to the object only exists because of its metonymic connection to an agent in the sacred space. Nevertheless, this kind of ritual agency should at least be analytically separated. It is an open question whether participants, in a given ritual using an object connected to a sacred agent, will have any representation of that agent as the efficacious agent, or whether the object *in itself* will be ascribed such agency by virtue of the metonymic connection. Like religious rituals, magical rituals can be embedded in each other, entailing that the agency or ritual power of a magical object is facilitated by another ritual changing the very essence of that object (Lawson & McCauley 1990). This points to the fact that metonymic connections, besides being facilitated by psychological essentialism, entail the generic space representation of a CONTAINER schema, connecting two elements as possible containers of a given essence. The CONTAINER schema ensures that essence, once transferred, can be retained and will remain inside the new object for some period of time. Presumably this is a feature somewhat dependent on other image schematic properties of the object in question. Thus objects can wield ritual agency by virtue of being containers of a given essence connecting them to the sacred domain. This will help explain why the origin of magical powers in objects is often not made explicit or even represented.

Other instances of object-based agency are not connected to any sacred agent, but are instead conceptualised as having magical potency by virtue of being a member of a certain category of magical objects. Brown (1985), working among the Aguaruna Indians of the Amazon, describes how certain stones are identified as magical. They are understood as belonging to one of three different exclusive classes of magical stones each with their own magical function. It is significant that no perceptual features distinguish them from other non-magical stones or even divide the three classes of magical stones. Instead they are identified according to two procedures. (1) According to the place they are found and where they are believed to have their origin. Certain perceptual qualities, not of the stone, but of its surroundings will be understood as indices of both the stones' essence and their origin. (2) Judgement of the magical performance of a specific stone, entailing an identification of whether a specific stone possesses a specific essence or not. This involves both indexical and iconic interpretations of perceptible features of actions involving the stone. Indexical in judging the outcome of a given endeavour as causally related to the essence of the stone (e.g. successful hunting), and iconic in comparing this indexical relation with the ideal model of a given type of sacred stones. It is important to notice that the judgement concerns the essential qualities of the stone, qualities believed to categorise the stone in an exclusive manner. The magical essence cannot be transferred, as the categories of stones are both exclusive and nonchangeable. Only the identification of the stones can change (Boyer 1994). Examples like these point to the importance of local conceptual structures identifying objects in the profane domain as really belonging to the sacred domain by extended and indirect perceptual indices and icons.

But how does this relate to basic domain-specific categorisation, with its intuitive ascription of ontological properties to material object? There are two compatible explanations. The first takes language as an example of the everyday character of ascription of agency and intentionality to material objects, as when people blame cars for not starting. Even if people do not believe objects to be intentional agents, they still *talk* as if they were. According to psycho-linguistic research, these expressions should not be understood as manifesting a system of belief in contrast to naive biology and naive physics, but rather as determined by situational factors: "[A]nimistic appraisals are most common and most persistent in connection with entities which are active, purposive, constitutionally complex, and causally enigmatic" (Cherry 1992). One might object that such linguistic phenomena do not tell us anything about the cognitive representations behind them. Even if this is the case, they do tell us something about the pragmatic circumstances in which animistic conceptions are more likely to be applied. The object will have a tendency to be ascribed non-mechanical agency due to both the special situation of magical rituals, and to special qualities of the objects used.

The second, and compatible, explanation argues that objects used in magical rituals are ascribed a certain number of counterintuitive properties, but that they actually uphold a number of intuitive properties as well (Boyer 1994). An Azande using magical medicine against a foe directs the inherent power of the medicine towards the target, in the same manner as when directing any other physical force based on mechanical causality towards a goal. In a number of ways he interacts with the medicine as with any other object. At the same time, properties of the objects clearly contradict very basic physical expectations. It understands vocal direction, it can act at distance, and it is even understood as having its own intentions (Evans-Pritchard 1929, 1937). The explicit combination of intuitive and counterintuitive properties in magical objects might be one of the reasons for the great proliferation of magical objects in all traditions and cultures. In contrast to agents and actions, objects easily change hands in economic transactions facilitating a spread of magical agency, possibly in opposition to institutionalised ritual efficacy. The counterintuitive content of such representation, however, can be further described as based on conceptual mappings from other domains, which, entails that *schematic* properties are transferred from other domains and used to make inferences about magical objects. Thus the Aguarunas have elaborate stories describing where and how one typically finds magical stones, and how these are to be kept, and all these things are intimately related to the counterintuitive properties of these stones (Brown 1985).

Finally, some objects are in possession of magical power solely by virtue of perceptual resemblance or similarity. Religious iconography, where icons are ascribed magical powers, is a prime example of this type of object-based agency. Pictures, statues and other material objects can obtain ritual efficacy simply by virtue of a similarity-based connection to elements in the sacred space. Again, this could be understood as parasitic upon the agent-based agency stemming from the sacred space. Once more I will uphold the analytic distinction because: (a) the object will be understood as a container able to retain the essence, at least for a period of time, but possibly for ever; and (b) icons will correspond not only to sacred *agents*, but also to objects, such as buildings or places, or to purely symbolic signs, such as geometric figures.

This representative function, based on perceptual resemblance, points to the complex problem of material (linguistic) signs used as objects in magical rituals, e.g. as amulets and talismans. Even though linguistic signs based on conventional reference are very common, purely iconic references are often exploited in material objects used as magical talismans or amulets. It can be drawings of a mythological scene, of a superhuman being, or even abstract geometrical figures representing divine structures.[3] In all cases, iconic reference, facilitated by image schematic structures in the generic space, establishes ritual agency by linking a profane object to the sacred space. Linguistic reference does play a significant role in talismans and amulets by facilitating the performance of ritual action through symbolic invocation of specific agents from the sacred domain. But as we have seen in the description of both agent-based, action-based, and the other types of object-based agency, purely symbolic, conventional connections are de-emphasised in magical rituals. They are replaced by iconic and indexical connections and interpretations based on basic cognitive mechanisms of perceptual similarity and ascription of essence. In most important aspects, the linguistic signs written on amulets and talismans have lost their symbolic reference. This is replaced with indexical references based on the conception of a direct connection between a given sign and its referent, in which the sign is seen as 'originating' from, or having 'power over' its referent. In this way, both symbolic and iconic signs can be understood as indexes—that is, as metonymic extensions of their referent. This is evident both in the widespread use of 'exotic' scripts in talismans and amulets (e.g. Egyptian hieroglyphs), but is also formalised in systematic elaborations of magic based on claims of an 'original' language in which words are perfect outer manifestations of the real nature of things and related by a causal structure (Ormsby-Lennon 1988).

In this presentation of object-based agency, I have not distinguished natural objects from artefacts. This is for two reasons. First, the distinction plays only a minor role in the ascription of magical agency. Magical agency ascribed to an artefact rests either on the assumption of a metonymic connection to its maker, belonging or connected to the sacred space, or on the ascription of magical agency to the original material from which the artefacts were made (or a combination of the two). Both falls within the mechanisms described above. Second, natural objects understood as wielders of magical agency will in fact be classified as instrumental objects, similar to artefacts. Thus both are capable of changing a state of affairs by virtue of functional qualities, even though the causal transparency of the change differs considerably. The degree of transparency, however, cannot in itself be the basis of a distinction between magical and non-magical objects, as humans use numerous artefacts with obscure causal relations to their result without ascription of magical agency.

To summarise, Agent, Action and Object are the basic constituents in the action representation schema utilised in magical rituals. Both situational and cultural differences influence what element is ascribed ritual efficacy or magical agency:

1. Agent-based agency appears in two forms: (a) as an integrated part of a role-value connection, based on formal, functional and essential criteria; (b) as a temporary or permanent possession establishing an identity connection between agents in the two spaces. In both cases, metonymic extension or identity will form the primary counterpart connection, enabled in the generic space by psychological essentialism and a CONTAINER schema ensuring the possibility of agents to contain essence. On a semiotic level of description, both symbolic and iconic signs are de-emphasised and instead interpreted as indices of an essential counterpart connection (e.g. the actions and formal status of Jesus as indices of his identity with Christ). This emphasis on indexical relations and de-emphasis of iconic and symbolic elements can give rise to new ritual forms.

2. Action-based agency depends on the notions that the more or less exact reproduction of a prescribed ritual sequence creates a connection between the sacred and the profane space. Thus, the important factor is the procedural unfolding of a ritual frame that precedes any semantic or causal interpretation of the action. Spells are included in this category as a special type of speech-act almost devoid of ordinary communicative function and symbolic content. Common for both are the metaphoric or iconic counterpart connections between sacred space frames and profane space instantiations. Generic space image-schemata and force-dynamics enable these counterpart connections. On a semiotic level, symbols are de-emphasised and indices are interpreted as space-internal relations having an iconic relationship to similar relations in the other space, e.g. ritual success (indexical) judged as a result of correct iconic replication. The emphasis on iconic relations and de-emphasis on symbolic and indexical relations enable import of ritual forms from other cultural and symbolic systems.

3. Object-based agency rests on the notion that an object can be responsible for the ritual efficacy, no matter who wields it, and almost in whatever manner it is wielded. Of course, magical objects have to be handled in a specific manner in order to work. This, however, does not distinguish them from ordinary instrumental artefacts. What I want to stress is the *non-formalised* character of action in which the primary agency is placed solely in the object. The investment of magical agency in objects can be based on both metonymic and similarity-based counterpart connections. Among the first are objects connected to a sacred agent, by *pars pro toto* metonymy or contagious transfer, and objects classified or identified as belonging to a conceptual class of magical objects. In both cases essentialism constitutes the most important generic space schema. Object agency based on connections of similarity rests on perceptual resemblance to agents or other elements in the sacred space, enabled by generic space image schemata and often entailing an automatic ascription of common essence. Again, the symbolic meaning of objects, specified through their symbolic relation to other symbols in systems of classification, is de-emphasised, strengthening both iconic

and indexical relations. The focus on both indexical and iconic interpretation of the object will enable both invention of new, and import of 'foreign' magical objects. Magical objects are in fact often subject to commercial exchange over socio-cultural borders (Evans-Pritchard 1929, 1937).

4.1.4 Time, Location and Participants

Although Agent, Action and Object are by far the most important ritual elements, the other parameters on the generic space list in fig. 4.1 will, to a varying degree, influence the ascription of magical agency. *Time* plays an important role in the performance of many magical rituals. Not only are religious festivals almost everywhere considered auspicious periods to perform magical rituals, but any other time spans can be understood as having a special quality, for instance, determined by astrological constellations. In both cases, a special period, ascribed sacred properties, is mapped onto the profane time in order to produce a ritual frame in which certain actions can be performed, that could not otherwise be (as successfully) performed. *Location* is also intimately connected to both magical and religious rituals. All over the world, certain physical locations are understood as sacred either as a permanent quality or by virtue of a mythic or a ritual action at a specific point in time effecting the sanctification of the place. Such more permanent locations may contain structures like temples, churches, shrines and mosques. Modern New Age beliefs in "vortexes", places on the earth emitting or receiving special or particularly strong energies, are based on a similar notion of a bounded area with a special quality allowing special kinds of actions and interaction. Sacred space can also be constructed each time a particular ritual is performed as an exact copy of the spatial relations in the sacred domain. William Hanks describes exactly such a procedure among the Maya Indians of Yucatan. Each time a ritual is performed an altar is constructed as an exact miniature model of the cosmological order (Hanks 1984, 1990). It is important to recognise that, as with religious festivals, the concrete physical location as a bounded space is itself a blend, in which the sacred and the profane space interacts. The special power of the place is, of course, a result of the contact with the sacred domain, but profane elements, like gravity, physical materials and so forth are still present. The elements of Time and Location refer to cases in which sacred periods of time or bounded physical areas are either a prerequisite of performing magical rituals, or elements that will endow the actions performed with extra force (cf. J. Z. Smith 1987).

The quality and status of *Participants* often play a secondary role in the establishment of magical agency. Participants in the ritual will not be the primary wielders of direct magical agency, but their special connection to the sacred space might be a prerequisite for the magical ritual to have any effect. This is most evident in negative examples, where magical rituals are judged as unsuccessful because of the presence of 'non-initiates' understood as blocking the connection to the sacred space. This is, of course, especially evident in esoteric or initiation-based groups, but is also common in the widespread notions of 'ritual cleansing'. Participants must bring themselves into the correct ritual state in order to promote or avoid being a hindrance to the connection to the sacred space. In some cases it will be profitable to distinguish between *Patient* and Participants. Compared to passive participants, the direct patient of a magical ritual might be subject to special ritual constraints in order to facilitate the transfer of agency from the sacred space. This difference is, however, more in degree than in kind.

Before turning to empirical examples of the three most important types of agency described above, a summary of these positions, as they are instantiated in a conceptual blend, is in place. Magical agency is established through a *genetic blend* that accounts for the origin of individual elements, frames and models present in any given magical ritual as the ascription of a specific origin of each element in the ritual space correlates with ascription of power and agency.

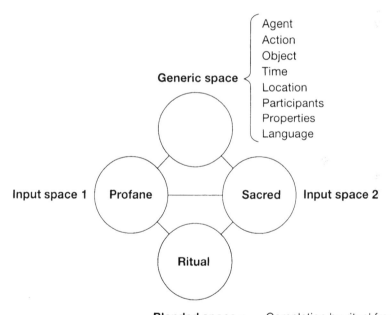

Figure 4.1: The genetic blend

Figure 4.1 is an abstract illustration of how a ritual space is constructed through the selective projection of elements from the input spaces into the blended space, which is then completed by the ritual frame. The input spaces are temporary spaces created from elements of the profane and the sacred domains respectively, and they are constrained by both pragmatic considerations and conceptual models. Pragmatic, in reference to the importance of the local purpose and motivation driving the specific ritual and the element present in it, and conceptual in reference to the pre-established conceptual connections that promote the evocation of whole conceptual clusters from a given domain. The elements in the generic space are described above as general instances that enable, but do not determine, the connection between elements of the profane and elements of the sacred space. It should be noted that in the following analysis of concrete magical rituals, the generic space will not only contain such abstract categories, but also image schemata, force-dynamics and psychological essentialism that specify each category and its respective mappings. As described above, all the elements listed in the box need not be present in any particular magical ritual. Rather, the ascription of magical agency will be constrained by both tradition and by pragmatic opportunism. Thus, even though a ritual tradition might delimit ascription of magical agency to a specific source, this will not mean that other types of agency cannot be ascribed in a particular situation.

A few other features of magical agency in the blended space constituting a ritual must be discussed at this point. First, the different kinds of agency will seldom appear alone. Different kinds of magical agency are often combined, either to strengthen representations of ritual efficacy, or as a prerequisite for the successful outcome of the ritual action. As we shall see below, different cultures and different ritual types gravitate towards specific formations of magical agency. Magical agency is thus one of the prime parameters in establishing a typology of magic rituals. Second, one should keep in mind that the ritual blend, including the genetic blend, is a temporary and local construction. Thus, counterpart connections, whether metonymic or metaphoric, are only evoked when prompted by the construction of a ritual blend in order to perform a magical action. Most agents, actions and objects will resume a position in the profane domain when the ritual is terminated, but are likely to undergo a procedure of cleansing, severing the connection to the sacred space. However, certain elements, related to the sacred domain by identity connectors or permanent metonymic connections, retain this connection. These elements have a special position in the profane domain, as is evident in certain ritual objects and actions considered taboo, and in most agents with more permanent connections to the sacred domain. Thus, ascription of magical agency often entails violation of domain-specific ontological assumptions, transforming for instance objects into genuine agents with a will of their own, belief-desire psychology etc. In this view, anthropomorphism can be seen as a result of the ascription of magical agency. Thirdly, there is a diffusion of sacred power in the blended space—one could call it the contagious character of magical rituals. More peripheral elements projected into the ritual space from the profane space can be contaminated (positively or negatively) by their sheer presence in the ritual blend. This has two entailments: (a) the ontological status of elements used in the ritual has changed or has become unclear; (b) ordinary procedures following magical rituals are either rituals of cleansing in order to sever the connection to the sacred, or its opposite, the avoidance of cleaning in order to retain this connection. Besides severing the direct connection to the sacred space, cleansing rituals can also restore the 'normal' ontological status of the elements in question. This severing of the contact with the sacred domain is in fact seldom fully accomplished. There will often remain a 'sacred residue' attached to the elements used in the magical ritual, temporarily or permanently changing the position of particular objects in local classificatory systems.

In general, the ritual blend is a temporary and bounded construction enabling a contact between the sacred and the profane domains. This is a basic and often-reported function of all rituals. What the methodological tool of conceptual blending facilitates is: (a) the conceptualisation of rituals as a 'zone of convergence' between a sacred and a profane space, locally constructed by recruitment of elements from the respective domains, and not as a transgression into the sacred domain; and (b) the analytical description and typology of different types of magical rituals based on a difference between kinds of magical agency, on the general level, but, as we shall see further on, also based on a difference between types of magical action.

4.1.5 Empirical Examples

In order to substantiate this rather technical description, I will analyse three empirical examples of ascription of magical agency in ritual. It is crucial to recognise that these function as *examples* of more general theoretical and methodological hypotheses of the function of conceptual blending in magical rituals. They are not necessarily representative for the practice of the whole tradition. The examples are taken from the Trobriand Islands, described by Malinowski, the Azande, described by Evans-Pritchard, and the Catholic Eucharist. The reason for comparing these materials comes from historical precedent. In 1929, Professor E. E. Evans-Pritchard published the paper "The Morphology and Function of Magic" in *American Anthropologist* (1929). The paper is a comparative analysis of magic among the Trobrianders, based on Malinowski's material, and of Zande magic, based on Evans-Pritchard's field studies in Africa in 1926-27. The main purpose of this comparative analysis was to illustrate the difference in emphasis on elements used in magical performances in both societies. Based on his Trobriand material, Malinowski had claimed that the single most important part of magic, as a general phenomenon, was the spell. But evidence from the Azande, among whom the material element is the most important, made Evans-Pritchard question this theory. He explains this by reference to difference in social structure: that is, knowledge of, ownership of and access to ritual agencies on the one hand, and the relation between magical power and social power on the other. Not denying that social structure plays a role in the formation of magical ritual, this is not a sufficient explanation. We need to focus on the ascription of magical agency in the two societies, as this will reveal further differences between the two societies.

As both the Trobrianders and the Azande will appear in several examples below, each example of ascription of ritual agency will be preceded by short introductory remarks placing the examples in an ethnographic context. These are based on the works of Malinowski and Evans-Pritchard respectively, but as they are very brief, I refer readers to the original works by the two authors for greater detail.

In his famous monograph *Coral Gardens and Their Magic*, Malinowski analyses the elaborate system of magic surrounding agriculture on the Trobriand Islands (Malinowski 1935a, 1935b). The Trobriand Islands are a small group of flat coral islands about two hundred miles northeast of Papua New Guinea. Malinowski carried out his field study between 1915 and 1918. In the present analysis, I will use this material without considering possible cultural changes, as the material is used to exemplify more general propositions. Therefore, I will use "the ethnographic present tense" as referring to the population and their culture at the time of Malinowski. The Trobrianders' source of nourishment is firstly from agriculture and secondly from fishing. The most important crop is *taytu*, a form of yam. *Taro* is also important, but due to its poor storage qualities it must be eaten immediately, in contrast to *taytu* that can be kept for a long time. Fishing and sailing in order to trade also plays an important part of Trobriand culture, and good canoes are regarded with considerable pride, as are well-kept gardens (small agricultural fields). The fields or gardens are connected to the villages by hereditary ownership based on matrilineal descent, and they are cultivated with the slash and burn method. It is not entirely new land cultivated each year, but there is a rotation of which fields are cultivated—a decision made at the *kayatu* meeting between the local headman and garden magician. Trobriand society is matrilineal and patrilocal. This means that the hereditary line follows the mother; a boy has to move to his maternal uncle's village when he grows up, and women have to move to their husband's villages (away from their hereditary village). This is combined with an elaborate system of exchange, according to which a man has to give a huge share of his *taytu* harvest to his sister's household. The taytu is therefore not only the primary source of nourishment but also a very important symbolic object.

Magic plays an important role in most aspects of Trobriand life, as it is deeply intertwined with most practical affairs such as gardening and fishing. The same clans that yield political power also own Garden magic and, as in the case of political power, it is with a few exceptions handed down through matrilineal descent. In principle the headman and the garden magician should be the same person, but usually the headman transfers the position as magician to a male in his matrilineal kin or to his son (which is regarded as more problematic). Even though magic is owned by specific groups and the most important rituals are performed exclusively by the magician, most spells are generally known. Despite the widespread knowledge the important spells are still used only by proper magicians (1935a: 105). Other spells are known exclusively to their owners—an exclusive right zealously guarded and strengthened by the intricate linguistic forms of the spells. Malinowski refers to two myths explaining the origin of garden magic among the Trobrianders (1935a: 68-75). The first states that the ancestors brought magic with them when they first emerged from underground. This is related to the Trobriand myth of emergence, according to which villagers are connected to their soil by a specific hole of emergence. Magic and people are, according to this myth, connected to the soil by a common metonymic link. In the second myth, magic was a gift to the first magician from the culture hero Tudava. Both myths have the common theme that magic is a cultural possession acquired in mythic times. In both cases there are mappings between a mythic or sacred space and a present or profane space with its magician and spells. Magic in general and spells in particular came into the world as the exclusive property of magicians. This mapping is illustrated in figure 4.2 below:

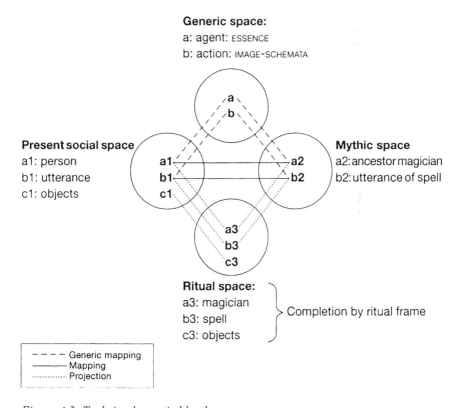

Figure 4.2: Trobriand genetic blend

The person in input space 1 and the magician in input space 2 are connected by a metonymic link (blood) that makes the present person a magician with the right and authority to use magical spells and the hereditary relation to use them correctly. Diverse paraphernalia, such as the hereditary magical wand, *kaylepa*, strengthens this connection, by functioning as an icon confirming the indexical connection. Thus, the magician takes part in a common essence, materially expressed in the genealogical bloodline eventually all the way back to the culture hero, Tudava, and this essence is intimately connected to the land through the metonymic link between each local group or sub-clan and the local land (Malinowski 1935a: 64-70). The spells, on the other hand, are mapped by iconic identity connectors as their expressions are believed to be exact replicas of the spells given to humans in mythic times. In figure 4.2, the spell is represented as a type of action (a speech-act), and the identity of the profane and sacred spell will be judged on the basis of certain perceptual or iconic features, leading to a judgement of image-schematic identity.

Magic among the Trobrianders thus combines the Agent-based and the Action-based origin of ritual efficacy and magical agency. Both the magician and the spell are believed to have magical power, the magician through his metonymic role-value relation to the ancestral magicians (who all had magical power), and the spell through its iconic identity with the primordial spell. This seems to correlate to the population's attitude toward both spells and magicians. It is only the magician who dares utter the spells, and the magician must not only know the spells but recite them correctly in order for them to have any efficacy (Malinowski 1935a: 105; Senft 1985). Further, the magician must obey certain taboos associated to the specific ritual. According to Malinowski, these are usually connected to the purpose of the ritual in a sympathetic manner, for instance by the magician abstaining from food made out of plants whose growth is promoted in a given ritual.

The garden magician has a considerable power. Not only does he belong to the same lineage as the headman. By controlling the magical powers associated with gardening, he controls "the work of men" via the organising force of the magical actions connected to specific parts of the agricultural calendar. The metonymic connection between the present magician and the sacred space magician is not necessarily made explicit in all magical rituals. But the single most important magical formula, the *vatuvi* spell, always incorporates an invocation connecting the present magician to his predecessors (Malinowski 1935a: 96-98).

The generic space AGENT that enables the metonymic connection between the present and the mythic agent is based on both "psychological essentialism" containing specific notions about properties of human agents, and diverse image-schematic representations of common origin, line of descent and containment of essence. The connection of similarity between the present spell and its mythic model is based on image-schematic representations of iconic features such as pronunciation, intonation, prosody etc., giving an abstract representation of the (speech-)act. These iconic features enable the judgment of whether a given expression had success or failure in establishing a connection between the profane space and the sacred space.

So, the Trobrianders invest magical agency primarily in the spell, due to image-schematic properties enabling the exact iconic reproduction of the original spell, and secondly in the magician, due to ascription of an essence-based role-value connection to the sacred space:

> In every act the magician's breath is regarded as the medium by which the magical force is carried. The voice—and let us remember it must be the voice of the accredited and fully instructed magician, and that his voice must correctly utter the words of an absolutely authentic spell—"generates" the power of the magic (Malinowski, 1935a: 216).

The importance of the spell as an iconic representation of the "sacred spell" is evident in the elaborate linguistic mechanisms used to distinguish the spell from other types of language, and by the role it plays in other types of magic, like love magic. In love magic, one need not be a magician to be the agent of the rite, but the spell must still be correct in order to carry any magical efficacy (Malinowski 1937a: 445). Uniting all kinds of magic among the Trobrianders is the assumption that the primary magical agency lies in the utterance of the correct spell, and only in magic related to important communal endeavours, such as gardening, does the magician play any role as a source of magical agency.

Among the Azande, the ascription of magical agency is altogether different. In the anthropological classic, *Witchcraft, Oracles and Magic among the Azande*, Evans-Pritchard gives an elaborate description of Zande ritual practices, including notions of magic and magical efficacy (this short introductory remark derives from Evans-Pritchard [1937] and, once again, uses the "ethnographic present tense"). The Azande live on the savannah dividing the Nile and the Congo River in Central Africa. Traditionally, political authority is based on several kingdoms spatially divided by unpopulated bush but all ruled by a member of the royal *Vongara* house. Each kingdom forms a political unity based on patrilineal descent and inheritance, with local authority given to the relatives of the king. Until British colonial rule, the basic sociological unit was the family. These were living in separate homesteads placed close to a stream and with up to several miles to the closest neighbour. More recently, people have been moved to small villages placed at the government roads, a measure presumably motivated by a wish to fight the widespread sleeping-sickness. Azande farm small gardens with crops like eleusine, maize, bananas and sweet potatoes. Besides they fish, hunt and collect wild fruits berries, roots and insects.

Zande magic is an overwhelmingly private affair. Most magical rites take place at home, or as a part of everyday behaviour—as in the ingestion of magical medicine. As pointed out in the title of Evans-Pritchard's monograph, magic form one side of a triangle, the other two being belief in witchcraft and sorcery as the source of almost all negative events, and the practice of poison oracles, by which witches and sorcerers are identified. Both oracles and magic can be seen as ritual means to combat witchcraft and sorcery. Witchcraft takes the form of a psychical attack without any outward or visible ritual manifestation, whereas sorcery is the morally reprehensible performance of ritual magic. It should be noted that magic is not deemed to be either good or bad based on its results. Such judgement is made on the basis of whether the medicine is "good" or "bad" medicine and whether the people it afflicts deserve punishment due to some transgression of morality. Thus, after the British colonial authorities outlawed direct physical revenge grounded on witchcraft allegation, vengeance-magic has taken over much of this function (Evans-Pritchard 1937: 26).

The Azande ascribe magical agency to the material objects used in the ritual. The only thing the human agent needs to do is direct the essential tendencies of the medicine in the right direction, by what Evans-Pritchard calls a "saying-spell", distinguishing them from the Trobriand "formula-spell" (Evans-Pritchard 1929: 625). One could argue that the medicines are not natural objects, that they are objects brought together and cooked by human agents, and that it is this mixing, cooking and uttering of accompanying spells that infuse the magical properties into the objects. But, according to Evans-Pritchard the Azande represent the properties as essential qualities of the objects. Cooking and mixing only 'heats' the medicine (making it active)[4] and directs it toward the desired goal:

> It is this material substance which is the occult and essential element in the rite, for in the substance lies the mystical power which produces the desired end. It is useless merely to wish an event to happen. A rite must be performed, i.e. a portion of a tree or a plant must be treated and manipulated in certain ways. It is likewise useless to utter spells by themselves, for the spells have no specific virtue. They are words of direction uttered to medicines linking them with desired ends (Evans-Pritchard 1937: 441).

Two features further support this description. (1) Most Zande spells explicitly address the medicine as an active agent able to direct its power in certain directions. The importance of this "giving direction" can be illustrated by cases in which medicine is used against an innocent. In such cases the medicine will instead turn against its owner. It is, however, a bit unclear whether this property is judged to be an intentional act performed by the good medicine, or an automatic effect resulting from the inability of the medicine to attack its appointed target. But there is no doubt that magical agency rests in the object. (2) Most medicine can be sold and bought like any other type of object, accompanied by knowledge of how to prepare and use the medicine. The efficacy rests in the objects and, like other types of instruments or tools, the buyer only need know how to use it properly.

The material focus in Zande magic also finds its expression in myths. Both agent and spell can be changed, and only the material object must remain the same (1929: 626-27). According to Evans-Pritchard, the Azande have no myths explaining the origin of magic in general, and only a very few myths relating the origin of specific medicines, often believed to originate from foreign people. Instead, beliefs in the efficacy of specific types of medicine are spread by rumours and anecdotes, relating the efficacy of a given medicine to a specific episode (629). The special essence of certain substances, extracted from trees and plants, is believed to be a defining element of magical objects. But the 'sacred' character of the material substances used in magic is not only a question of classification, but is also expressed in stories and anecdotes describing the gathering of the plants, roots and bulbs cooked into magical objects. In fact, there seems to be a direct correlation between the perceived danger in collecting the ingredients and their potential power: the stronger the magic inherent in the substances, the more dangerous it is to collect the necessary ingredients, hidden as they are in caves and surrounded by snakes and ghosts (Evans-Pritchard 1937: 215-219). Figure 4.3 illustrates the origin of magical agency in Zande magical rituals.

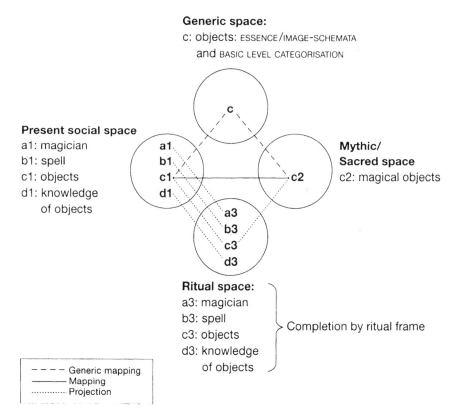

Figure 4.3: Azande genetic blend

The combination of magical agency placed in the object, and the transformation of these objects into magical medicines through an instrumental process, poses a problem. Evans-Pritchard strongly emphasises that the efficacy is placed solely in the material object, but only as a potential that can be made potent by knowledge of the correct treatment. The object is transformed from a natural to a cultural object by means of a ritual. As I have looked in vain for any description of how the Azande understands the knowledge necessary to manufacture magical objects, I have chosen to represent this knowledge as itself stemming from the profane domain. Knowledge of the right construction of magical medicine is placed on the same level as other less central aspects of the ritual, like the saying of spells, the status of the magician etc. All these are necessary ingredients in the ritual, but they are not responsible for the transfer of magical agency from the sacred to the ritual domain. I do not say that these matters are not important—they are—but only that the magical agency is placed in the magical medicine or cultural object, by virtue of their direct relation to the natural object believed to contain magical power.

The mapping between an object in the profane and the sacred space is established by an identity connector, identifying an object as belonging to a class of magical objects. Contrary to the magical stones of the Aguaruna, Zande magical objects are categorised by perceptual characteristics, such as appearance and place of growth, all functioning as indices of a common essence of magical potential residing in an object that only needs refining in order to be effective. Psychological essentialism, image-schemata and basic-level categorisation are active in the generic space enabling the establishment of an identity connector between the object in the sacred and in the profane domain.

These two examples illustrate the cultural and possibly situational differences of ascription of magical agency. Whereas the Trobrianders ascribe agency to the spell uttered by a human agent authorised by virtue of a metonymic connection to former values of his role (ancestor-spirits), the Azande believe magical agency rests in the material object, which is then subject to commercial exchange. The difference is reflected in the terminology. On the Trobriand Islands 'magic' it is called *megwa*, meaning 'magical formula' and among the Azande it is called *ngwa*, generally meaning wood and only in special contexts 'magic' (Evans-Pritchard 1929: 626). Evans-Pritchard explains this difference by reference to the social structure in question. The Trobrianders invest magical efficacy in agents belonging to the ruling class because of weak secular and physical powers. Magic is in this respect a strong instrument of socio-political control. The Azande, on the other hand, have very strong secular power enforced by the ruling aristocracy, and they need no magical authority in order to enforce their authority. Thus, magic only solidifies into formula-spells and myths of legitimacy when used by a ruling segment of a social structure with weak secular power, and both myth and the formulaic format of the spells will in that case protect the ownership of the magical agency. If this social pressure is not present, these structures will not solidify, and the magical agency will be placed in media facilitating its role in economic exchange (Evans-Pritchard 1929).

There is no doubt that social structure, and especially relations of power, influence the ascription of magical agency to specific individuals. There are, however, certain problems attached in the causal connection between political structure and magical agency. First, it is questionable whether social structure should be seen as *determining* the morphology and function of magic. Containment of magical agency is in itself a strong argument for political authority, so causation might go in the opposite direction, from ascription of magical agency to political power. Secondly, ascription of magical agency to formulas or other kinds of actions—owned exclusively by the ruling class—does not always coincide with weak secular power. Strong political power can *in itself* be a reason for the ascription of magical agency, e.g. in the healing power of the "monarch's touch" observed in Europe until at least the nineteenth century (Thomas 1991). Of course, a weak ruler would be a fool to disregard beliefs that would strengthen his power, but it is likely that a strong ruler will attract more ascription of magical agency. Thirdly, social structure should not be seen as unchanging and static, and the ascription of magical agency might play a role in social change. R. Firth (1967) describes how spirit mediums on Tikopia have gained influence at the expense of the local chiefs during a period of about 50 years, primarily as a result of rapid social change involving the diminished *secular* power of the traditional chiefs. Whereas magical agency was formerly placed in formulas owned by local chiefs, much as on the Trobriand Island, the authority of spirit mediums is an example of agent-based agency. This illustrates that notions of magical agency can change over time, and that several factors might influence such change. Ascription of magical agency is based on ordinary cognitive abilities connecting elements in two spaces by means of symbolic, metonymic and similarity-based connections. Several notions of magical agency might coexists and even in cases where one is dominant, it is better to talk about the *proclivity* of a to ascribe magical agency to specific elements in a particular cultural context.

The third example of ascription of magical agency is the investment of magical agency in the rituals of Roman Catholic Church. Figure 4.4 models the ascription of magical agency to elements in the Catholic Eucharist.[5] Both the priest and the ritual action, including the spell, are depicted as connected to the sacred space, and therefore invested with ritual agency as both elements are deemed to be necessary in order to perform the transubstantiation of bread and wine. Contrary to the Trobrianders, among whom the spell is the primary bearer of magical agency, both the ritual agent and the correct performance of the ritual yield the necessary magical efficacy. The action is based on an iconic reproduction of a mythical act of Christ, thus creating an identity connector to the sacred space (Matt 26: 26-29, Mar 14: 22-25, Luke 22: 14-23,1 Corinthians 11: 23-34), and its efficacy rests in the correct performance of the ritual action as prescribed by the Church. Thus, although correctly ordained, a deaf-dumb priest cannot perform the consecration of bread and wine (McCarthy 1956: 9).

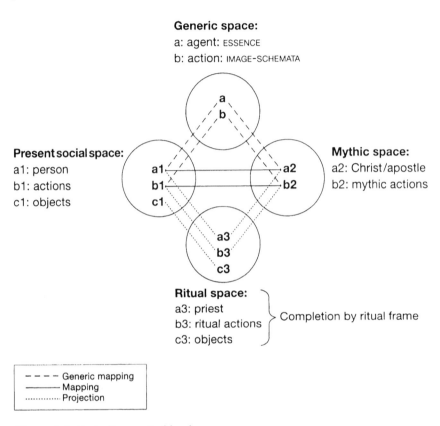

Figure 4.4: Catholic genetic blend

The counterpart connection between the priest and Christ/apostles is even more significant. A central element of the ordination of the priest is captured in the dogma of apostolic succession according to which the bishop ordaining the priest is directly connected all the way back to the apostles, if not, to Jesus himself. An important part of the ordination of priests and bishops is the laying on of hands, by which a 'line of touches' can be reconstructed, from any present priest all the way back to the apostles. Thus, a 'pseudo-genealogical' lineage is formed connecting the present day priest with the sacred authority of the apostles. This lineage is an important legitimisation of magical or ritual efficacy of the priest (McCarthy 1956: 340). However, a more direct counterpart connection between the sacred and the profane space is also constructed. The transubstantiation of bread and wine into the flesh and blood of Christ cannot succeed without the proper intention of the priest, making him "the instrumental cause" voluntarily performing the action of "Christ whose agent he is" (McCarthy 1956: 98). So, with the right intention to perform the action as prescribed by the Church and by performance of the correct ritual procedures, the priest functions as an instrumental agent invested with magical agency, transferred through both a metonymic connection, and a elaborate kind of role-value connection, understanding the value (the priest) as an instrument of the sacred role (Christ). Image-schemata ensuring the right iconic representation of the ritual action, essentialist notions establishing a metonymic link by apostolic touching, and psychological essentialism ensuring the right essential disposition of the priest to function as a value of the sacred role, are all present in the generic space facilitating the counterpart connections linking the sacred and the profane space.

This third example illustrates the importance in recognising that magical actions are not a characteristic of so-called primitive or pre-literate people, or of people of pre-modern historical periods. The practice of ascribing magical agency to various elements can be found all over the world, in all historical periods, and in relation to all kinds of religious and political systems. Ascription of magical agency is a fundamental prerequisite for representations of efficacy in ritual, when these are not only understood as purely symbolic expressions, but are believed to change or uphold a state of affairs either by ritual means alone or in combination with technological action.

4.2 The *Linguistic* Blend

In discussing the transfer of magical agency into the ritual in the genetic blend, I refrained from an analysis of the role of language. Language is only one parameter in the genetic blend, but as language has traditionally been given special treatment in literature on magic and ritual, it will be treated in some depth below. Language plays an important role in magical rituals but some of the features traditionally treated as special linguistic effects are more fruitfully described as a part of a larger class of ritual elements. Spells and magical formulas are a certain type of speech-act almost devoid of direct reference and communicative effect, equivalent to ritual action with its lack of direct instrumental effect. Besides their more or less transparent referential meaning, linguistic signs are also a sort of material objects ascribed magical agency by metonymic or metaphoric connections. In the following section, the role of language in general and of special linguistic devices will be analysed, first in the construction and demarcation of a ritual space and second as a social marker.

4.2.1 A Ritual Marker: Linguistic Anomaly and the Construction of a Ritual Space

Linguistic anomalies have always been described as one of the distinctive marks of magical rituals. Think of *abracadrabra* and *simsalabim* of the stage magician. These linguistic deformations are spread all over the linguistic register and have a very distinct effect used to mark off the ritual space from everyday communicative interaction. Language in magical rituals can profitably be understood as a blend between natural, everyday, profane language (input space 1) and idealised sacred or magical language(s) (input space 2). Cultures and even individual rituals within a culture can use different linguistic parameters in the construction of a ritual space, so, like the genetic blend, the linguistic blend should be understood as an abstract model depicting the relationship between natural and sacred language found in magical rituals.

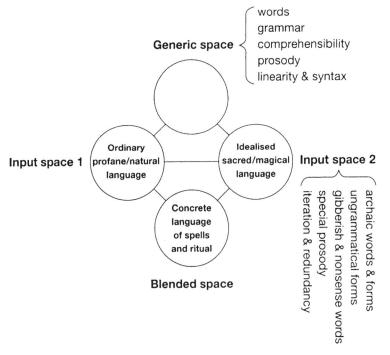

Figure 4.5: The linguistic blend

Figure 4.5 is an abstract illustration of the linguistic blend genres found in magical rituals. The top right bracket contains the general linguistic parameters taken into consideration and constitutes the content of the generic space. The lower right bracket contains the content of input space 2.

Archaic linguistic forms are a typical trait in the language used in religion, magic and in ceremonial language in general. The most natural explanation for this 'conservatism' in relation to magic is the intimate connection, if not identity, between word and reference. This postulated property of the idealised magical language is projected into the ritual frame, effecting that words will function as a special type of speech-act. Sympathetic relations between word and object of course strengthen the tendency for archaic forms to proliferate in ritual language. But this transfer of magical agency by word-reference identity is not the only reason archaic forms proliferate in magical rituals. Old-fashioned language will, inevitably, give rituals an aura of tradition and 'old wisdom' handed down through generations. Participants in a given ritual will meet a linguistic usage predating their own existence pointing to the existence of a 'transcendent' realm of cultural facts, such as conceptual systems or language as an expressive and communicative medium. In this aspect, it does not matter whether this archaism is genuine or fake, as long as participants consider themselves to be participating in something extended far beyond their own life. This aspect of archaic word usage is also in different degrees exploited in all kinds of ceremonial language not imbued with any notion of word-object identity or other type of magical agency. *Ungrammatical* forms might be explained by the same mechanism of direct connection between word and reference, placing the stress on the correct reduplication of a spell irrespective of its grammatical form compared to spoken language. Magical rituals often use dead or foreign languages. Tambiah describes how Sinhalese mantras contain a hierarchy of languages: Sanskrit, when Hindu gods are invoked; Pali, when Buddha and Buddhist myths are referred to; Classical Sinhalese, when origin myths are narrated in the spell; and, finally, a polyglot mixture of several languages when the demons are addressed (Tambiah 1968: 177-8). In more extreme cases, *nonsense words* or pure *gibberish* play a substantial part in magical rituals. In that case, words do not have any semantic reference for the participants (or this is 'hidden' or 'forgotten'). Instead, they are believed to be a compelling force alone by their material or performative aspect, as a sign or a sound, or by their ascribed function as a communicative medium of the sacred space. Knowledge of special words and languages enables the magician to communicate with elements belonging to this space and enable these elements to be active in the ritual space. Archaism, ungrammaticality and senselessness are all dependent on the default understanding of natural language as a medium of communication. By breaking this cultural expectation (at least for the participants not understanding) three things follow: (1) the highlighting of indexical and iconic aspects of language, described in the last section, (2) the creation of a pragmatic context marked off from everyday language, and (3) a social differentiation, based on possible access to understanding of the sacred language.

Words and grammar are not necessarily deprived of their referential and logical function. The expressive side of language can also mark off ritual use of language from everyday natural language. The *prosody* of magical spells is an important expressive marker. Spells and magical formulas are often recited in a very special manner with specific rhythm, intonation and stress. Other linguistic utterances in the ritual, not considered to be efficacious spells, also make use of a special prosody immediately marking off the ritual context from ordinary language. Thus, magical rituals can be delineated as a pragmatic genre with special prosody, rhythm and iterative effects (for instance at the Trobriand Islands, see Senft 1985: 73; Malinowski 1935b: 213). *Iteration* and *redundancy* are common linguistic traits found in magical rituals. These are effective means to distinguish ritual language from everyday natural language with its lineal structure and communicative intention. The length of many magical spells is thus totally out of proportion with the information and meaning contained in the utterance. According to an influential anthropological theory, iteration and redundancy strengthens the communicative function of ritual (Tambiah 1968, 1979). It is, however, by no means clear that iteration and redundancy have this effect. On the contrary, this praxis in fact de-emphasises the purely symbolic meaning of words repeated. Iteration and redundancy ensure that words are more or less deprived of the meaning they obtain through symbolic reference in a network of other words. Therefore the cognitive system looks for other clues to the 'meaning' or purpose of the linguistic utterance, i.e. either direct perceptual features, or indexical relations relating linguistic elements to superhuman agents. These effects will be addressed in further detail below.

4.2.2 A Social Marker: Ownership, Transmission and Accessibility

Spells and formulas marked off from ordinary language by the above-mentioned linguistic devices play an important role in the construction of the ritual space. The special features of ritual language directly influences the ownership and transmission of magical formulas and spells and, in relation hereto, ritual participants' access to knowledge concerning the magical language and the sacred space this language is believed to refer to. As noticed by Evans-Pritchard (1929), linguistic parameters can be an important factor in limiting the access to and spread of magical procedures. Long, complicated and iterative spells, abundant with archaic and nonsense words, ungrammatical forms and a strange prosody, are much more difficult to learn and transmit, features that considerably limit unauthorised use. When combined with explicit or implicit beliefs in the magical agency of the spells uttered (necessitating its correct pronunciation) and myths and doctrines delegating the knowledge to a specific class or profession, we will have a system with very limited access for most participants. Ritual language is therefore an important social marker, differentiating participants into roughly two groups: one with access to the magical language, and the other without. The question, then, concerns the opaqueness or transparency of the magical language space as a subspace of the sacred domain. In the most extreme cases, not even the ritual agent will understand the words used. In less extreme cases, the ritual agent understands the words used but ordinary participants do not, and at the other end of the continuum, all participants might understand the language.

This parameter is connected intimately to the social status and function of magic—whether being a magician is a 'protected title' based on esoteric knowledge and hereditary rights or initiation-based transmission of spells. 'Secret' or archaic language, unknown by anyone besides the ritual agent, functions as an index of the real authority of the agent, no matter whether this agent knows the meaning of the words uttered or not. The use of a special sacred language in magical rituals not only sets the ritual apart from normal interaction and communication, but also functions as an index of the status of the ritual agent. Thus, it is intimately related to the types of magical agency present in the ritual—whether the magical efficacy is invested in actions, objects, or ritual agents. In case agency is invested in either the object or the ritual agent, language only plays a minor role as a communicative device used to direct magical agency residing in object or the agent towards the desired goal, an objective that can be obtained by using ordinary language. This is the case among the Azande, in which the role of the "saying spell" is to direct the magical power of the objects in the right direction (Evans-Pritchard, 1929: 625, 1937). Or it might be the case that magical language has not yet been crystallised by the personal agent wielding the magical agency, a process connected intimately to the institutionalisation of new rituals seen in the emergence of new religions (discussed in chapter 7).

Rituals always consist in a blend between ordinary and magical language(s). Often the spells themselves will contain both contemporary and archaic forms, and at least the practical instructions will be carried out in ordinary language. So, when participants have no or very limited access to the sacred space, it constitutes a deliberate breach with the default mechanisms normally ensuring the possible unpacking of both input spaces from the blended space (see chapter 3.3). Participants have only unlimited access to the natural language space and its referential potential, whereas access to the sacred language space and its esoteric elements of reference is blocked. This deliberate breach of expectations concerning free access, however, is parasitic on more everyday blending depending on this access. This has an important effect: an input space containing a sacred language is constructed. This contains words about whose reference participants have very limited knowledge, but which will be believed to contain such reference, whether or not it is potentially obtainable for participants. Secrets are not secrets if not believed to be about something, and in principle the sacred space can be unfolded, revealing its secrets. In this way, opaque reference to the sacred space is one of the important constituent factors in the construction of a sacred space. Strange linguistic forms used in magical rituals will not only be involved in the construction of a ritual space. Their implicit referential function helps to construct a sacred space about which little or nothing is known.

The importance of reference without content points to the classical anthropological notion of "floating signifiers" with "zero symbolic value" proposed by Lévi-Strauss (1987). Linguistic blending might shed further light on this problem. Magical rituals can contain words devoid of any meaning in the traditional symbolic sense of the term (i.e. definable by other symbols). But this does not stipulate that they can be used for any possible interpretative purpose. They are bound to a discursive register (magical ritual), in which they have the semiotic function of referring to a sacred space, and thereby to a hidden potentiality of symbolic meaning. Ascription of symbolic meaning to a term will be constrained by other elements ascribed to this sacred space in the pragmatic situation in particular, and ascribed to the sacred domain in general. The ascription of symbolic meaning by reference to other symbols placed in the sacred space will combine both intuitive and counterintuitive elements as described by Boyer (1994) and can potentially form more systematised clusters of symbolic meaning. These words, however, might have other, non-symbolic, 'meanings.' Iconic features present in the utterance of the word, such as tone, intonation and stress entail a very basic schematic ascription of meaning based on linear scales, such as positive/negative, big/small, and friendly/aggressive. Indexical features, such as the 'origin' of the word and its enunciator, will in a similar fashion entail a basic ascription of meaning by relating the word to a given conceptual domain and pragmatic situation. It might be that these kinds of meaning should be described as 'affective' and thus not the object of traditional 'cognitive' theorising. But recent cognitive theorising suggests that such a demarcation would be a mistake (e.g. Damasio 2000), and that these affective features not only form a context to words and concepts otherwise defined by symbolic relations but effectively constrain symbolic meaning. Thus, linguistic elements with zero symbolic value are not only culturally underdetermined (Boyer, 1994), but symbolically underdetermined. Their possible meanings are, however, loosely constrained both by schematic structure inherent in their iconic and indexical features, as well as by symbolic elements in the immediate pragmatic context.

In this chapter I have presented a model of how a ritual space is constructed through conceptual blending. Magical rituals are blended spaces consisting of elements originating in either a profane and a sacred domain. Two aspects of this process have been shown to be of major importance. The first aspect is the ascription of magical agency necessary in order to infuse efficacy into the ritual action. Several types of magical agency have been described, with agent-based, action-based and object-based as the most important ones. Second, linguistic blending between a sacred language and a profane, natural language is active both in the construction of a ritual space, and, by virtue of the default referential function of all language, in the construction of a symbolically underdetermined sacred space. This is not intended to be an adequate theory of ritual in general, even if the elements outlined, and the method described could form a part of such a more general and comprehensive theory. By postulating a "ritual frame" that will complete the structure of any concrete ritual blend, it is argued that humans will have a more or less universal structure framing particular episodes of human behaviour as 'ritual' or 'ritualistic'. A hypothesis regarding this universal ritual structure is presented in chapter 6.

Notes

1. The blending theory originated as a mean to address certain problems in relation to linguistic and artistic expressions, but recently the scope of the theory has been broadened to cover numerous other instances of human cognition. See Fauconnier 1994, 1997; Fauconnier & Turner 1996, 1998, 2002; Grady, Oakley & Coulson 1999; Sweetser & Fauconnier 1996; Turner 1996, 2001.

2. Gächter and Quack (1989) describe an extreme, but no way isolated, example of such iconic aspects of speech-acts. In India, a Durga-ritual was performed in order to secure the welfare of some industrialist families. The ritual entailed a thousand recitations in honour of Durga. During one of these, a formal failure was made (in intonation, length, stress etc.), and as a result, elaborate ceremonies had to be performed in order to avoid unwanted effects and ensure that the results of the ceremony would prevail.

3. For a comprehensive if outdated comparative description of the use of amulets and talismans, see Budge (1961).

4. This notion of 'heating' as equivalent to making active is paralleled by Zande beliefs in witchcraft. Witches contain a witchcraft-substance, and the witches themselves might be ignorant of their true being, and involuntarily perform witchcraft. Allegations of witchcraft are therefore met by an apology and a 'cooling' of the witchcraft substance rendering it inactive (Evans-Pritchard 1937). It is likely that this related to a cultural model connecting 'heat' to activity, and 'cool' to inactivity or dormancy, cf. the equivalent found in Western cultures.

5. The description is primarily taken from J. C. McCarthy (1956): *Problems in Theology I: The Sacraments*. This book is a well of information of Catholic ritual practice, as it is a compendium of questions about special cases (such as whether a dumb-deaf priest can perform the consecration of bread and wine) from readers of the *Irish Ecclesiastical Record*.

5
Transformation and Manipulation: A Typology of Magical Actions

Typologies of magical actions and rituals are by no means a new endeavour. Among the many typologies and distinctions, Frazer's has proven to be among the most persistent. As described in chapter 2, Frazer defined magic as the erroneous application of the association of ideas, resulting in the understanding of relations of thought as real sympathetic relation between objects (Frazer 1911: 53). Of particular interest in relation to a cognitive theory of magic is Frazer's observation that two basic principles of thought are at work in magical actions and thought: the principle of association by contagion or contact, and the principle of association by similarity or imitation. These principles give rise to two types of magical procedures: contagious magic, and imitative or homeopathic magic. Even though Frazer has been severely criticised for his evolutionary approach and intellectualist bias, the distinction has persisted in many anthropological studies of magic, even if judged to be of varied importance and fruitfulness (e.g. Skorupski 1976).

More recently, the principles of thought underlying this typology have been the subject of psychological studies in modern North American culture. As an answer to questions raised by studies of disgust, Rozin, Nemeroff and associates found Frazer's typology to be of explanatory value as "descriptions of a consistent pattern of beliefs, thoughts, and practices observed across a wide range of traditional cultures." (Rozin & Nemeroff 1990: 105-6; see also Rozin, Markwith & Nemeroff 1992; Nemeroff 1995; Nemeroff & Rozin 2000). The occurrence of these patterns of thought basic to sympathetic magic are widespread in all cultures, and can as such be seen as fundamental structures of human cognition. Like Frazer, Rozin and Nemeroff (1990) distinguish contagion and similarity. Contagion is based on the notions that (a) an essence is transferred by means of contact (by smelling, touching or ingesting) and (b) once in contact, elements will keep some connection even if the spatio-temporal relation is terminated. The central representation facilitating this connection is therefore common essence. This leads Rozin and Nemeroff to distinguish between contagion based on forward and backward causation. Forward contagion—that an element can transfer some essence or quality by touching another element—can be explained by reference to adaptive mechanism in evolution, both socially and biologically (e.g. microbial contamination). Backward contagion—the representation that manipulation of an element once in contact with another element can influence this second element after the contact has terminated—has no similar apparent adaptive advantages, and can thus not be explained as an extension or side-effect of cognitive procedures with an evolutionary adaptive function. Both positive and negative effects are ascribed to the two directions in contagious transfer (Rozin & Nemeroff 1990: 208). Similarity is also expressed in both forward and backward causative directions and as having both negative and positive effects. In 'forward similarity', benefit or harm is represented as a result of the iconic likeness to some element, whereas 'backward similarity' implies the possibility to influence an element by another element of its likeness (224). Relations of forward similarity can be exemplified by the purported effect of an icon of the Holy Virgin in Catholic Christianity, in contrast to the effect of backward similarity by a voodoo effigy manipulated in order to harm its referent.

Rozin and Nemeroff do not attempt an explanation of how and why the apparently irrational beliefs in backward causation, in both contagious and imitative magic, arise (228). The theory of conceptual blending can be of assistance in this respect, as the counterpart connections between the two spaces do not contain any causal direction in themselves, but rather a mereological principle of part-whole structures and a metaphorical principle of conventional or perceptual likeness. Once the link is established between two mental spaces, it can be manipulated in either direction, even if it implies 'action at a distance-like' causal connections. The work of Rozin, Nemeroff and colleagues is important as it presents psychological evidence suggesting that aspects of the performance of cultural ritual can be explained by reference to underlying cognitive procedures.

Whereas Frazer's typology in reality only covers cases of similarity and backward contagion, the present typology aims to cover instances of forward contagion crucial in the analysis of transfer of essence. When analysing magical ritual from the perspective of conceptual blending, it becomes clear that relations of similarity (metaphor) and contagion (metonymy), or iconic and indexical relations, should be seen as means used to establish connections between mental spaces rather than distinct types of magical actions. Based on the pragmatic intent ascribed to the ritual and the cognitive processes involved in their performance, two types of magical actions are distinguishable. The first type is *Transformative Magical Action*. It covers magical actions contrived to transfer essential qualities from elements belonging to one domain to elements belonging to another domain. The second type I call *Manipulative Magical Action*. It designates magical practices aimed at changing a state of affair inside a domain by means of manipulating elements in another domain. In this case only schematic properties organising the relation between elements in a mental space are transferred from one space to another, whereas the essential qualities of elements in each space remain unchanged.

This typology enables scholars to distinguish ritual actions aimed to change essential properties of elements from ritual actions aimed to change schematic properties organising the relation between elements. At this point it should be noted that these two types do not designate separate types of ritual sequences as a whole but different kinds of mental representations involved in performing and participating in specific magical actions. Real-world rituals often combine different elements into one ritual sequence that involves both transformative and manipulative processes. Further, it is important to realise that the description of types of representations basic to magical action are all situated at another descriptive level than the analysis of ascription of magical agency and creation of a ritual space described in chapter 4. The performance of magical rituals has as a prerequisite the creation of a ritual space and the ascription of magical agency to some element found in the ritual. Whereas ascription of magical agency is a necessary condition for representations of ritual efficacy, the present typology concerns types of conceptual blending used *inside* the ritual space produced in order to effect a transformation or change in a relevant target domain.

5.1 Transformative Magical Action: The *Essence* Blend

In chapter 3, I stressed that *psychological essentialism* is crucial in the cognitive process of categorisation, and in chapter 4, I explained its importance for the ascription of magical agency to elements otherwise belonging to the profane space. As an essential quality, magical agency can be understood as either (a) an 'inborn' or ontologically ascribed aspect of the element in question, (b) a result of a metonymic relation to the sacred space, or (c) a projection of magical agency to the element obtained through the performance of another ritual. Such "embedded rituals" (Lawson & McCauley 1990, McCauley & Lawson 2002) facilitate the transfer of 'sacred essence' to an element stemming from the profane domain that formerly did not contain any magical agency. The latter case (c) is an essential *transformation*, changing some or all ontological assumptions ascribed to the element. Most, if not all, initiation rites of ritual agents contain procedures ensuring an essential transformation of the novice. As the cultural formats of magical agency differ to a substantial degree, the form and importance of this transformation will also vary. It might entail the ingestion of magical medicine in order to become a witch-doctor (Azande), the appropriation and internalisation of spells and formulas in connection with hereditary rights to become a garden magician (Trobriand) or the transfer of magical agency from one human agent to another to become a ritual agent invested with magical agency (Christianity).

The ontological assumptions of single elements are not only changed in rituals investing elements with magical agency, but also in cases where the relationship between perceptual appearance and inner essence is substantially altered. Magical rituals are performed in order to change the ontological status of elements that are not in a position to become the wielders of magical agency themselves. Elements eligible to be invested with magical agency are treated as are other types of element involved in a ritually instantiated ontological transformation, and therefore these will make use of the same ritual procedures in order to facilitate a transformation. This is the case even if rituals investing elements with magical (or superhuman) agency are understood and represented as central in a given ritual complex, as shown by Lawson and McCauley (1990). It is the cognitive mechanisms involved in the *modes of transformation*—not the relative status of any single ritual—that are of importance in this context. Thus, the same cognitive mechanisms are present in both important and less important rituals.

I propose two types of representations of transformative magical action. The first type contains representations of manipulation of the relationship between perceptual appearance and essence. The second type contains representations of the contagious transfer of essential qualities.

5.1.1 Essence Change / Essence Retention

The fundamental relation between perceptual appearance and essential qualities is a basic feature of magic in the broadest sense of the term, including stage magic as pure entertainment. The first type of transformative magic concerns the change of an element's essence by virtue of a ritual action. The transformation of bread and wine into the flesh and blood of Christ in the Eucharist as it is represented in the Catholic doctrine of transubstantiation will serve as an example. Neither the ritual agent invested with magical agency (the priest), nor the (speech)-actions involved in the ritual are represented in the model below. The investment of such magical agency is a prerequisite for the successful performance of the ritual (see chapter 4). The primary aim of this model is to illustrate the conceptual blending of two elements in order to produce a change of essence effected through the performance of a specific part of a ritual sequence, i.e. the 'sanctification' of bread and wine.

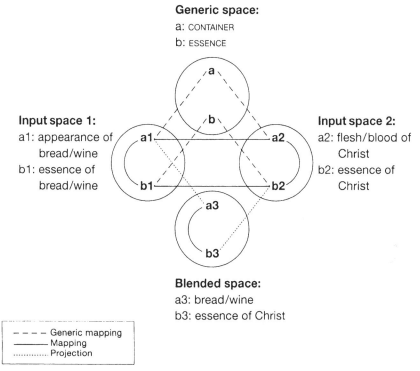

Figure 5.1: Sanctification of bread and wine

In the blended space, representing the result of the ritual action, the material appearance of bread and wine are ascribed the essence of Christ, an entity classified as belonging to the sacred domain. Inside the ritual, the material substances of bread and wine present are explicitly identified as the flesh and blood of Christ, thereby de-emphasising their own automatically ascribed essence (marked by the curved line in Input space 1). The explicit reference to the material appearance of Christ (flesh and blood) directly provokes the representation of an underlying essence contained in this material manifestation (marked by the curved line in Input space 2). As the bread and wine do not change their outer appearance despite the explicit identification, the ascription of a new essence (of Christ) to the bread and wine is the only way the participant can relate the two conceptual spaces. Thus, the identification can only refer to the essential qualities, as the perceptual appearance is unchanged. This is theologically elaborated by the Aristotelian distinction between *accidens* and *substance* (Watt 1912), echoing the cognitive distinction between categorisation by perceptual and by essential qualities. After a certain point in the unfolding of the ritual frame, the material appearance of bread and wine will work as indices, not of 'the wineness of wine' or 'the breadness of bread', but of the essence of Christ (the curved line in the blended space). Through the ritual, new complex concepts of sanctified bread and wine are constructed through the connection established between cognitive models belonging to two conceptual domains. This complex concept contains both intuitive and counterintuitive elements and can therefore be seen as a typical religious concept (Boyer 1994). Intuitive, as the bread and wine is still subject to gravity, can be consumed, and generally physically manipulated. Counterintuitive, as a familiar appearance of bread and wine are represented as containing the essence of a superhuman agent thus creating an attention-demanding tension between appearance and essence.

The counterpart connections, both established through relations of identity, are strengthened by the direct perceptual similarity between blood and (red) wine, and the more indirect similarity between flesh and bread (both having outer 'skin' and inner 'meat'). Both similarities, however, are vague and cannot serve as an explanation for the correlation in the first place, even though both can be described as belonging to the 'culinary domain' of things humans eat (a commonality basic to the potential interpretation of the communion as a cannibalistic sacrifice).

The primary generic space image-schemata enabling the identification of the counterpart element is the CONTAINER-schema, which permits both elements to function as containers for a given essence. In the case of the wine, this schema is emphasised by the ritual importance of the chalice containing an otherwise evasive fluid. The importance of the generic space CONTAINER-schema is illustrated by the fact that the essence of Christ, once projected into the bread or wine, will stay there. This gives rise to problems and numerous theological speculations about what to do about crumbs and the leftovers of the sacrificial meal, and to the possibility of using the bread for non-sanctioned ritual purposes (e.g. as protection against theft, see Thomas 1991: 51). In itself, however, the CONTAINER-schema is a very loose constraint on the possible elements connected by identity. In this case, the ritual action and the identification of bread and wine as the flesh and blood of Christ are both legitimised by a mythical narrative. The ascribed efficacy of the ritual action arises by virtue of it being an iconic reproduction of the mythical action of Jesus Christ if performed by a legitimate ritual agent. The elements connected in the ritual might be chosen for wholly pragmatic reasons or based on historical precedents of connecting these specific counterparts. It is a *conventional identification*, by now deeply entrenched in the conceptual system of most cultures under Christian dominion, and this entrenched conceptual connection can subsequently give rise to all sorts of symbolic interpretations and elaborations. So, symbolic interpretations of ritual actions will be constrained by the ritual in itself only in limited ways. In the ritual performance, participants are presented with an elaborate sequence of actions and elements, connecting and manipulating cultural conceptual structures. The most important cognitive constraints, inherent in the consecration of the bread and wine analysed here, is the CONTAINER-schema allowing the representation of the essence of Christ residing in bread and wine, and the notion of

ESSENCE, understood as an underlying property residing in all physical objects.[1] Other important constraints are located in the ritual itself as it is an iconic reproduction of the mythical event represented in the ritual as a whole. These constraints will be analysed below. Finally, the rich and complex history of symbolic interpretations of the central ritual of the Eucharist, and its relation to other rituals and dogmas of the church impose certain cultural constraints and influences on possible interpretation of the ritual itself. This interpretative discourse, however, is reserved primarily for the religious intelligentsia manoeuvring in a universe of symbolic relations and can therefore not in itself constitute an explanation for the widespread performance of the ritual.

Thus, we find three 'gravitational points' for individual and systematic interpretations of the complex conceptual model of the Eucharist: (1) an indexical interpretation emphasising the transfer and dissemination of sacred essence through transformative actions, and de-emphasising the iconic and symbolic representations; (2) an iconic interpretation emphasising the reproduction and reiteration of the mythical action and de-emphasising the indexical and symbolic representations; and (3) a symbolic interpretation, emphasising the purely symbolic aspects of the ritual and de-emphasising both indexical and iconic representations. These interpretative strategies are basic to interpretations of rituals in all religions, but very few, if any, interpretations are pure examples of one of these interpretative strategies and most will contain a mix of representations from all three gravitational points. In the study of magic, indexical and iconic interpretations and representations are the primary locus of interest, as these directly address the questions of magical agency and ritual efficacy.

Another group of magical actions utilising the relation between essence and appearance is based on representations of the *retention* of essence despite radical change of appearance. These representations are mostly known from fairytales and stage magic in which objects radically change their perceptual appearance, but retain their essential qualities. Take the example of the prince changed into a frog by an evil witch. An implicit, or even explicit, presupposition is that the prince still possesses his own essence, that only his physical appearance has changed, and that the prince will reappear when the spell is lifted (e.g. by a princess kissing the frog). Often, but not necessarily, the prince will even remember events that happened to him while having the form of a frog, entailing that not only does he retain his essence, but also some or all of his human cognitive abilities. This is not the place to enter into the complex and fascinating study of the narrative functions of such interplay between essence and appearance in the myriads of narratives—religious, mythological or secular—in which such change of appearance is a fundamental theme.[2] Of importance in this context is that the ascription of power to change the external appearance of oneself or others in a radical way—often crossing the border between intuitive ontological domains, for instance from human to animal or plant—is a very strong indication of and argument for the possession of magical agency. Thus, idealised cognitive models of ritual elements might contain notions of such perceptual changeability, by which aspects of two otherwise distinguished conceptual domains can be combined into one complex concept.

Besides cases involving conjuring tricks as a means to persuade participants of the genuineness of the magical agency ascribed to a given element, the theme is seldom explicitly used in magical and religious rituals. It is, however, a very common theme in allegations of sorcery and witchcraft, where witches and sorcerers are described as having a common essence with some animal (a 'familiar'), and in descriptions of the great magical powers of gods and magicians (e.g. the notion of using other peoples' or animals' slough in old Norse mythology). The representation has great evocative power because of its explicit counterintuitive character, violating representations of object permanence, of borders between cognitive domains structured by intuitive ontological assumptions, and of the intimate relation between perceptual qualities and ascription of essence. As notions of slow or minor change of perceptual appearance while retaining essence are not counterintuitive in themselves (e.g. ageing, getting a haircut), several factors can be involved in making these representations counterintuitive. The speed of transformation (e.g. directly from young to old), the direction of the transformation (e.g. from old to child), the crossing of borders between ontological domains (e.g. from human to animal), the change of bodily scale (e.g. from human to small frog) and the gross discrepancy between perceptual appearance and the essence (e.g. frogs with human intelligence).

To summarise, essence retention and essence change both function as indices of magical agency and, in the case of essence change, as a process facilitating further manipulation of sacred essences by their infusion into objects people can manipulate. In a direct and explicit way, the practices confront two basic cognitive mechanisms of human categorisation, namely recognition by perceptual appearance and automatic ascription of psychological essentialism. By juxtaposing essence and appearance—in ascribing either novel essence to familiar appearance or novel appearance to familiar essence—counterintuitive representations are created, representations that are hard to categorise as belonging to a specific domain organised by ontological assumptions. Is it bread or flesh? Is it a prince or a frog? These counterintuitive elements and objects function as highly salient items of memorisation and transmission (Boyer 1990, 1994). They are also important in ritual procedures, not only by facilitating the manipulation of and interaction with sacred essence inside a ritual space, but as pragmatic signs marking off the special character of the actions, thereby emphasising the difference between ritual and profane mental spaces.

5.1.2 Forward Contagion (Essence Transfer)

A second type of transformative magic concerns transfer of essence between ritual elements by means of contact. This is intimately related to representations of contagion and, as discussed in the beginning of this chapter, we find two modes of contagion, forward and backward, which can be seen as temporal inversions of each other (see figure 5.2 below). In forward contagion, the physical contact or contiguity of two otherwise distinct elements ensures a transfer of essence. In backward contagion, *prior* physical contact between two elements is believed to have created an essential link that can be used to manipulate elements in one domain in order to affect elements in another domain. This will be analysed in detail in the section on manipulative magic. What these practices have in common is the mental and social representation that some sort of physical contact facilitates the establishment of an essence link, enabling either the immediate transfer of essence or the future magical manipulation of one element by means of an essential link to the other. It is important to recognise that, despite its negative connotation, both types of contagion exists in both positive and negative versions, and that valorisation to a substantial extend depends on viewpoint.

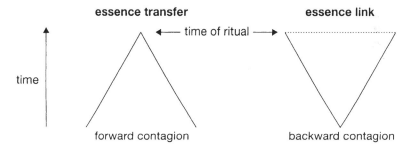

Figure 5.2: Essence transfer and essence-link

As seen in the model, time and spatial distance are the primary parameters distinguishing the two types. Each line represents a ritual element. In forward contagion, the elements start out as separate and are connected at the time of the ritual, whereas in backward contagion the elements are represented as once connected but separate at the time of the ritual. Whereas forward contagion is based on physical or pseudo-physical contact and spatial proximity in the actual ritual, backward contagion is based on an earlier contact between the two objects and current spatial distance.

Representations of forward contagion are found in practices such as inhalation, ingestion and touching, but metaphorically extended to cover instances of seeing and hearing. As an example, the analysis of the Catholic practice of the ritual of Eucharist or Holy Communion is extended. Above, we saw how the perceptual appearances of bread and wine had their corresponding essences changed into that of Christ through the ritual act of transubstantiation. The following part of the ritual is an instrumental action that enables the main purpose of the ritual as a whole: the dissemination of sacred essence to all correctly initiated participants in the ritual. The model below illustrates this essential transfer. The ritual agent (the priest) is not depicted, as he has no active role, but one should keep in mind that the whole ritual sequence is structured by an action representation schema, according to which an agent performs an action on one or several objects. Thus, contrary to the act of transubstantiation, a deaf-dumb priest can perform this ritual in case of emergency (McCarthy 1956: 9), as the sacred essence has already been transferred into the bread dispensed, and the object can be understood as carrier of the magical agency. The model focuses on the interrelation between a subject participating in the ritual and the ritual object ingested.

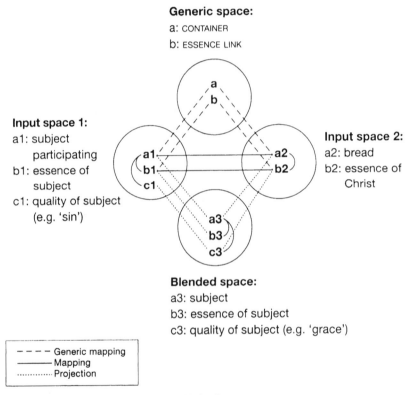

Figure 5.3: Forward contagion in Holy Communion

Figure 5.3 models some of the possible active connections in the representation of Holy Communion. For the subject participating in the ritual it is a prerequisite that he or she has undergone another ritual—baptism—that changes the essence of the individual, as it is "reborn" in the community of the church, the metonymic extension of Christ and the Trinity. It is telling that this embedded ritual of baptism (Lawson & McCauley 1990) follows a similar procedure according to which a material element is consecrated—an action changing the essential qualities of the material—which in turn is used to change the essence or quality of a ritual participant by contagious transfer. Thus, by virtue of baptism, the counterpart connection between the ritual subject and the bread is not entirely dependent on a correspondence of space internal structures (both elements being containers containing an essence), but also by a direct metonymic LINK between the essence of the subjects and the essence of Christ/the Church present in the conceptual model of a member of the congregation. The formal or symbolic qualities of the subject expressed in baptism are, however, not the only prerequisites. The ritual subject's intentional recognition that the essence of the bread and wine contains the essence of Christ is also necessary for the efficacy of the ritual. In fact, according to explicit doctrine, the ingestion will have a negative effect without this recognition (1 Corinthians 11:27-39). To what extent explicit doctrine has cognitive effect is an open question, but in any case it strengthens the understanding that the status of the individual participants is based on an ascription of essence rather than mere formal initiation.

The most significant part of this model is that the essence of Christ, present in the bread, is transformed into a quality of the subject ingesting the bread. Ritual participants are not subject to a change of their fundamental essence, but receive a quality that can be interpreted in different ways, for instance as entailing the remission of sins performed after baptism. In that light, communion is a recurring ritual having effect on the quality of the subject, in this instance by replacing the quality 'sin' with that of 'grace.' However, in this context the importance lies not in the actual interpretation of the quality. Rather it rests in the representational structure that by the ingestion of a substance a specific essence is transferred and that, by virtue of this particular action, the essence is transformed into a quality of the participating subject. The ingestion of the ritual bread does not supplant the already existing essence but transforms the quality of the subject. This is a theme found in many examples in the history of religion and ethnography, in which a desired quality is obtained by contagious interaction with an element in possession of the desired essence or quality, or a negative quality is acquired by pollution stemming from unintended contagious interaction. Of course, this is tightly connected to cultural conceptual systems ascribing certain qualities and essences to elements in the world and delimiting which of these are eligible for ritual manipulation. Does this imply that these connections are purely arbitrary? Two answers can be given to this question: First, participants experience aspects of conceptual models found in a given ritual as containing *real* essences or qualities. This points to the fact that even if languages and conceptual systems of a given culture are largely arbitrary and conventional in a diachronic perspective, the synchronic relationship between subjects and cultural systems is more adequately described by the notions of participation and motivation. Words and concepts are experienced as "experiential natural" and "transparent" rather than arbitrary and conventional (Shore 1996: 331-32). Second, even if the interpretation of what is transmitted will most likely change through time, the very basic representation of receiving something through a contagious action cannot change, but can only be eradicated. In a comparative perspective, magical rituals are therefore profitably described by principles of how essences, qualities and structures are transmitted and manipulated, and by the role played by certain aspects of conceptual structures in this process.

In the case of the communion, the ingestion of the bread is an act in which one container (the subject) absorbs and dissolves another container thereby releasing the essence it contains. This is, of course, a very basic schema of forward contagion, relevant in all representations of nutritional value of foods, of transfer of diseases by close contact with infected people, as well as in representations of more symbolic values attached to elements, such as bravery of the bear, believed to be transferred by ingestion or other types of contagious interaction (for several examples see Douglas 1995; Kirkland 1994). It is important to notice that such representations are very common in areas not traditionally covered by the terms 'magic' or 'religion.' The special status of objects formerly owned by famous peoples, such as John F. Kennedy, Elvis Presley or Princess Diana, are excellent examples of 'non-religious' notions of forward contagion. Even if these representations do not contain any clear and expressed notion involving the transfer of essence between the desired person and the person now in possession of the material media, it is unlikely that an Elvis fan would allow the dry-cleaning of a jacket formerly worn by the idol. The studies of Rozin and Nemeroff already cited give clear evidence that such essentialist connections are even stronger in relations of repulsion, exemplified by such things as eating a food once in contact with a cockroach, even if it was both dead and disinfected (Rozin & Nemeroff 1990). The examples of both Elvis and the cockroach point to a general hypothesis: that the epistemic judgement of the belief in or likelihood of a certain connection, whether based on indexical contagion or iconic similarity, is a symbolic operation *succeeding* the cognitive processing and establishment of counterpart connections, as are the judgement whether an influence is desirable or not. This will be further treated below.

To summarise, we have seen how magical actions based on representations of forward contagion involve a strong notion of essence that can be transferred by means of 'physical' contact. By bringing two elements in close contact, essence is represented as being transferred between containers belonging to two separate mental spaces in a direction specified in the ritual. Thus, unidirectional transfer of essence is usually schematised by the action representation in which the object of the action is understood as the destination of the transfer and the element containing the desired essence will be either the agent or the instrument of the action. In the transfer of essences, these are transformed into qualities of the receiving subject, whose fundamental essence is unchanged, distinguishing these ritual actions from those of essence change or retention. Representation of forward contagion can be seen as an extension of causal representations of things like the nutritional value of foods, the experience of a burning sensation of the skin after getting burned on a hot object etc. There are countless numbers of everyday experiences that support notions of forward contagion. Based on the work of Rozin, Nemeroff and associates referred to at the beginning of this chapter, Pascal Boyer argues for the evolutionary origin of a domain-specific inference module primarily used to avoid contaminated food. Basic principles of this inference module are "that the dangerous substance is not necessarily visible, that the dose does not matter, that any contact with the original source of danger transmits the whole pollution" (Boyer 2001: 135). When applied outside its proper domain, for instance to the interaction between people, it will lead to apparently irrational notions of polluting kinds of people, either based on origin or occupation. It is an open question whether notions of forward contagion have their origin in a single specialised cognitive module. First, we experience instances of forward contagion in several different situations besides contaminated food, e.g. in the transfer of cold or heat between objects and the body (invisible substance), or in behaviour spreading through groups of people, such as laughing and yawning. Second, it is unlikely that notions of pollution are not graded. Thus, cleansing rituals will differ in correlation to the type of contact with a polluting object or agent (e.g. prescriptions for Brahmins that have been in contact with polluting material, see *Vishnu Purana*, Ch. 17), and this is in correspondence with another possible source of schemata for ritual contagion, that of physical pollution and cleansing.

5.1.3 Principles of Transformative Magical Action

If notions of contagion are not based on a single domain specific inference module, which principles are then responsible for the widespread notions of transfer of essential qualities through physical contact or spatio-temporal contiguity? Is it possible to unearth some underlying cognitive structures uniting these otherwise diverse beliefs? Above, I have described two types of magical actions that involve strong representations of essence. The first group covers the instances of essence change and essence retention. The most basic generic features expressed in representations of these actions are all based on psychological essentialism and, related to this, the image-schematic structure of CONTAINMENT. An important aspect of this focus is the complex interaction between essence and appearance, resulting in all sorts of counterintuitive representations combining perceptual appearance with very unlikely essences. The second group is representations of magical actions based on the transfer of essence by contact.

The first area of interest is the importance of the element invested with magical agency in respect to both essence change and essence retention. As noted, essence change and essence retention can be understood as strong indices of an element's (often the agent's) possession of magical agency and form part of the cultural and idealised cognitive models of the element containing that agency. This can be expressed in the principle that *the greater ontological dis-*

crepancy between an element's physical appearance and its ascribed essence, the stronger attention on the possessor of magical agency able to bring about this discrepancy. Not everybody can change the essence of bread into that of Christ, change the appearance of a prince into that of a frog or make a broomstick fly into the air. It demands strong magical agency and the greater the ontological discrepancy between essence and appearance, the more powerful this agency has to be. As described in chapter 3, basic-level categorisation utilises a combination of perceptual features and ascription of essence in order to form experiential gestalts. Therefore, a strong discrepancy between the two approaches will trigger a search for a reason for this and for an agent responsible.

Another important feature is the designation of things, events, and psychological dispositions violating causal expectations based on ontological assumptions as 'magical' by pre-school children.[3] The basic problem is posed by developmental psychologist Jean Piaget's description of young children as understanding many events in a quasi-magical (Johnson & Harris 1994: 35), pre-operational or even pre-logical fashion (Zusne & Jones 1989: 26). According to Piaget, such early understanding is supplanted by a rational, causal and operational approach in the course of development. In order to test this hypothesis, several psychologists have investigated even very young children's causal expectations of objects in the world, and found that children seem to have a predominantly rational understanding of the world, even if limited by lack of knowledge in some domains. Very early, children subscribe to most of the ontological assumptions described in chapter 3.1.1, but simultaneously describe certain events as 'magical' when prompted by contextual and motivational factors. In these psychological studies, both psychologists and children use the concepts of 'magic' and 'magical' to designate events violating causal expectations or involving strong discrepancy between essence and appearance. In both cases there is a strong ascription of special agency to a 'magician' making these otherwise impossible events possible.

> Thus, the dominant mode of children's causal reasoning about events in the natural world appears rational, not magical. Young children do, however, accept magical mechanisms for changes and do not make a distinction between possible and impossible outcomes *if a magician is involved in the transformation*. Thus, children seem to have access both to normal, everyday mechanisms and to extraordinary, magical ones to make sense of their experience (Rosengren, Kalish et al 1994: 80, emphasis added).

It is likely that such events are not only better understood by reference to cognitive models of magical agents but, more concretely, that explicit counterintuitive or inexplicable events trigger the development of representations of such magical agents in the first place. Children will search for a magical agent as an explanatory factor in events breaking causal expectations. Of course, all things being equal, this search for a magical agent will exploit external cultural models already found in a given culture. This process is strengthened by the role played by contextual factors—such as grown-ups acting on the basis of a story containing magical elements—in children's judgements of the possibility of certain events (Woolley & Phelps 1994: 63; Subbotsky 1994: 105). The construction of a ritual space and ascription of magical agency has fundamental influence on the judgement of possibility of events also by adult participants (Sørensen 2002).

In the second type of representation involving essence as a contagious element, there is no such necessary focus on magical agency. Agents, objects and actions invested with magical agency will be represented as repositories of desirable or feared special essence (either as a result of an idiosyncratic or cultural designation), and thus function as containers one can interact with in order to receive (or avoid) an essential quality. Two important principles are at work in facilitating notions of forward contagion. The first principle is obvious and involves the generic space image-schema of CONTAINMENT understood as the bearer of internal essence. In notions of contagion involving the human body, the body is understood as the primary container carrying a human essence and as able to receive other essences and qualities as a new quality of its own. In order to transgress the border of the body, some 'vehicle' is needed that will often itself have the schematic structures of a container. This might explain the prevalence of mediating objects such as the bread and wine in rituals involving transfer of otherwise 'non-embodied' essence. The understanding of the body as a container implies a whole range of schematic entailments as to the exact nature of both positive and negative contagion. The skin is the BOUNDARY between an inside, containing an essence, and an outside with all kinds of objects containing essences of varying FORCE that are either desired or feared. But this boundary, the skin, has several openings allowing foreign essences and qualities to be transferred from other containers. A principle structuring the conception of the body as a container in relation to contagion is, *(a) the deeper a penetration into the receiving bodily container, (b) the more open / fragile the yielding container, and (c) the more powerful the transmitted essence, the more efficacious the contagious transfer*. This means that eating or inhaling something will, all other things being equal, produce a more contagious transfer than merely touching or looking at it, and that eating an object that passes right through your digestive system will be less contagious than eating an object dissolving inside it (Rozin et al 1995). A forceful essential quality, however, might effect a stronger transfer—for instance, by merely looking—than a weaker force effects by ingestion. Thus, contagion can be understood as a system involving force-dynamic representations of the relative strength of the borders of two containers, of possible entries, and of the power of essence or quality transferred.

If this principle holds, we must explain why there is a discrepancy between the relative importance of rituals involving different kinds of contagious transfer. Why, for example, is Christian baptism regarded as at least equally important to communion, when baptism only involves water touching the outer skin, a case in apparent contradiction to the principle stated above? Why is the water not consumed? One possible reason is that contagious transfers are constrained by the basic schemata underlying the performed action. Where communion is based on a CONSUMMATION-schema, baptism is based on a combination of a CLEANSING-schema, a CONTACT-schema and explicit symbolic representations of rebirth. This has obvious consequences for participants' evaluation of the relative importance of the two rituals. Baptism is represented as an essential transformation, in which the old individual dies and makes room for a new essence. The old person is cleansed away, and a new person emerges in its place, facilitated by the transfer of new essence effected by contact with the sanctified water. In contrast, communion must be repeated, just as consummation of food must be repeated, in order to renew its otherwise temporary effect. The ritual only effects the qualities of the recipient, whereas the essence (already transformed by baptism) is unaffected. Harvey Whitehouse's theory of two different modes of religiosity based on two types of ritual transmission offers another and complementary explanation. Often repeated rituals, such as communion, are related to what Whitehouse defines as the "doctrinal mode of religiosity", with a relative heavy emphasis on the transmission of propositional knowledge. These are subject to a "tedium-effect", as they are stored in semantic memory, are strongly scripted (one cannot remember one communion from another), and repeated with a low level of sensory pageantry. When focusing on representations of ritual efficacy, this entails a relative downsizing of its directly experienced efficacy of the ritual action. In contrast, (for the direct participants) baptism is an "infrequently performed ritual" related to the "imagistic mode of religiosity" stored in the episodic memory (Whitehouse 2000). This points to the fact that the frequency of transmission is an important parameter both for the cognitive processing of the ritual actions, as well as for subsequent evaluations of their relative importance and magical efficacy. Finally, the wide range of ways to perform baptism points to the importance of the above mentioned principle. The ritual can be performed as a mere cleansing of the head or as a total submerging of the whole body—the latter mostly performed in cases of conversion and adult baptism. This indicates that in baptism of young or adults the action must reflect its relative importance, in contrast to infant baptism, where the direct recipient is indifferent. Thus, the principles presented above are valid descriptions of basic cognitive intuitions governing evaluations of ritual actions, even though they are constrained by other parameters, such as frequency, memory and the relative weighting of individual rituals in larger ritual complexes.

The discussion above indicates that elements used in contagious transfer are embedded in both episodic and narrative schemata organising the recent past of the elements employed, as well as in cultural models and conceptual systems, directing attention towards elements containing desirable or unwanted essences. The bread and wine of the communion will not work if not ascribed essence via the prior event of transubstantiation, and this temporal organisation is intimately connected to the diagnosis of events and the prognosis of effect that surrounds most ritual actions. This will be discussed in detail in the following chapter. Bread functioning as a container of the essence of Christ, the healing effect of relics, and, to a certain extent, the health value of vitamin pills, are all based on cultural models specifying these objects as containing positive qualities that we should have contagious interaction with. Cultures, cultural systems and cultural models all play an important role in both emphasising and limiting different elements understood as bearers of contagious essence, even if cognitive mechanisms responsible for the mental representation of contagious transfer is independent of and underdetermined by culture, and emerges on its own accord.

5.2 Manipulative Magical Action: The *Schematic* Blend

Manipulative magical action covers ritual procedures aimed at changing schematic properties in one domain by the active manipulation of elements in another domain. This is achieved either directly by physical interaction (e.g. by manipulating an effigy), or indirectly by using natural language or other symbolic features. Broadly speaking, a structure or a frame from one mental space and elements from another space are projected into the blend. This makes it possible to manipulate elements belonging to one domain by means of a structure projected from another domain. Blends appearing in this type of magic are often based on one-sided shared topology networks, in which only a few elements originate in one space, and a whole frame structuring the blend originate in another (see chapter 3.3; Fauconnier & Turner 1998). The active use of image-schematic properties, in relation to the transfer of magical agency through iconic reproduction of ritual action, has already been described. At this descriptive level, iconic representations are used in order to produce a change in a specific area of experience by virtue of image-schematic connections to element in another domain. Analogy, similarity and metaphor all play a central role in the performance of manipulative magic, but metonymic relations are also active in the construction of counterpart connections between mental spaces especially in cases of backward contagion.

Three sub-types of manipulative magic can be distinguished according to the counterpart connection used to relate the two domains: (1) backward contagion is based on *pars pro toto* relations, in which the essential connection between an element and its (former) parts enable a mapping between two otherwise distinct domains; (2) blending of object schemata covers the widespread usage of perceptual and conventional similarity in order to manipulate objects in magical rituals (Similarity of Objects); and (3) blending of action schemata is related to the fact that the performance of iconic actions often are central elements in manipulative rituals (Similarity of Actions). This distinction is analytic. Real world rituals do not follow such neat distinctions, but there will be a tendency to emphasise one of these aspects depending on which types of counterpart connection is evoked.

5.2.1 Backward Contagion (Essence Link)

Ritual practices based on representations of backward contagion have traditionally been seen as the primary example of the 'irrationality' of magical practices. In backward contagion, manipulation of one element is understood as influencing another element that it was once in contact with. Examples of this type of contagious influence in the ethnographic historic literature are *legio*. A footprint can be used to manipulate the person whose foot made the imprint, hair cut off from someone's head can be used to influence that person etc. Whereas forward contagion is an extension of ordinary principles of mechanical causality, according to which an element will influence another element by direct mechanical interaction (Leslie 1994), practices based on backward causation seem very 'irrational' as they break with the basic intuitive assumption concerning action at distance. This leads Skorupski (1976) to define these actions as based on a former contagious connection later transformed into a symbolic relation. The element once in physical contact with another element is later merely a symbol of the thing it was in contact with. In this manner, Skorupski seems to avoid the problem of irrationality, as the action is only symbolic and does not claim any actual influence and thus upholds the no-action-at-a-distance constraint. But the many practices aimed to protect subjects against sorcery involving backward contagion—such as the ritual destruction or hiding of bodily residues like hair, teeth and nails—indicate a much more direct and effective understanding of the connection between elements connected by contagion. If we instead presume that the symbolic evaluation of the 'likeliness' of the *causal* connection implied by a ritual action only follows the cognitive mechanisms establishing the connection, we can postpone the problem of the rationality of a given causal connection, and instead focus on the internal logic of the counterpart connections established between the elements. Backward contagion plays an important role in magical rituals, as one of the basic representational links established between two conceptual spaces, and representations of backward contagion often appears in manipulative magic as a metonymic counterpart connector enabling interaction with one space through manipulative action in another.

An example of beliefs in backward contagion is the procedure invented during the search in seventeenth century England for a method of exact measurement of the navigational longitude. This is, in the strict sense of the term, not a ritual use of backward contagion, but the example has the merit of removing the representation from notions of primitivism and at the same time explicates the more general cognitive ground for representations of contagion. The proper designation of the exact position of a ship at sea would be of great advantage for navigation, and thereby give a lead in trade and politics for the nation first possessing such a method. The whole problem was basically the impossibility of exact time-keeping on ocean-going ships. A precise chronometer was yet to be invented, and the exact knowledge of the time in Greenwich compared to local time was a prerequisite for determining the longitude. A determined search led to several competing theories, as well as ardent competition, especially between astronomers and clock-makers. A more odd, yet serious, theory was conceived based on backward contagion. The theory was based on a negative inversion of the widespread belief in 'weapon-salve', that is the possibility of treating a wound through the manipulation of the weapon used to inflict the wound, and, more specifically, the blood remaining on the weapon (Frazer 1991: 202ff; Thomas 1991: 225, 266). In an attempt to designate a method of measuring the longitude, a dog was wounded with a sword. The wounded dog was taken on an ocean-going ship, and its wound prevented from healing, whereas the sword was kept in Greenwich. In Greenwich, everyday at noon, a powder was applied to the sword that wounded the dog (and still having the dog's blood on it). According to the theory, the dog on the ship would then howl in pain at the exact same time, because of an essential link between the sword and the wound, and the blood on the sword and the blood in the dog. By determining the local time by measuring the position of the sun and comparing the result to the Greenwich time indicated by the howling dog, the navigator could determine the exact longitudinal position of the ship.[4]

Figure 5.4 illustrates how the manipulation of a sword with the dog's blood on it is believed to influence the dog, even when hundreds of miles separate the two elements. There are two possible bearers of the counterpart connection. The first is the metonymic connection between the instrument and the result of an action, the weapon and the wound it inflicts. This is an example of the widespread belief of the continuous relation between (instrumental) cause and effect. In the framing of an event, the designation of elements to different roles in the desired causal unfolding is a prerequisite. It is obvious that a special 'windowing' of attention is active in this case, as focus is directed to the material instrument, i.e. the direct mechanical force and the result it inflicts. This need not be the case. In examples of witchcraft, for instance among the Azande, the material instrument is often all but ignored and the connection to the ascribed intending agent—the witch—is emphasised. The witch found by means of divination must 'cool' his or her witchcraft, in order for the connection to be terminated, or if none is found, the victim must protect himself by magical medicine and vengeance magic (Evans-Pritchard 1937).[5] The reason for bringing in the Zande example is to emphasise that the connection believed to exist between different parts of a causal frame is too a large extent locally determined and strongly influenced by cultural dispositions connecting certain effects to certain causes and intentions. The framing of several elements into a single event-frame (wounding the dog with a sword) is the generic space schema that facilitates the connection, subsequently enabling the metonymic connection between the sword and the wound. Metonymic connections based on causal framing, however, are limited to interacting within the same frame and they retain the causal direction specified by that frame. Weapon-salve can be used to heal or worsen a wound already inflicted, but not to bring for instance richness to the wounded, and by manipulating the weapon the wound can be influenced, but the opposite is not the case.

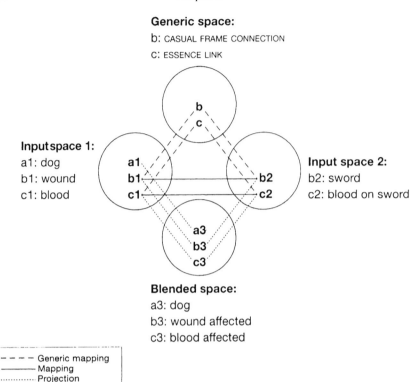

Figure 5.4: Backward contagion

This constraint does not apply in the second type of counterpart connection: the direct metonymic relation between the blood on the sword and the blood in the wound. This is an example of the belief in the continuous connection between a part and the whole from which it originates (*pars pro toto*). The metonymic connection is an example of the Neoplatonic understanding of the universe as interwoven by correspondences between essences, and parts and wholes. The neoplatonic theory held that "the vital spirits in the blood congealed on the weapon would be drawn along the air to rejoin the body" (Thomas 1991: 266). According to Thomas, however, such systematised belief in weapon-salve was an elitist development of a widespread 'folk-belief' in the essential relation between a wound and its blood on the one hand, and the weapon used to create the wound and the blood remaining upon it on the other (Thomas 1991: 225, 266). In the framework given by a cognitive theory of magic, such an explanation of the essential connection is a secondary symbolic interpretation based on pre-established and cognitively more basic indexical and iconic connections. The generic space schema that facilitates the metonymic connection is based on essentialist representations connecting part and whole by an ESSENCE LINK. Unless the belief enters into a more systematised system of representations demanding an explanation of the causal connection, the exact nature of the causal connection relating the whole to the part need not be represented at all as the connection is automatically ascribed.

To summarise: contrary to forward contagion that works by direct interaction, backward contagion works on the essential link established through prior physical interaction. The metonymic counterpart connections established thereby are based on several cognitive schemata, such as a PART-WHOLE schema or EPISODIC schemata that interrelate elements of the same causal frame. No matter which type of metonymy, the importance lies in the essential link relating the two elements and their respective mental spaces. An experiential basis of backward contagion is less obvious than in the case of forward contagion. Good candidates are emotional attachment, relating a part to a whole, an indexical sign relation between the two element, according to which one element will 'point to' the other element, and the experience of a PATH-schema relating present elements to past interactions as an imaginary line.[6] However, the experiential basis only strengthens the counterpart connection facilitated by essentialist assumption that underlie identity and metonymy ("it is the dog's blood on the sword"), the framing of sequences ("this wound was made by this particular sword"), and the local, pragmatic and motivated explication of these possible connections for some ritual purpose.

5.2.2 Object Schematic Blending

Magical rituals involving objects that have some sort of similarity to elements that a particular agent wants to influence are widespread and has long been considered one of the defining characteristics of magical procedures (e.g. Frazer 1911). This, however, is fraught with serious problems, especially if similarity is taken as *the* defining feature of these actions. As Mauss and Hubert convincingly argued, connections based on similarity or contagion do not just appear out of the blue, but are conventionalised connections tightly related to a given culture's classificatory systems: "they [sympathetic rites] are performed, not because they are logically realizable, but because they are prescribed." (Mauss 1972: 51). Lakoff and Johnson make the same point concerning the foundations of metaphor. Metaphor cannot be explained by reference to perceptual similarity alone, but depend on experience, conceptual structures and conventional connections (Lakoff & Johnson 1980, and chapter 3). This, however, does not change the fact that comparison based on similarity and difference is the main focus of interest once the connection has been established. Cultural models embedded in conceptual systems to a large extent decide *which* elements are alike, but only to a limited extend *how* they are alike. The likeness is relevant from a cognitive perspective, relative to the perceptual features facilitating the establishment of counterpart connections between two mental spaces. The widespread performance of magical action by using effigies (voodoo magic) can be taken as an example of this. A person is represented as afflicted because a magician is manipulating a doll representing him by resemblance. Mauss and Hubert are obviously right in claiming that the doll does not resemble the man to any great extent, and that the production of 'magical dolls' are prescribed and conventionalised (Mauss 1972: 68). Still, the doll cannot have any possible form. It will have an overall structure resembling the schematic structure of a human being, and these schematic properties inform the magician's interaction with the doll. When piercing the leg of the doll, this interaction will most likely be represented as influencing exactly the leg of the man represented by the doll. Other elements would have to be applied in order for the doll to represent a specific person, and not just any human being that resembles the crude schematic form of the doll. This can be done by various means containing a *motivated* link to the person in question, such as by metonymy, by contagious materials like clothing or hair, by symbolic means, like the name of the person, or finally by the magician just directing his attention towards that specific person. This illustrates how both metonymic and symbolic connections are used in representations of schematic manipulations in order to direct these to their designated goal. Further, essence-based metonymic connections are used to establish the contagious interaction of the two domains through what both Evans-Pritchard and later Tambiah described as the *materia medica* (Evans-Pritchard 1935: 448; Malinowski 1968: 193). This practice might be even more pertinent in practices where linguistic mapping alone establish a connection between two domains, giving to the ritual some degree of materiality.

My first example of object schematic blending used in magical rituals comes from the Trobriander *Yowota*-ritual, which is the inaugural ritual of the agricultural calendar and, more specifically, the part involving the *Vatuvi* spell described by Malinowski (1935a: 93-102; 1935b: 255-65). The *Vatuvi* spell is one of the central spells in Trobriand magic and is recited on several occasions during the agricultural cycle. In relation to the *Yowota* ritual it is recited in the magician's hut the day before the clearing of the bush presently occupying the selected garden-sites. The recitation is performed by 'breathing it' in between two coconut mats that contain the axes used in the coming clearing and a magical mixture attached to these. Thus, the spell is 'connected' to the axes and when the axes touch the ground the next day the efficacy of the spell as a whole is transferred to the garden by contagious interaction. The legitimacy of the magician is invoked in the beginning of the spell by a reference to the genealogical connection to ancestors previous in office (as we saw in the last chapter). Immediately hereafter follows the part of the spell that is of interest in this context, namely the procreative part aimed at enhancing the fertility of the garden:

"The belly of my garden [hereafter ...] leavens, ... rises, ... reclines, ... grows to the size of a bush-hen's nest, ... grows like an anthill, ... rises and is bowed down, ... rises like the iron-wood palm, ... lies down, ... swells, ... swells as if with a child" (Malinowski 1935a: 96-97).

In this case, the schematic blending of objects is only expressed linguistically. The ritual procedures, however, involve both some of the materials mentioned above and others in the magical mixture that function as a *materia medica* attached to the axes with a leaf and used in a contagious fashion. These are equally based on motivated perceptual similarities such as colour, strength or form (summarised in Tambiah 1968: 193-94). The use of the materials mentioned in the spell strengthen the metaphoric connections already established in the linguistic blending, and in effect this material action will tend to 'materialise' the blended mental space presented below as a concrete action using direct mechanical interaction of forwards contagion. Consequently, a purely metaphoric connection is changed into one of metonymic contagion (Tambiah 1968: 194).

"The belly of my garden", repeated throughout the spell, is a conventional metaphor of widespread usage in Trobriand spells other than the *Vatuvi*.[7] In the Trobriand conceptual system, there is a direct relation between humans and the land and soil of their gardens. A given sub-clan, dominating a village politically and owning the garden magic, is believed to have originated out of a hole in the soil cultivated by this particular village. Thus, we find a metonymic relationship between people (represented by the leading clan by metonymy) and soil, according to which the people were 'born' from the soil at a specific spot through a hole ('birth canal') (Malinowski 1935a: 64, 341-42). This connection is further strengthened by a conventional conceptual mapping describing yams (*taytu*) as the "children of the garden" (263). Keeping in mind that land is owned by women and inherited by matrilineal descend, even if cultivated by male descendants and their family, a direct metaphorical connection is established between women and land. So, like yams, humans originate from the soil, and, like human children, yams are born. This is related to the deep-layered intuition that common origin entails, if not identity, at least common essence. As a result, the garden soil will be equated conceptually with a woman in two ways: (1) humans originate from it, and (2) yams are the children of the garden soil. In the metaphor of "the belly of my garden", this is further strengthened by image-schematic representations of 'inside-outside' connected to both human belly and soil, and the possible movement from inside to outside in birth and harvesting respectively.[8] This is illustrated in figure 5.5:

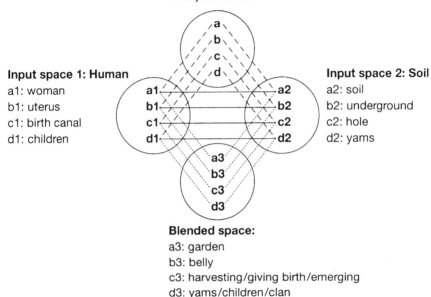

Figure 5.5: Trobriand mapping between women and garden

Figure 5.5 illustrates the importance of basic image-schemata such as INSIDE, OUTSIDE, CONTAINER, BORDER, SURFACE, SOURCE, PATH and GOAL. In combination, these image-schemata supply a very rich structure to the mapping and facilitate all sorts of force-dynamic interpretations, elaborations and creations of idealised cognitive models. The complex mappings between 'woman' and 'soil', and 'humans' ('children') and 'yams' can be extended to a wide range of counterpart connections, for instance in the elaborate rituals following pregnancy, in which the woman, on behalf of her unborn child, avoids 'daylight-like' yams, and is dyed in white colour (the same colour as good yams tubers have when thinned, see Malinowski, 1935a: 152, Tambiah 1968). Thus, a general cultural model is generated organising diverse, but interrelated, mappings between humans, women, soil and yams (tubers). It is used actively in several domains (myth of origin, child birth, gardening), it is poly-directional (e.g. yams are like children, children are like yams), and it is embedded in the conceptual system by homonyms that are motivated by metaphorical mapping.[9] This cultural model is utilised in the spell by using metaphors to describe the desired development and future condition of the yam garden. "The belly of my garden" is mapped onto several other domains described in figure 5.6:

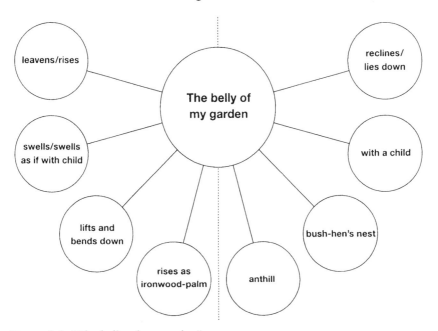

Figure 5.6: "The belly of my garden"

Figure 5.6 illustrates the mapping present in the spell. It is, apparently, quite easy to understand. The blending (not represented) between the target-domain (belly of my garden) and all these other domains makes it clear that the magician wants the garden to prosper and that he gets that message through by using several metaphors all describing this development and the following result. The mappings involved, however, are not as simple as that. A complex cognitive activity ensures that only a very few of the possible counterpart mappings are actually entertained. Making this kind of list of metaphors compresses a combination of mappings into a single mental representation, which again has two interrelated results. First, unwanted inferences are removed through the combined mappings leaving only a few common image-schemata intact. The belly of my garden cannot both contain a baby, be an anthill and rise like an ironwood palm, but the basic image-schemata present in these metaphors combine finely (CONTAINER, BULGING OBJECT, EXPANSION, UPWARDS TRAJECTORY). Second, the combined mappings result in a strengthening of the desired transfer of properties through schematic repetition. This is a feature found in most Trobriand spells and a common feature in spells and magical rituals in general. The repetition results both in a de-symbolisation, i.e. the removal of all unwanted symbolic meaning of the elements mapped, and in a strengthening of specific, directly experienced meaning based on image-schematic structures. The metaphors are divided into two groups: a predominantly dynamic schematism to the left and a predominantly static schematism to the right. The dynamic schemata refer to the *process* of the surface of the soil rising (EXPANSION, UPWARDS TRAJECTORY) as a result of the growing tubers, whereas the static schemata refer to the end result of this process (CONTAINER, BULGING OBJECT). The static domain is further emphasised by the otherwise rather enigmatic references to "reclining" and "lying down". It is possible that this feature can be explained by reference to other aspects of the agricultural cycle, such as the matured crops. By presenting a great number of metaphorical instances of these image-schemata, the "meaning" of the ritual is to ensure that the desired image-schematic properties in the garden domain are unfolded. Remember, these words are spoken directly to the axes used later to strike the ground, and in this manner the desired quality is transferred by contagious interaction. The following part of the *Vatuvi*-spell will be analysed in the next section (5.2.3), as it is an example of action schematic blending.

Before getting to that, a second example of object schematic blending is useful, as it is based on the direct physical manipulation of objects, rather than linguistic representations of these. Evans-Pritchard describes how a Zande man places a stone in the fork of a tree in order to delay sunset, an action apparently quite normal among the Azande (1937: 468-9). While placing a stone in a fork of a tree, the man addresses the stone saying:

> "You stone, may the sun not be quick to fall to-day. You, stone, retard the sun on high so that I can arrive first at my homestead to which I journey, then the sun may set" (Evans-Pritchard 1937: 469).

Before analysing the ritual, a precautionary remark is in place. In itself, the mapping illustrated below says nothing about the epistemic status of the behaviour described. It is merely a description of the mental operations necessary to have a meaningful comprehension of the behaviour. Whether each and every agent performing this rite has the representations in question is, of course, an open question. Some might do it just because others do it, applying an accepted cultural model to a pre-specified situation. It would, however, be very difficult to explain the origin and the persistence of the rite without these mental operations.

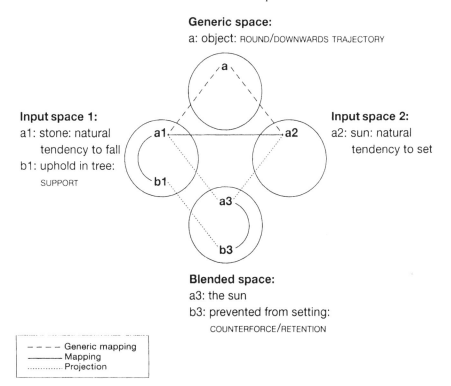

Figure 5.7: Zande spell delaying sunset

The two elements, connected in this mapping, are structured by a common shape (ROUND object) and a common image-schema and force-dynamic pattern (DOWNWARD TRAJECTORY). The common shape constitutes a very superficial similarity as stones are seldom perfectly round as is the sun seen from earth. It is the common image-schema that is of primary importance. Both the sun and the stone have a conceptual structure involving a DOWNWARD TRAJECTORY. The sun exposes this image-schematic structure every day at sunset and a stone when released from above the ground. This generic space schemata facilitates the construction of a metaphoric counterpart connection between the stone and the sun, necessary in order to influence one element (the sun) by manipulating and addressing the other (the stone). What happens is that the image-schema used to facilitate the metaphoric connection in the first place (DOWNWARD TRAJECTORY), is opposed in the domain containing the stone with another image-schema that works as a COUNTERFORCE. This second image-schema is the SUPPORT-schema structuring the ritual action of placing the stone in the fork of a tree performed by the agent, and thus opposing the effects of the DOWNWARD TRAJECTORY schema by SUPPORTING the stone. This SUPPORT-schema is projected into the blend together with the stone. The sun is projected by its metaphoric relation to the stone and connected to the SUPPORT-schema, which should then produce the desired result of the ritual action, the delay of sunset. The ritual creates the ambivalent situation that the schema connecting the two objects in the first place is the one the ritual seeks to abolish by the introduction of a second schema. It is unlikely that participants 'believe' that they actually stop the sunset, as it would be extremely easily falsified by experience. As Tambiah observes, the relation between the sun and the stone more likely replaces a relation between the traveller and the sun, in which the sun is winning 'the race' of getting home. By performing the ritual action, the agent replaces one relationship (the sun is travelling faster than the traveller) with another (the stone is retaining the sun). According to Tambiah's analysis, the ritual is 'performative' and, therefore, mainly serves as an expressive gesture of the man's desire to be home before dark (having the side-effect that he moves faster), rather than involving any belief in the efficacy of the ritual (Tambiah 1985: 74). I propose a middle way between such an expressive understanding and an interpretation based solely on notions of magical efficacy. In the ritual, an unwanted image-schema (DOWNWARD TRAJECTORY) is opposed by performing a ritual action involving a SUPPORT-schema that will function as a COUNTERFORCE. Therefore, DOWNWARD TRAJECTORY and SUPPORT enter into a force-dynamic interaction in which the SUPPORT-schema can only counter the effect of the DOWNWARD TRAJECTORY-schema to a limited extend, thus 'holding' or RETAINING the progress of the sun. This has to do with representations of relative power of the image-schematic tendencies of the objects concerned. There is, of course, an expressive side to this (in the performance of the ritual action), by which the relation to the sun is transferred from the traveller to the stone, but also an ascription of efficacy, without which one would ask why any participants would bother in the first place and actually use valuable time to perform the ritual. One should bear in mind that the epistemic judgement as to the possibility of the stone delaying the sun is a secondary cognitive procedure not necessarily provoked by the ritual performance and not in any way necessary for its performance.

In both the Trobriand and the Zande examples of object schematic blending, we see the extreme importance of image-schemata structuring both form and expected behaviour of the objects in question. In both cases, it is these abstract yet fundamental and basic aspects of human cognition that are active in connecting otherwise separate conceptual domains in local mental space interaction. Also, in both cases image-schematic qualities are represented as transferred between the two domains, thus influencing one domain by manipulating objects belonging to another domain.

5.2.3 Action Schematic Blending

The third type of manipulative magic is based on the practice of manipulating one domain of experience by performing certain actions in another domain. In this case, the similarity is not primarily between objects in the two domains, but between actions performed in one domain that should effect similar actions or results in another. Thus, even though object similarity may play a role in establishing a connection between the two domains, the schematic representation of an action transferred between the two domains is in focus. Again, Frazer can provide a short illustrative example ascribed to the Dyaks of Borneo. Two magicians help a woman in hard labour. One tries to help by manipulating the body of the woman, while the other simulates the birth of the baby by attaching a large stone to his stomach in order to manipulate it in a way similar to the one desired in the woman (Frazer 1911: 73). In this case, neither the stone nor the magician resembles the baby or the mother respectively. Instead, the action is represented schematically by a simulation, and connected to the space of the woman by: (a) a structural similarity between the image-schematic and force-dynamic patterns in the two spaces; and (b) the spatio-temporal contiguity ensuring that the right woman is affected. Again image-schematic features play a major role both in connecting the two spaces (the woman's and the magician's), and in the attempt to alter development in one space by manipulating image-schematic qualities in another space.

The example I analyse below is the continuation of the *Vatuvi*-spell analysed in the preceding section. This part of the spell is called the *Tapwana* or middle part of the spell (literally the 'body' or 'trunk' of the spell). It is the longest part of the spell and, in the important case of the *Vatuvi*-spell, recitation of the whole spell can last approximately 45 minutes (Malinowski 1935a: 98). It is the protective part, following the procreative part analysed above, and it consists of an almost endless repetition of exorcising words aimed at protecting the garden and its (future) crop against pests and diseases of the garden:

> "I sweep, I sweep, I sweep away. The grubs I sweep, I sweep away; the blight I sweep, I sweep away; insects, I sweep, I sweep away; the beetle with sharp tooth, I sweep, I sweep away; the beetle that bores, I sweep, I sweep away; the beetle that destroys the taro underground, I sweep, I sweep away; the marking blight, I sweep, I sweep away; the white blight on taro leaves, I sweep, I sweep away; the blight that shines, I sweep, I sweep away;......" (Malinowski, 1935a: 97).

The formula reproduced above is repeated with several other verbs filled in, such as "blow", "drive thee", "send thee" and "chase"—and Malinowski has not even reproduced the whole of this part of the spell. The spell is characterised by an extreme degree of redundancy, all aimed at emphasising the exorcising theme. This is represented in the figure below:

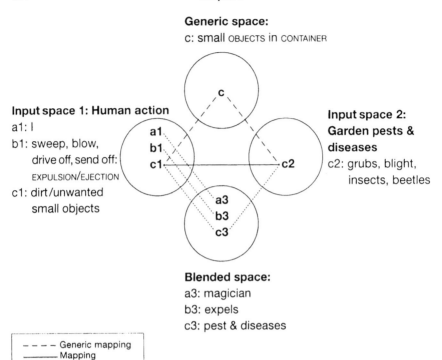

Figure 5.8: Trobriand garden exorcism I

In figure 5.8, the linguistic expression of the exorcism of garden pests and diseases is represented. The mapping is generated by the metaphoric counterpart connector between, on the one hand, objects functionally related to the human actions belonging to the domestic/social domain, involving expelling objects out of a bounded area (CONTAINER) where they do not belong. On the other hand, similar small objects of grubs, blight, insects and beetles are structured in a corresponding way to the rest of the domain of the garden—as unwanted objects in the bounded area of the garden domain. In the blend, the mode of interaction is projected from the domestic/social domain of human actions, and the objects of this action are projected from the domain of the garden. Thus, the blend enables the magician to manipulate physically things that are otherwise difficult or impossible to manipulate in the real garden. It is an example of a mapping between a relatively static domain characterised by a very specialised mode interaction (the garden) to a dynamic domain characterised by a very general mode of interaction (human action in the domestic/social sphere). We see a high degree of iteration of all the modes of action stemming from the domain of human action, a redundancy that strengthens the schematism of a movement away from the agent and that removes unwanted inferential extensions. The blend is an example of a one-sided topology network, in which the frame of the blend comes exclusively from one space that structures the interaction of elements projected from the other space. The basic image-schematic properties of EXPULSION and EJECTION are both examples of image-schemata present in a general class of magical actions that can be subsumed under the heading of exorcism, whether it is from a body or from another type of spatial CONTAINER, such as a garden. The juxtaposition of image-schemata such as the ones present in this example results in the creation of a force-dynamic field in which the strengths of EXPULSION and EJECTION are judged relative to the difficulties of crossing the BOUNDARY of the CONTAINER and the COUNTERFORCE exercised by the objects. Repetition and redundancy thus strengthen the relative power of the expelling schemata facilitating the expulsion of the designated objects from the unwanted area. This can be described as an iconic representation, in which strength is relative to time spend reciting this part of the spell and the amount of repetition present.

Exorcism rituals such as this are logical inversions of magical rituals aimed to attract positive or negative influences *into* a CONTAINER. As negative pollution seems to overshadow and overpower positive pollution (one drop of sewerage spoils a barrel of wine, but one drop of wine does not change a barrel of sewerage, Rozin & Nemeroff 1990), the need of exorcising evil forces might equally overpower the need to attract positive ones.

The *Vatuvi*-spell continues with another example of a one-sided topology network. Here, the pests and diseases are sent away by boat using a paddle, and travelling by a specific route towards the north-west, the direction all exorcised material and the spirits of the deceased go and that babies come from (Malinowski 1935b: 264). The following extract immediately succeeds the iterative second part analysed above:

"I split for thee thy sea-passage of Kadilaboma, O garden blight. Laba'i is thy village, Ituloma is thy coral boulder. Sail on a *de'u* leaf, that is thy boat. Paddle with a coconut leaf rib" (Malinowski 1935a: 98).

This extract of the *Vatuvi*-spell is an example of a conventional conceptual mapping between the domain of gardening and the domain of seafaring permeating both magic and mythology (Malinowski 1935a: 249). In several spells, concepts describing actions and elements of seafaring are used to describe actions and elements belonging to gardening. The *kamkokola*-sticks used to fence the garden and the log cabin used to store yams are all "anchored" or "moored". The log cabin, the important storehouse of yams, is also described as a "canoe" firmly "anchored" (248-49). In the exorcism, the garden blight is contained in a canoe that is not firmly anchored, but rather set on a specific course away from the village. This is represented in the figure below:

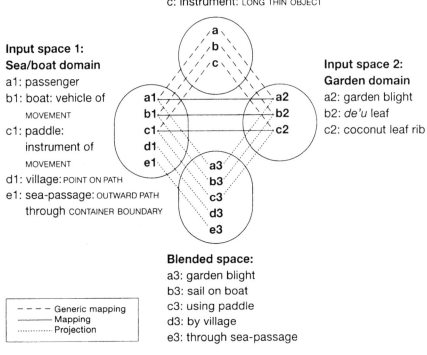

Figure 5.9: Trobriand garden exorcism II

In this blend, the frame of a sea-voyage—going by boat, using a paddle, following a specified route through the coral boundary—structures the pre-emptive interaction with the garden blight. The boat and the paddle both have their counterparts in the garden domain, thus facilitating that the garden blight can be understood as the passenger in the boat on this trip, despite the fact that there is no explicit creation of a direct connection between passenger and blight. The generic space contains basic image-schemata facilitating the construction of counterparts connections: LONG THIN OBJECT between paddle and coconut leaf rib, CONTAINER between boat and *de'u* leaf, and the possibility of something being CONTAINED mediates between passenger and garden blight. The mapping is coherent, which enables the possible extension of further mappings between elements in one domain and elements in the other. Explicit counterpart connections facilitate that the garden blight is understood as a passenger in the canoe crossing the BOUNDARY of a CONTAINER represented by the "splitting of a sea-passage", and that it embark on an OUTWARDS PATH that leads away from the garden and, by route of a village and a coral boulder (POINTS ON THE PATH), away from the island altogether. Again, image-schemata of one domain are used to interact with elements belonging to another domain, in this case resulting in the transfer of a stationary element, the garden blight, to a path leading away from the garden through a hole in the boundaries surrounding the bounded area of the garden. As in the preceding example, the mapping between two domains enables the ritual manipulation of a relatively static domain (garden) by means of structures and elements belonging to a more dynamic domain (seafaring). This should be understood in opposition to the "anchoring" (keeping) of the "boat" (storehouse) containing the harvest inside the boundaries of the village found in several other magical formulas. In this case a dynamic or fleeting domain (amount of food) is manipulated and controlled in the same way as a boat are controlled in the seafaring domain, that is by static image schemata.[10]

Near the end of the *Vatuvi* spell, the relation between garden pests and diseases and the garden is compared to the prescribed behavioural relation between a sister and her brother. The extract of the spell goes like this:

"Be lost, begone ! Thou art my sister, keep off me ! Be ashamed of me, get off me ! Begone, slink away ! Slink away bending" (Malinowski 1935a: 98).

This structural mapping can be illustrated like this:

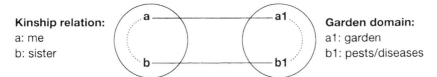

Kinship relation:
a: me
b: sister

Garden domain:
a1: garden
b1: pests/diseases

Figure 5.10: Mapping between the domain of kin relations and the garden domain

The figure illustrates the relations implied in the cultural model prescribing the normative understanding of the relationship between sister and brother. The model is not fully unfolded as it focuses on the *relation* between the two elements (represented by the dotted curve) regarded as similar to a relation between two elements in the other domain. The similarity is based on a common image-schema of REPULSION, which structures the counterpart mapping between sister and pests (bold line). Therefore, in the strict sense, this is not a schematic representation of *action*. I nevertheless include it here as it points to two features. First, culturally prescribed models of social interaction can function as iconic models working as action schemata in the conceptual blend active in the spell. Avoidance between sister and brother can be used to manipulate a domain in which no such prescribed rules govern the interrelation between the elements. Second, the relational structures deeply embedded in the conceptual systems of a given culture can be utilised to organise relations in other domains of experience (as noted by most structural interpretations of culture, notably Lévi-Strauss 1966). This leads to the construction of new frames of expected behaviour or causal unfolding in target domains and, through the poly-directionality of conceptual mapping, in the source domain as well. A stable relation governed by a prescriptive rule, such as a strict rule against intimate or incestuous relations between sister and brother, can be expressed by applying it to another domain of experience, in which possible causal unfoldings can be experienced without any great risk for the social structure. The use in the spell of the strict taboo on intimate relations between brothers and sisters not only expresses a wish that the relation between crops and pests will be the similarly discreet, but also exemplifies possible results of both compliance and breach of the incest taboo. As intimate relations between crops and pests will destroy the harvest, so intimate contact between brother and sister will destroy the social fabric.[11]

All examples of action schematic blending are taken from the Trobriand material presented by Malinowski. This is for two reasons. First, it completes the analysis of the most important parts of the *Vatuvi*-spell. Figure 4.2 described the ascription of magical agency in general, and figure 5.5, 5.6, 5.8, 5.9 and 5.10 are illustrations of different parts of the spell making use of both object-schematic and action-schematic blending. As the ritual, in which the spell is a part, contains several contagious transfers expressed in the physical manipulation of objects, this is an example of how elaborate rituals combine several of the different types and sub-types of magical action representations described above. Second, it gives at least a superficial impression of how magical practices are related to cultural models and the conceptual system of the culture they are performed in, even though the scope of a comparative and phenomenological project like this one does not allow a more thorough investigation of this connection. The Trobriand examples illustrate that even though the relation of two conceptual domains frozen in complex cultural and cognitive models might be a matter of convention, once this connection is established all sorts of counterpart connections based on metaphor, metonymy and essence facilitate and enable their use in the performance of magical rituals based on direct physical or indirect linguistic manipulation of image-schematic properties and transfer of essential qualities. Thus, the choice of the Trobriand material should by no means be understood as an expression of the lack of rituals based on action schemata in other cultures and historical frames. These structures are present in magical rituals in all cultural and historical settings.

5.2.4 Principles of Manipulative Magical Action

Above, we saw how the representations involved in manipulative magical action can be divided into three analytical types: the first type is based on an essence link connecting two otherwise distinct conceptual spaces. This is also referred to as backward contagion. The second type is based on blending of object schemata and the third on blending of action schemata, both being examples of iconic connections between spaces. The division has its merits in pointing to the difference in relative importance given in the ritual to essence, objects or actions.

Concerning the first type, i.e. manipulation facilitated by the an ESSENCE LINK, the same principle found in forward contagion applies in a slightly modified version: *The more central or essential the element used in backward contagion is to the element it should influence, the more efficacious the contagious link will be.* Blood will be better than a fingernail that in turn will be better than clothing that in turn will be better than a footprint etc. The link is thus not just an arbitrary symbolic relation, but based on the relative centrality of its anchoring, as the essence of an element is probably represented as an emanating force weakening as it extends outward from a central source. It combines the CONTAINER schema with a CENTER-PERIPHERY schema, which illustrates that the body boundaries are not always strictly defined, but can be extended to cover hair, nails, excrement, sweat or even a footprint.

If we turn to the similarity based blends, the first thing that appears is the relative importance of the agent in the ritual performance. In object schematic blending, the ritual agent does not necessarily play an important role, whereas in action schematic blending, the actions transferred are usually performed by the ritual agent or described as having the ritual agent as the subject of the action. This can be formulated as a first principle of manipulative magic: *Action schematic blending will, all things being equal, entail a greater emphasis on the role of the ritual agent and effect a tendency to invest magical agency in that agent. In object schematic blending, the interest and focus of the ritual are invested in the counterparts connecting the two domains, effecting a tendency to invest magical agency in objects containing these or to search for agents responsible for the efficacy of the objects.* This principle connects the type of blending used inside the ritual frame to the more general blend ascribing magical agency to elements otherwise belonging to the profane space, as described in chapter 4. The Zande practice of magical medicine is an excellent example of magical agency ascribed to objects, of which a substantial part is directly motivated by image-schematic counterpart connections. The Trobriand examples are more problematic as they seem to illustrate both tendencies. Through actions expressed as having the ritual agent as acting subject ("I sweep..."), pest and diseases are exorcised from the garden. At the same time, however, objects are referred to and used as physical substances in the procreative part of the ritual in order to establish similarity based blends aimed at transferring schematic properties to the garden and crops from these ritual objects. Malinowski refers to the physical material as a "magical mixture" (Malinowski, 1935a: 105-6), and they are all based on perceptual metaphors relating desirable features to the crops in the garden (such as green foliage, white tubers etc.). They are neither secret, nor a they ascribed any efficacy independent of their ritual use, but the Trobriand magician still uses a substantial amount of time to collect the different ingredients and mix them into the correct mixture. How do we explain this apparent contradiction between the ascription of magical agency to the magician and the spell, and the use of magical mixtures made from physical objects with sympathetic relations to the garden? Why do the Trobrianders bother to produce magical mixtures when the magical efficacy of the ritual is exclusively invested in an accredited magician reproducing the correct spells? The main reason is that these objects are physical manifestations of the metaphorical connections used in the spells that enables the magician to effect, through physical manipulation, a transfer of desirable properties to the recipient. The physical symbol is thus a metonymic extension of a metaphorical connection (Tambiah 1968: 194). Rephrased in the terminology of this book, the physical objects 'materialise' the conceptual blend and thereby make it possible for the magician to make a direct physical transfer of schemata between the two domains by contagious interaction. The objects are infused with the spell and thus function as a *materia medica* that enables the magician to manipulate the inherent schemata physically. In this perspective, the physical materials function as mere *indices* of the iconic relation prescribed by the spell and recited by the magician. Thus, the cross-modal character of elements used in the ritual strengthens the overall structure of the conceptual mapping. Trobriand magic is based on ascription of magical agency to the action (the iconic reproduction of the spell) and to the magician (as the legitimate wielder of magic by indexical connection to former wielders), and the material objects in the ritual are indices of the conceptual mappings present in the spell and strengthens these conceptual mappings.

Not all magical rituals based on schematic manipulation involve such physical mediums of transfer, or other obvious physical means of transferring the schematic content between conceptual spaces. This points to a salient feature of the relation between similarity-based iconic representations and essence-based indexical representations. The identification of perceptual similarity between two objects seems to trigger off an automatic ascription of essential qualities common to the similar elements. As we saw in chapter 3, this is for good reasons, as perceptual similarity is one of the two cognitive approaches used in basic-level categorisation, theory-driven essentialism being the other. An interesting example of this intimate relation between perceptual features and essence is how a newborn baby is described as sharing physical features with its alleged father. Thereby the essential genealogical relation between father and baby are established, an ascription not necessary with the mother, as she has a direct essentialist connection by being the observable physical 'source' of the child. In relation to magic, the same cognitive procedures play a role in the second principle of manipulative magical action. *Mappings and counterpart connections based on perceptual similarity will tend to entail the ascription of common essential qualities between the similar elements, thereby facilitating the possible transfer of schematic properties not used to establish the counterparts connection in the first place.* Thus, an icon of the Holy Mary can easily be understood as an outwards manifestation of the essence of the Holy Mary, just like an effigy of a person might be understood as an outward manifestation of the essence of that person, enabling influencing the person through manipulating the effigy. Just think of the Western folk-belief banning destruction of pictures lest that particular action should harm the person(s) depicted. Most people would definitely deny entertaining any belief in a causal connection between the picture and the person, but would nevertheless still feel uncomfortable with tearing up the picture of a loved one. This points to the fact that judgements concerning the ontology and epistemic status of the connection between picture and person is a secondary symbolic processing, that possibly overrule, but does remove, causal intuitions based on the perceptual link.

In manipulative magical actions, great importance is invested in an elaborate system of image-schemata that are compared, transferred and exchanged between conceptual spaces and domains. This facilitates a desired change or development in one domain by the manipulation of objects or actions performed in another domain. Image-schemata play two important roles in manipulative magical actions: first, they are very important in the establishment of counterpart connections between two conceptual spaces. The connections might be conventional mappings embedded in a given culture's conceptual system, but even in that case, the image-schematic properties are active as abstract and fundamental cognitive representations underlying the conventional connection. Second, schematic structures are transferred from one domain to another. They either just add to schemata already present (the rising and swelling garden) or they replace present, but undesirable, schemata, even if these were the ones used to establish the counterpart connection in the first place (as in the Zande case with the stone halting the sun). This can be expressed as the third principle of manipulative magical action: *Manipulative magical action works on the basis of a conceptual blending between elements belonging to at least two conceptual spaces. The counterpart connections enable the adding to, or even replacement of, the schemata used to establish the connection with a more desirable image-schema transferred from one space to the other.* Thus, in all the examples given in the preceding sections, image-schemata are transferred from one conceptual domain to another in order to affect the target domain. Often this results in the representation of a force-dynamic field constructed by opposing image-schemata (e.g. between a setting and a supported sun) or relations of relative force between dynamic and static schemata (e.g. the force needed to cross the boundary of a space, e.g. a garden). This force-dynamic field is even more evident in cases of witchcraft and sorcery, in which magic and counter-magic can wage war. Representations of relative power, however, are always present in magical rituals, as they are intimately connected to the relative force of the ascribed magical agency (strong magician v. weak magician, strong spells v. weak spells, strong medicine v. weak medicine) as well as to the successful performance of the ritual. This notion of force-dynamics in relation representations of magical actions points to the fact that magical rituals can be both exhaustive and time-consuming activities. It further indicates the existence of underlying mental representations entertained by participants that an effort must be put into the ritual project in order for it to overcome some degree of inherent opposition. Thus, cognitive representations of force and counter-force are an inherent part of both religious and magical rituals, even if they sometimes only play a minor role in the explicit cultural representation of the ritual.

Whether it is possible to provide a more general description of the direction of conceptual mapping in manipulative magic, and whether this can be defined as a distinctive feature of conceptual mapping in magical rituals is a pertinent question. In the Trobriand examples analysed above, there is a tendency towards mapping elements from a dynamic domain (e.g. seafaring) onto elements belonging to a more static domain (garden). This direction, however, might be a result of the examples chosen and of the purpose of the ritual involving a desire for a dynamic interaction with elements belonging to the static domain. In other cases it would be the opposite way around. In magical rituals aiming to control a chaotic situation, static image-schemata would be evoked in order to replace chaotic dynamism (e.g. in calming a violent storm). A more general and applicable principle is that *conceptual blending in magical rituals involves the mapping of image-schemata belonging to a manipulative domain onto a less manipulative domain in order to enable the agent to interact with this domain*. A domain can be difficult to interact with for several reasons. Distance (both social and physical), size, power, proper technology and several other factors can all make a domain more or less impossible to interact with directly. Several scholars of magic and religion have noticed this instrumental aspect of magical action and it is a widespread explanation of magical actions. Frazer claimed that magic is a (false) explanation of things yet unexplained (wherefore magic is the "bastard sister of science"), and its aim is to manipulate events in the world by a false equation between relations in thought and relations in reality. Malinowski claimed that the primary function of magic is to furnish the individual with some sense or feeling of security over affairs beyond its direct (technological) control. This is to refer to just two of the scholars emphasising this instrumental character of magical action.

This approach has its justification. Magic *is* used to explain otherwise unexplainable events, like sudden death or bad harvest, and is also used to control events of emotional uncertainty and danger. This, however, points to a much more general cognitive mechanism that is exploited in different pragmatic settings and to different ends. According to Lakoff and Johnson (1980; Lakoff 1987; Johnson 1987), one of the primary functions of conceptual metaphors is to facilitate the understanding and structuring of a less known and more abstract domain, by mapping elements from a better-known and perceptually salient domain that is directly meaningful. Conceptual mapping, structuring more abstract and less coherent domains by reference to experientially salient and highly structured domains, is the result of quite ordinary cognitive procedures whose products are deeply entrenched in the conceptual system of all cultures. This has two entailments for conceptual mappings in manipulative magical ritual: first, the tendency in magical rituals to map domains containing schemata of highly structured interaction onto domains or sub-domains with less structured experiential interaction should be seen as an expression of a general tendency in conceptualisation to map structured domains onto more unstructured domains. This movement is constrained by: (a) the motivation guiding the judgement of structural adequacy, implying that an import of structures from another domain is motivated by what the agent of the actions wants to do with the domain in focus; (b) possible conceptual connections based on deep-level cognitive processing facilitating the transfer; and (c) influences from socio-physical environment and the conceptual system limiting the scope of meaningful connections. Second, as many of these mappings are deeply entrenched in conceptual systems, individuals performing manipulative magical actions have a large repository of already established connections at hand that can be reinterpreted and tailored to current needs. This can be done by de-emphasising the symbolic and indexical aspects of the elements involved and emphasising the iconic aspects. This facilitates the establishment of counterpart connections that enable manipulation of one domain by actions performed on elements belonging to another domain, and thereby revitalise otherwise conventional relations by actively recognised image-schemata.[12]

5.3 Transfer and Manipulation, Essence and Similarity

In the preceding part of the chapter, I have analysed two ideal types of conceptual blending in found in magical rituals. *Transformative Magical Action* concerns the change and transfer of essence by virtue of a ritual blending of two mental spaces made out of broader conceptual domains. *Manipulative Magical Action* describes how counterpart connections are used to manipulate one domain by actions performed in another domain. The two types, however, are almost always combined in rituals. As both perceptual similarity and essentialist assumptions are productive cognitive mechanisms utilised in basic-level categorisation, contagious transfer of essences and perceptual manipulation by similarity are present and actively used in most magical rituals. Forward contagious transfer involves physical interaction between elements. This aspect gives a material dimension to ritual actions that otherwise might only involve linguistic expressions of conceptual blending (as we saw in the Trobriand examples). Perceptual similarity, on the other hand, gives an almost limitless repository of possible conceptual mappings enabling the transfer of multiple types of image-schematic structures. It also directly involves the senses and the individual's imaginative capacity in order for him/her to grasp, which structures are transferred and which are not in each single ritual. Therefore, very basic cognitive mechanisms are actively utilised in magical rituals in order to produce persuasive and cognitive salient procedures for changing a state of affair in a desired direction. At a semiotic level of analysis, this is done by emphasising indexical and iconic relations at the expense of conventional symbolic interpretations based on the relative position of elements understood as symbols—that is, the interpretation of conventional symbols by means of other conventional symbols. Symbolic materials, such as words, are 'deconstructed' entailing a relative heightening of the inherent iconic and indexical material.

The reasons to propose a new typology of magical actions are twofold. The first problem is that Frazer's old distinction of Homeopathic and Contagious Magic does not include forward contagion. Including a class of Transformative Magical Actions amends this deficiency. The second reason is that the distinction between backward contagion (metonymic connections) and similarity (metaphoric connections) is fuzzy, whereas the distinction between transformative and manipulative magic is based on pragmatic purpose and difference between essentialist and schematic transfer, rather than by the nature of the counterpart connections. A short example can illustrate the fuzzy distinction between similarity and contagion. Frazer quotes Plutarch's description of how a person suffering from jaundice can be cured by looking a stone-curlew steadily in the eye. By virtue of its golden coloured eye, the bird will draw out the yellow jaundice from the afflicted person (Frazer 1911: 80). Neither the man nor the bird is categorised by the yellow colour. Yellow is an unnatural and unwanted property of the person, but a natural property of the bird, namely the colour of its eyes. It is quite evident that the similarity of colour between the symptoms of the diseased person and the eyes of the stone-curlew are fundamental to this practice, even if there are other, more conventional reasons as well. It is also evident that there is an image-schematic representation of a LINK or PATH between the person and the bird's eye allowing the disease to pass from one to another in a semi-contagious manner (it will not work if they do not both look). But is it really a question of similarity or a question of common essence? Is the bird's eye believed to attract the disease because of its likeness or because of the ascription of a common essence underlying both physical manifestations of the colour yellow? Whereas the perception of similarity only needs to be pointed out, it is more difficult to estimate whether any essentialist notions are behind this belief. The example illustrates the fuzzy boundary between metaphoric counterpart connections entailing relations of similarity, and metonymic counterpart connections entailing relations of common essence or identity. It is fundamentally a question of whether a connection is understood as a member of two different conceptual categories with some properties in common, or as a member of a third conceptual category, believed to have its own essence, and present as a non-defining characteristic in the two other conceptual categories. In the first case, we have a metaphor; in the last case, a metonymy constructed by linking all elements containing this third category (like yellow). Conceptual categories and cultural classifications might, in contrast to basic-level categories, be divided by principles relatively strange to persons belonging to another culture. Lakoff cites the wonderful example of the novelist J. L. Borges' description of a taxonomy of the animal kingdom from an ancient Chinese encyclopaedia, the

Celestial Emporium of Benevolent Knowledge, from the book *Other Inquisitions*.

> On those remote pages it is written that animals are divided into (a) those that belong to the Emperor, (b) embalmed ones, (c) those that are trained, (d) suckling pigs, (e) mermaids, (f) fabulous ones, (g) stray dogs, (h) those that are included in this classification, (i) those that tremble as if they were mad, (j) innumerable ones, (k) those drawn with a very fine camel's hair brush, (l) others, (m) those that have just broken a flower vase, (n) those that resemble flies from a distance (cited in Lakoff 1987: 92).

This is, of course, a work of fiction, and it is unlikely that any culture could have a classificatory system that is as 'unnatural' as this fantastic example. One might also argue that no essence will be ascribed conceptual categories so far removed from, and indeed, in opposition to basic domain-specific categorisation. But as we have seen, essence can be transferred, and one of the characteristics of religious concepts is that they are ascribed essential properties that are in more or less direct opposition to the essence normally ascribed in relation to perceptual categorisation (Boyer 1993). The bread and wine might look like bread and wine, but in essence it is Christ. The Borges example illustrates how magical procedures can take advantage of the human capacity to construct new conceptual categories and connections 'on the fly' in order to achieve a specific goal, and that these new concepts and connections can stretch across ordinary classificatory boundaries, as long as they achieve their objective—to connect otherwise distinct conceptual domains in order to produce a specific result. These new complex concepts can be structured by both ascription of essence to already existing categories, such as yellow, or by focusing on some perceptual similarity, not noticed before. Rozin and Nemeroff have conducted a study that illustrates the human potential to make such new conceptual connections:

> Subjects (a few hundred undergraduate students) read a half-page vignette describing a hypothetical culture. There were two versions of the vignette (unknown to the subjects), which were identical except that in one case, the people were described as eating a marine turtle, and hunting wild boar, but only for its tusk, whereas, in the opposite case, wild boar was eaten and marine turtle was hunted, but only for its shell. So the two vignettes differed with respect to what was eaten (and fabricated), and not in terms of other contact with the two animals in question. After reading the vignette, subjects were asked to rate male members of the culture on a number of personality scales, including good swimmer versus good runner, irritable versus good-natured, phlegmatic versus excitable, long-lived versus short-lived. Many of these traits had been selected to discriminate boar from turtle. We found that subjects reading the boar-eating vignette rated people in this culture as more boar-like than those rating the turtle-eating culture. We obtained similar findings, with other subjects, using a contrast between an elephant-eating culture and a vegetarian culture that hunted elephants for their tusks (Rozin & Nemeroff 1990: 215-16).

These findings illustrate how a wide range of perceptual and essentialist assumptions used to characterise a given element (e.g. a "wild boar") can be understood as influencing both essential qualities (e.g. "irritable") and perceptual characteristics (e.g. "good runner") of other elements with whom they interact (in this case by contagious transfer). The purpose of the test was to show that essential and perceptual properties, ascribed to an animal, were both unconsciously used by subjects to characterise the persons eating that particular animal. One could argue that the subjects lacked other parameters, besides food and hunting, from which to make a balanced judgement concerning the abilities of males of this fictitious culture. This is a fair critique, but the example does illustrate how easy it is to facilitate belief in the transfer of essential and perceptual properties by manipulating the context in which judgements are made. Ritual is such a strongly manipulated context in which participants are presented with selected perceptual inputs in order to constrain the possible meaningful interpretations of the actions. This "meaningfulness" of ritual action, however, should primarily be looked for on a very basic cognitive level involving representations of essence and image-schemata that are only subsequently constrained and influenced by culture-specific symbolic interpretations.[13]

This points to the relation between these basic cognitive mechanisms and cultural systems and models as they are expressed in representations of magical actions. It should be remembered that cultural systems and models are constrained, but not determined, by cognitive mechanisms involved in basic-level categorisation. Essentialist and image-schematic representations are deeply embedded in all conceptual categories and facilitate numerous conceptual mappings and the construction of complex concepts. As we saw in the Trobriand examples, cultural models relating conceptual domains are actively utilised in the construction of counterpart connections in representations of both transformative and manipulative magic. The conceptual counterpart connections between elements belonging to the domain of the garden and elements belonging to the domain of seafaring is a pertinent example of such a ritually instantiated cultural model. Often, cultural models and conceptual mappings are linguistically expressed as conventional metaphors and extensions of these. They can therefore be seen as conventional symbolic connections not necessarily evoking any commitment to the ontological proposition(s) contained in the metaphor (as in "time *is* money") or any notions or beliefs in the possibility of transfer of properties between the two domains. But something happens when such conventional mappings are utilised in magical rituals. Through ritual and linguistic procedures, the symbolic and conventional nature is de-emphasised and the image-schematic and essentialist connections are relatively emphasised, which facilitates representations of transfer of both essential and schematic properties between conceptual domains. This is intimately related to the notion of ritualisation treated in the next chapter. Magical actions *revitalise* conventionalised conceptual connections (by virtue of the emphasis placed on the schematic and essentialist properties based on direct perception and directly meaningful bodily interaction that facilitates the connection in the first place), and *de-conventionalise* meaning of concepts by emphasising perceptual and essentialist aspects of the conceptual mapping. This has the intriguing effect that it enables individual participants in the ritual to make subsequent symbolic reinterpretations of the ritual and the concepts contained in this, in relation to themselves as individuals or as a group, including representations of self, actions, and the context or praxis they are a part of. Such idiosyncratic interpretations are constrained only by cognitive structures of basic-level categorisation and to a varying degree influenced by more or less orthodox cultural interpretations. The *viability* of these idiosyncratic interpretations in a social discourse, however, is strongly constrained by the extent to which they relate to already existing cultural models and frames of interpretation occupying the same conceptual domain. Not all novel interpretations will be externalised, and among those that are, only a few will gain a wider support ensuring their transmission. The immunology of cultural systems (Sørensen 2004) understood as relatively stable structures of discourse, is a constraining factor on the epidemiology of conceptual representations (Sperber 1994, 1996). Therefore, even if rituals themselves do not convey cultural proposition in a direct manner, the chances are good that participants will employ culturally sanctioned modes of interpreting these actions, at least in public discourse.

Some concepts are deeply constrained by conventionalised symbolic interpretations and are therefore very difficult to reinterpret. In these cases, the cognitive mechanisms responsible for the ascription of magical efficacy to the ritual can be over-ruled by symbolic interpretations. The magical efficacy will be strongly limited and restricted to implicit individual representations, or the ritual will cease to be ascribed any magical efficacy altogether. This can lead participants to look elsewhere for magical efficacy, eventually in other cultural contexts. As the basic cognitive procedures underlying representations of magical actions involve the active de-emphasis on the symbolic aspects of concepts and conceptual mappings, imports of ritual structures from other conceptual systems are relatively easy, as these can be appropriated without their local symbolic interpretations. Thus, both ascribed and inherent iconic and indexical aspects are open for ritual usage and new symbolic interpretation. I shall return to this point in chapter 7. It is raised in this section in order to summarise the argument that ascription of efficacy in both ideal types of magical actions depends on the de-symbolisation of elements and signs used in the ritual, allowing their iconic and indexical aspects to be emphasised and manipulated. This enables participants to create the conceptual connections necessary to make both individual symbolic interpretations and eventual judgements concerning the probability of the alleged ritual effect. By removing ritual elements from their everyday interpretative frame—in which they have conventional meanings according to symbolic interrelations—their direct perceptual qualities and ascribed essentialist assumptions are foregrounded, allowing for the manipulation of these basic aspects in the ritual frame. Of course, such a theory of magical efficacy entails a theory of how rituals accomplish this feature, a problem we shall turn our attention to in the next chapter.

Notes

1. Other constraints imposed are based on non-ritual properties of bread and wine: that they are edible and drinkable; are relatively easy produced in vast quantities; are not of excessive value etc.

2. See, for instance, Propp, 1968[1928]; Greimas, 1966; Greimas & Courtés, 1988.

3. Children's understanding of magic and magical events is the theme of an edition of *British Journal of Developmental Psychology*. See Baillargeon 1994; Chandler & Lalonde 1994; Harris 1994; Johnson & Harris 1994; Rosengren, Kalish, et al 1994; Subbotsky 1994; Woolley & Phelps 1994; summarised in Elksnis & Szachara 1996. See also Subbotsky 1985.

4. This example is taken from the general exhibition on navigational history at the Royal Observatory at Greenwich, June 1997.

5. It is interesting that the Zande belief of witchcraft does *not* entail any notion of an object or *materia medica* through which the witch works. If medicines are involved in such immoral endeavours, it is black magic performed by a sorcerer.

6. Thus in several languages, such as Danish and Kwaio (an Austronesian language of the Solomon Islands), the same word is used to designate a person's 'imprint' (as in foot print) and a marked direction (a path or a track). *Spor* in Danish and *tala* in Kwaio (Keesing 1993).

7. See, for instance, its direct appearance in Magical Formula (MF) 5, p.101; MF 12, p.130; MF 23, p.154; MF 24, p.155; MF 24a, p.156; MF 25, p.165; MF 27, p.169; MF 38, p.284 (all Malinowski 1935a).

8. See Keesing (1993) for a related description of the cognitive model of *wado*, 'earth', among the Kwaio of the Solomon Islands.

9. See Sweetser (1995) for a linguistic analysis of the diachronic relation between metaphor and homology.

10. E.g. MF 28 and 29 (Malinowski 1935a: 221, 223-24).

11. A recent analogy to this relationship is the overall reaction to the outbreak of BSE (popularly known as Mad Cow Disease) in Great Britain. The widespread explanation has it that the disease is caused by involuntary cannibalism, as the cows were fed with feeding stuff partly made of bone meal and marrow from cows. The evocation of the notion of cannibalism was primarily meant to express a condemning judgement of this practice, but it works the other way around as well. Even though the taboo against human cannibalism hardly needs strengthening, BSE could still function as an example of the possible causal entailments of breach of such a tabooed practice. Thus, the notion of cannibalism would properly not have been evoked had this practice resulted in big strong cows, as this would have undermined the taboo.

12. This resembles what Glucklich (1997) calls a "magical experience". This term, however, is more obscuring than clarifying, as the mechanisms responsible for the de-symbolisation are not restricted to magic, but are a more general feature of ritualisation (Bell 1992; Humphrey & Laidlaw 1994). See chapter 6.

13. This is related to the arguments presented by Bell (1992) and Humphrey and Laidlaw (1994). All express strong scepticism towards the view of ritual as a kind of communication and instead see the central purpose of ritual in the concept of the 'ritualisation' of certain agents and actions. See chapter 6.

6
Frames of Ritual Action: Causation, Diagnosis and Prognosis

Previous chapters have dealt with the construction of a ritual space, the ascription of magical agency, the role of language in magical rituals and usage of conceptual blending in facilitating representations of essence flow and image-schematic transfer. This chapter will focus on the embedding of magical rituals and actions in pragmatic contexts. Magical rituals and actions are not performed in a contextual void. They are extremely dependent on mental and cultural representations of two sets of relations: (a) between the ritual action performed and the event-state immediately preceding the magical action (diagnosis); and between the ritual action and the resulting event-state (prognosis). Thus, magical actions are deeply embedded in at least a single *event-frame*, in which the ritualised actions are represented as the instrumental component aimed to control the direction of the causal unfolding of events. A stress on such temporal representations is a distinctive feature of magical rituals, whereas other types of rituals do not necessarily evoke such representations even if they can be interpreted as containing transformative or manipulative potential. To be more specific, certain rituals are exclusively directed at facilitating the emergence of some pre-specified state of affair (e.g. restoration of health, good harvest, or winning love), whereas, at the other end of a continuum, some rituals do not contain any prescribed goal and will only impose very loose constraints on the possible interpretation of the ritual made by participants (e.g. Catholic Mass, Jain *Puja*). Malinowski (1992: 88) was right in distinguishing 'magical' from 'religious' rituals by reference to the mental and/or cultural representation of concrete, practical, and more or less immediate results involved in magical rituals, whereas 'religious' rituals need not have any such direct utilitaristic aspects (but possibly more distant ones, like salvation). He was wrong, however, in claiming this to be an inherent quality of the particular ritual. Even if representations of ritual goals might influence the actions performed in the ritual, it is a distinction of both the event-frame and the pragmatic repertoire in which the ritual action is embedded rather than the ritual actions themselves. The employment of a ritual as the instrumental cause in an event-frame is based on participants' intentions and their interpretations of the ritual, which means that it is nearly impossible to judge the purpose of a ritual without knowledge of its position in locally constructed event-frames.

In order to understand the importance of magical rituals in pragmatic repertoires, it is necessary to analyse two aspects of rituals at a more general level before proceeding to a tentative typology of pragmatic repertoires of magical rituals. The first aspect concerns the relation between intentions of the agents performing the ritual and the actions involved. The pragmatically motivated embedding of rituals into event-frames is facilitated by the transformation of the instrumentality of actions at the core of rituals. Most of the actions contained in rituals do not in themselves have direct instrumental effect. The ritualisation of an action de-emphasises the instrumentality inherent to representations of the actions when performed outside the ritual frame. The ritual *as a whole*, however, and, through their embedding in this whole, individual elements used in the ritual sequence, can subsequently be ascribed instrumental qualities, which facilitates their utility in several different event frames (Boyer 1994: 202-11). This subsequently ascribed instrumental efficacy is dependent on the process of "ritualisation" of actions (Bell 1992; Humphrey & Laidlaw 1994), as this new instrumentality can only be ascribed when the direct everyday instrumentality of an action is removed through its performance inside the ritual frame. Such special instrumental status of ritual actions, as well as ritual agents and ritual objects, points to the role of the *intentions* of individuals performing or participating in a specific ritual.

The second aspect concerns the cognitive representations of event-frames and how event-frames containing magical rituals differ from non-ritual event-frames. Ritualisation not only entails the transformation of the relation between intentions and actions, but also radically alters the causal representations involved. This subsequently results in the emergence of two hermeneutic strategies employed by participants in representing the purpose of magical rituals. Finally, a typology of magical rituals based on both internal and external parameters is proposed. This introduces a third hermeneutic strategy based on the embedding of magical rituals in locally constructed networks of interrelated event-frames.

6.1 Intention and Meaning in Magical Actions

The question of the intentionality of subjects performing ritual actions in general and magical actions in particular is extremely complex, both from a philosophical and epistemological angle. It plays a central role in most theories of ritual and magical actions, epitomised in the so-called "rationality-debate" of the late 1960's and early 1970's. The rationality-debate centred on two related problems.

The first problem concerned the relationship between the observation of apparently irrational behaviour of people in the performance of ritual actions and the rational behaviour observed in other behavioural contexts. Why do, for instance the Trobrianders, perform rituals grounded on apparently irrational beliefs, obscure causality and 'magical' agency, in intimate relation to practical actions based on apparently rational beliefs and 'normal' causal unfolding? In short, how do we explain the almost simultaneous existence of both irrational and rational beliefs and actions in relation to the same intentional purpose (for instance building a canoe)? The second question concerns the relation between the reasons and purposes participants give for performing the ritual and the actions contained in the ritual. That is, whether there is any relation between the expressed intention behind the performance of a ritual action (if there is any) and the actual actions performed in the ritual? This is an important question as it is the apparent disjunction between expressed intention and performed action that provokes the classification of an action as a ritual action in the first place.

In the rationality-debate two views opposed each other. Proponents of the *symbolist* approach claimed that one should disregard the expressed or explicit intentions of participants and instead look for a deeper, more fundamental, and implicit reason (or intention) for the action, either in socio-cultural or in psychological structures. The purpose of ritual performance is thus to *communicate* something else, something hidden below the surface of explicit action, a feature that can explain their coexistence with non-ritual, practical actions. This solves (or dissolves) the second problem, as the relationship between participants' purposes and reasons expressed and the ritual actions is a mere epiphenomenon. The latter is instead seen as outward symbolic (in this context indirect) expressions of the hidden structure independent of participants' explicit intentions.

The *intellectualist* approach is in opposition to this view. Its proponents claimed that the observer has to take the explicit reasons expressed by participants performing a given ritual seriously, as the legitimate intention behind its performance. Rituals are prescribed instrumental actions used to obtain certain specified states of affairs, and the reason people perform them is that ritual actions are grounded in a local explanatory system that gives a rationale for the actions performed. Therefore, ritual actions are not irrational if the observer has knowledge about the local explanatory context that informs the performance of ritual actions, and practical and ritual actions should both be treated as rational manifestations of underlying explanatory structures. According to the intellectualist approach, ritual action can be distinguished from other types of actions only by addressing the character of the abstract explanatory system to which they refer.[1]

There are serious problems connected to both of these approaches. The symbolist approach allows for an extremely wide range of possible interpretations, as participants' expressed intentions are practically disregarded (or seen as further symbolic expressions that should confirm the structures found by the observer and otherwise regarded as 'noise'). Reasons or intentions expressed by participants are instead understood as a feature of the underlying system expressed or communicated in the ritual actions. As this system or structure is hidden or unconscious, the job of the observer is to uncover it through an interpretation of the symbols expressed. This "cryptological" view has been severely criticised by Sperber (1975) and Boyer (1994). The main point of Sperber's critique is that it unclear whether the system uncovered really exists outside the anthropologist's head, and that there is a very problematic relation, not explained by defenders of the symbolist approach, between the system claimed to underlie the ritual action and the mental representations of the persons actually performing it.

Compared to the symbolist, the intellectualist approach has the obvious advantage that it takes seriously the intentions expressed by participants performing the rituals. The problem with the intellectualist approach lies elsewhere. In claiming that the ritual actions are rational expressions of an underlying explanatory system, it follows that this system is *in the mind* of the (ideal) individual participants. Otherwise it would not be an explanation of ritual action in itself, but only of possible secondary interpretations of ritual action. The explanatory system must be the theoretical ground motivating a ritual response to a specific state of affair. Ritual actions are thus understood as expressions of not a symbolic system, but of a (possibly wrong) explanatory system. Participants, however, often state no theoretical reasons for performing ritual actions. Even when they do, the explanations expressed often diverge to such a large extent that it becomes doubtful whether they are constructed 'on the fly', and thus cannot be the reason for the action or expressions of a coherent and culturally prevalent explanatory system (Humphrey & Laidlaw 1994). Subsequent *interpretations* might be influenced by explicit explanatory systems (e.g. by theologies), but these are not the reason motivating the performance of specific ritual actions. Intellectualist approaches also fail to address the problem of why rituals are so complex if they merely wish to express an underlying explanatory system. Intellectualist approaches generally de-emphasis the special character of ritual and ritualisation. Their only distinctive feature is found in the type of explanatory system informing the actions.

A common problem in both symbolist and intellectualist approaches is the implicit assumption that rituals are expressions and communications of underlying systems or structures, in the intellectualist case accessible as participants' explanatory systems, and in the symbolist case as an unconscious psychological or a cultural system partly or totally unknown to the participant. As we recall, the central questions are why people perform rituals in relation to other actions and whether the reasons for doing so in any way determine the form of practises and actions actually performed in that ritual? Humphrey and Laidlaw observe that a fundamental aspect of ritualised action is the transformation of the agent's representation of the link between intentional meaning and actions performed (1994: 5, 71).[2] Whereas everyday, non-ritual actions are characterised by an intimate relation between action and intention, the performance of ritual actions does not expose the same kind of relation to an agent's intentions. Instead, intentions related by participants to prescribed, ritual actions are understood as an independent act of symbolic interpretation that is not constrained by the actions themselves. According to Humphrey and Laidlaw, the meaning of a ritual cannot be found in the actions that constitute the ritual. Meaning is a feature only subsequently ascribed by symbolic interpretation eventually made by individual participants. Addressing ritual recital in the Jain *puja* they argue that:

> the link between form and meaning is loosened to the point where the meaning attributed to the utterance is radically underdetermined in comparison with everyday language. These kinds of linguistic utterances in rituals, just like non-linguistic ritual acts, generally appear to call for interpretation, because no meaning, purpose, or intention can be either directly understood or uncontentiously inferred (Humphrey & Laidlaw 1994: 194).

According to this view, ritual actions should not be understood as acts expressing or communicating features that have meaning by their relative position in some underlying semantic structure (whether symbolic or explanatory). Rather, they constitute a distinctive type of action, removed from its ordinary frame of intentional meaning through a process of ritualisation. This 'meaninglessness' of rituals is exactly the feature that provokes the creation of more or less novel, systematised, and culturally informed interpretation by individual participants (and anthropologists). It is also this freedom from intentional meaning that makes ritual form so persistent through time, as it facilitates the utility of rituals for different purposes and in different interpretational endeavours. Seen in this light, the symbolists are right in claiming that there is no direct connection between the explicit intentions of the participants and the ritual actions performed, but wrong in claiming that the meaning of ritual actions can be found in a symbolic system. The intellectualists, on the other hand, are right in taking seriously participants' reasons or intentions for performing a ritual but wrong in claiming that ritual actions are explained by reference to an explanatory structure accessible to the participants. A theoretical explanation made by a participant of a given ritual action should only be seen as an informed subsequent interpretation, but not as the *raison d'être* for the actions of which the ritual consists.

There are, however, two problems in Humphrey and Laidlaw's argument. First, ritual actions are not totally devoid of meaning in themselves, even though this inherent meaning is neither a direct expression of a symbolic system nor of an explanatory system. The rejection of meaning in rituals is based on the flawed idea of meaning as an either-or property based on what Lakoff and other have called "objectivist" semantics (Lakoff 1987; Lakoff & Johnson 1980). In the objectivist view, meaning is understood as a property of the relative position of individual symbols in a system of symbols and of the symbols' references to elements in an objective, or possible world. Instead, ritualisation of actions facilitates the appropriation of non-symbolic or non-propositional meaning from essentialist and image-schematic features of the ritualised elements, and these will constrain subsequent symbolic interpretations. The ingestion of an object, for instance, is unlikely to be interpreted as an act performed in order to avoid influence ascribed that object, and kneeling in front of a statue of a god will not be interpreted as an act submitting the god, but vice versa. In the same way, material elements are often involved in the ritual action functioning as indexical or iconic signs relating the domain in focus to the actions performed. The fact that these elements are often an important part of a cultural symbolic system, has led anthropologists to overlook the radically altered function these elements have, once ritualised. Even though it is often their special position in cultural classificatory systems that justify specific symbols appearance in a ritual performance, once ritualised and embedded in a ritual event-frame, the symbolic meaning is de-emphasised and meaning is instead derived through much more basic cognitive operations (e.g. in pledging by putting a hand on the Bible as opposed to a phone book). Thus, culturally important signs can be described as having three functions in relation to magical rituals:

1. Either as bearers, indexes or icons of magical agency, intimately related to cultural models configuring relations between the profane and the sacred domain (e.g. in concepts specifying magical agency).

2. As referential devices linking the ritual performance to the domain in which the change resulting from the ritual is supposed to take place (thereby relating the ritual space to a non-ritualised or purely 'profane' space both before and after the performance).

3. As referents to a more or less limited range of interpretational frames, embedded in specific discourses or discursive genres, for instance organising cosmological ideas.

At a discursive level, the scope of interpretations can be further narrowed by taking into account: (a) what types of interpretational frames are available to participants as members of a specific socio-cultural group at a specific time, and (b) how these frames are related to elements appearing in the ritual. Even if one cannot rule out altogether novel interpretations, it is more likely that these will be transformations of culturally available interpretational frames. The very act of ritualisation, however, results in the emancipation or loosening of elements from the constraints imposed by their relative position in symbolic networks, thereby activating cognitive mechanisms used in basic-level categorisation. It is very possible that these basic cognitive features primarily work as negative constraints delimiting the scope for non-contradictory interpretations, which will make it practically impossible to deduce exactly what interpretations the performance of a given ritual will give rise to in individual participants. But, based on features of basic-level categorisation and the range of interpretational frames, it is possible to stipulate the *borders* of likely interpretations.

Thus, even if Humphrey and Laidlaw are right that symbolic and propositional meaning is radically de-emphasised in (magical) rituals, two points modify their hypothesis. (1) Ritualisation facilitates the evocation of essentialist and image-schematic meaning that not only constrains subsequent interpretations but also activates representations of essence-flow and image-schematic transfer. These cognitively basic constraints are without doubt looser than constraints applied to everyday action through directly related intentionality, and will therefore prompt the application of a much wider spectrum of interpretational frames. Nevertheless they will constrain the production of secondary symbolic interpretations. (2) Individual elements used in the ritual are, by virtue of their embedding in cultural symbolic systems, connected to a more or less limited scope of interpretational frames that are likely to influence individual interpretations of a given ritual.

The second problem of Humphrey and Laidlaws account is, that the transformation of the connection between intention and action also alters the role of representations of *agency* in ritualised action. Once actions are ritualised, the ritual agent's intentions are relegated to a superordinate level containing a representation of the ritual as a whole, positioned as the instrumental cause in an event-frame. This will be treated in depth below. This relegation has a specific purpose, at least in magical rituals, namely to facilitate the ascription of *magical agency*. As described in chapter 4, this can be done in numerous ways but the ritualisation of some element, whether an agent, an action, or an object, seems to be a prerequisite for the appearance of the magical agency responsible for the efficacy of the ritual actions. Humphrey and Laidlaw indirectly acknowledge this aspect when they propose that the success of shamanistic performance (contrary to stipulative liturgical rituals):

> is not really defined by control over disease or other afflictions. An excuse or alternative diagnosis can always be found if the patient dies. It is a matter, rather, of *creating and confirming personal shamanistic power*, and this is achieved through a discourse in which the audience is an essential partner (Humphrey & Laidlaw 1994: 10, emphasis added).

In this case, the agent is ritualised, and he/she is the element connected to the sacred space, channelling magical agency into the ritual. Therefore the actions performed in shamanistic rituals need not be ritualised to the same degree, as they are not represented as facilitating the transfer of magical agency. Instead, the actions are iconic signs that, by their reproduction of a repertoire of relatively unfixed ritual actions, function as indices of the magical agency invested in the ritual agent (the 'shamanness' of the shaman). In a similar way, the ritualised nature of linguistic utterances used in the Trobriand spells ensures the infusion of magical agency. The loosening of the connections between intention and action effected by ritualisation not only ensures that there are fewer constraints on subsequent symbolic interpretation, but also facilitates the ascription of efficacy to the ritual as a whole. This in turn enables participants to direct the ritual efficacy in a number of directions. Ritualisation transforms the ritual as a whole into a powerful instrument that can be embedded as the instrumental cause in several event-frames.[3]

Humphrey and Laidlaw studied the Jain *Puja*, a ritual performed very regularly in the morning by most participants and thus not directly related to any particular reason or explicitly ascribed efficacy, neither dogmatically nor personally. But, as described above, many rituals are performed in order to achieve some pre-specified goal, in reaction to a specific state of affair, or both. This implies that the intentions of a person performing magical ritual actions are intimately connected to the representations of the overall efficacy of the ritual actions, i.e. of the event-frame in which the ritual is a part. Usually this representation is culturally explicit in prescriptive models (e.g. "in case of y, perform ritual x, in order to achieve z"). This points to the next general aspect of magical ritual, namely the existence of mental and cultural representations of event-frames structuring inherent representations of causal relations in magical rituals.

6.2 Event-frames, Causal Unfolding and Cultural Models

Every ritual, performed in order to achieve a pre-specified goal, is embedded in representations of a temporally structured event-frame that can be analytically described as constituted by three distinct mental spaces each comprising a distinct event-state. A *Conditional* space organising representations of the event-state preceding the ritual action, an *Action* space organising representations of the ritual action, and an *Effect* space organising representations of the event-state believed to result for the ritual action.[4] The representation of these temporally connected spaces entails two cognitive operations: (1) the process of making a *diagnosis*, structuring the representation of the Conditional space in its relation to the actions contained in the Action space; and (2) the process of making a *prognosis*, mentally representing the effects that Action space actions will have on the Effect space. It is important to recognise that the spaces form part of one integrated structure—the event-frame—and that elements belonging to the spaces, are connected to each other through relations of identity, metonymy and metaphor, in the same way as we saw in the case of conceptual blending.

The ritual is defined as the instrumental action placed in the Action space connected to both a Conditional and an Effect space. The reason for this central position is the instrumental role ritual action is represented as playing in changing the state of affairs preceding the ritual action into a transformed state of affairs following the action. Rituals are, for the reasons discussed above, set apart as a special pragmatic repertoire, and it is in the sense of rituals organising event-states either preceding or following the ritual that the temporal unfolding of the event-frame should be understood. But one need not take the Action space as the vantage point for unfolding the system, as the whole event-frame can be represented using any of the interrelated spaces as the viewpoint.

As argued by Lawson and McCauley (1990), ritual actions are modelled upon representations of non-ritual actions. Inspired by models made by Fauconnier (1997), Brandt (2000) and Østergaard (2000), figure 6.1 attempts to capture a simplified event-frame of such non-ritual everyday action. This is needed in order to explain how ritual action differs from non-ritual action.

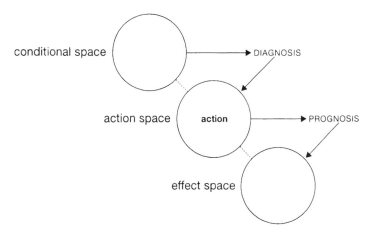

Figure 6.1: Non-ritual event-frame

The roles of diagnosis and prognosis are to relate the instrumental function ascribed an action to representations of event-states preceding and following the actions. This is done in an intricate manner involving a whole range of cognitive operations—such as perception, causal knowledge and expectations, memory of similar events, idealized cognitive models, cultural models, beliefs and intentions—all taking part in the processes involved in both diagnosis and prognosis. Causal knowledge and expectations are especially important in this context, as they relate the prior event-state to the present action, and the present action to the future event-state through causal connections, thus creating a unified whole integrating the event-frame into one causal unfolding.

Figure 6.1 is a simplified model of the event-frame of everyday non-ritual action, as an integrated whole of conditions, intentions, actions and results. In the mental representation of an action sequence expressed in the sentence "I smashed the window", the window was first unbroken, then, because of my actions involving the usage of a linguistically underspecified instrument (a hand, a stone etc.), it became broken. In both the diagnostic and prognostic process, all sorts of background knowledge are present. That windows can be broken by a sufficiently hard material, and that performing an action involving such a material ejected with a certain force towards the window, will most likely result in the breaking of the window, etc. (see related analysis in Boyer 1994: 133). Therefore the Conditional and Effect space are both represented as causally linked to the present action in the Action space and to force-dynamic representations of relative force, even if this is underspecified in the linguistic expression. As described in chapter 3, causal assumptions and force-dynamic representations are intimately connected to domain-specific categorisation. Windows are made of a physical substance, glass, with physical strength and I need to employ another physical entity with a superior strength or force in order to produce an effect by mechanical causality. In this model, the agent's intentions do not necessarily take part. I could be breaking the window on purpose or it could be a mistake. In most types of actions involving a *human* agent, domain-specific assumptions of belief-desire psychology are implied and the intention of the agent is intimately related to the action, making intentional action a default structure automatically applied ("I broke the window" [intentionally] v. "*Unfortunately*, I broke the window"). In case the intention is denied explicitly, the event change from being an action into a mere happening,[5] or the intentional agent is sought elsewhere (e.g. in the unconscious). So, in representations of non-ritual actions, the event-structure involves both causal and force-dynamic unfoldings, based primarily on domain-specific background knowledge, and an intentional unfolding based on the default ascription of intentionality to human action (cf. Leslie 1994, 1995).

Of course, more can be said about this complex problem,[6] but this should suffice to illustrate the difference between non-ritualised and ritualised action. We have already seen how ritualised action is distinctive by its transformation of the relation between intention and the actual actions performed. This is followed by a similar and related transformation of the representation of a causal link between past and future mediated by the present ritual. Not only are the particular actions constituting the ritual sequence intentionally underspecified but they are also causally underspecified, entailing that participants need not have any explicit representation of *how* a ritual work in order to believe *that* it works. Explicit representation refers to a consistent, propositional and symbolically explicable theory or worldview accounting for the causal chain between the recognition of a state of affairs, the ritual actions, and the resultant state of affairs. The preceding chapters should have made it clear that ritual participants hold implicit, coherent, non-propositional, iconic and indexical representations of some of the actions taking place and elements used in the ritual, and that these are necessary in order for participants to contain beliefs ascribing any type of efficacy to the ritual. Thus, two aspects should be recognised in this context. (1) Image-schemata and psychological essentialism provide a *weak* causal framework containing basic representations of image-schematic transfer and contagious flow. These are automatically emphasised when actions are ritualised and magical agency is to ascribed elements used in the ritual. [7] (2) The "windowing of attention" (Talmy 2000) ensures that the focus is exclusively on the intentional agent behind the action and on the result of the action, and that the causal means need only be made explicit due to contextual pressure.

Imagine that a specific magical ritual is performed in response to the recognition of a certain state of affairs—say a disease. The recognition of an disease as a specific type involves a diagnostic process classifying is as a type that can be manipulated by means of this particular ritual.[8] Classification of event-states is by no mean a simple process. It involves a complex interaction of several culturally specified models and conceptual categories of event-states, and abductive reasoning relating observable and induced phenomena to one or several of these models, as if the model could predict the phenomena deductively (see chapter 3; Boyer 1994: 146-48). Intimately connected to the cultural models used to classify an event-state are prescriptive actions believed to modify these event-states ('stay warm if you are catching a cold'; 'sacrifice to the ancestors if you unlucky'). Ritual actions, however, are distinct from prototypical non-ritual action in the relationship between the classification and models of interaction. As argued above, ritualised actions are recognised by the severing of the causal and intentional connections between recognition of event-states and actions performed in reaction to this recognition. This does not entail that the classification of an event-state fails to result in the performance of more or less pre-specified ritual action. It only entails that neither the intentions nor the causal assumptions connected to the classification of an event-state constrain the form or type of the resulting ritual action. So, there is no direct *causal* modelling relating representations of the Conditional space event-state to the subsequent ritual action. Instead, direct iconic and indexical connections between the spaces (dotted lines in figure 6.2) are emphasised, whereby the *strong* causal notions, inherent in domain-specific causal assumptions, are replaced by *weak* causal notions based on perceptual features and associative learning (Kummer 1995).

The same is the case in the other end of the event-frame that relates the ritual action to the represented future state by prognosis. The ritual action must necessarily be represented as causing the emergence or creation of a more or less specified future state of affair. This involves a prognostic classification relating the present action of the Action space to the Effect space of the future, represented as an alteration of the past event-state. But, again, *strong* causal assumptions, intimately connected by domain-specific inferences connected to the actual actions performed, are disconnected from representations of the result of the actions. These are replaced by *weak* causal connections based on associative learning and perceptual characteristics that ensure the relation between the ritual performed and the result represented to follow this performance. This altered event-frame is illustrated in figure 6.2:

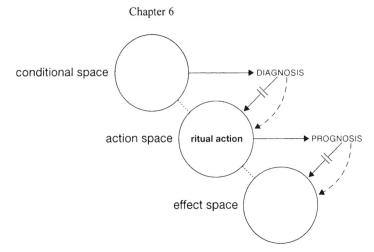

Figure 6.2: Ritual event-frame

Besides strengthening the indexical and iconic relations between the spaces, as well as internally in the ritual action, the severing of the causal and intentional connection between diagnosis/ritual action and prognosis/future event-state has another important effect. It results in the creation and crystallisation of new formal and symbolically expressed *conventional* connections between diagnosis/ritual action and prognosis/future result (curved arrow). This is the 'theological', symbolic interpretations and explanations of how a given ritual works, why it is performed, why it has the form that it has, why it has the result is said to have, etc. As these interpretations are made without the guidance of the causal and intentional knowledge usually connecting Action to both Conditional and Effect spaces, they must contain highly counter-intuitive ideas and representations that ensure their memorability and transmission (Boyer 1994). Thus, symbolic connections containing highly memorable counterintuitive concepts are established by referring to authoritative sources based on a wide range of cultural models, such as mythological traditions (oral or written), powerful religious figures or former experiences of a ritual performance. New explicit connections replace the implicit and automatically ascribed causal and intentional connections otherwise structuring the relation between action and event-frames.

To summarise: by embedding magical ritual action in an event-frame, as its instrumental cause, the event-frame is transformed. Both causal and intentional representations, connecting an action to the prior (diagnosis) and the following event-states (prognosis), are radically de-emphasised, leaving instead two interrelated hermeneutic strategies for ascribing purpose and meaning to the ritual. The first strategy utilises the direct meaning based on essentialist and image-schematic interaction between elements, both internally in the ritual and in relation to representations of elements belonging to the Conditional and the Effect spaces. This basic meaning will loosely constrain meaningful symbolic interpretations of the ritual actions, whether authorised, orthodox, illicit or idiosyncratic. The second hermeneutic strategy is based on the pre-existence of explicit and possibly 'materialised' symbolic interpretations in any cultural context. They constitute a supply of explanatory frameworks more or less relevant in the local situation, containing memorable counterintuitive propositions, testimonies of prior successful performance creating "current mythology" (Evans-Pritchard 1929) and reference to cultural models of authority. These two hermeneutic strategies always coexist in religious and magical rituals, sometimes in a symbiotic relationship of mutual reinforcement, and sometimes in a state of war based on a conflict between experienced meaning and authorised symbolic interpretation. This will be addressed in the next chapter. What should be noted at this point is that the magical use of ritual tends to focus on the first strategy, even while depending on cultural specifications of possible bearers of magical agency.

Neither participants nor observers understand all ritualised actions as magical rituals' or as having a 'magical potential', i.e. as an instrumental part of an event-frame. But even in cases of rituals not usually embedded in an instrumental event-frame, participants can utilise ritual elements in novel event-frames, whether individually constructed or prescribed by parallel traditions. Sanctified bread is used to protect against theft (Thomas 1991: 51), and water or paste formerly used to anoint the sacred *Jina* in the Jain *puja* is used to exorcise a demon from a possessed woman (Humphrey & Laidlaw 1994: 185-86). In both cases, the action is centred on magical agency invested in the element through authoritative ritual action, subsequently transposed into an alternative event-frame and transferred to a new recipient by contagious interaction. So, even rituals and ritual elements not ordinarily understood to have an immediate transformative or manipulative potential can be used as such: (1) if they are ascribed some sort of magical agency facilitated by a mapping between the sacred and the profane conceptual space; and (2) if they are embedded in an event-frame as the instrumental cause represented as facilitating or bringing about a change in the state of affairs.

The relation of magical rituals to event-frames is even more explicit in situations where a given ritual is the culturally prescribed (re)action, whether toward unexpected events, like disease, or expected events like harvesting. The embedding of the ritual into a locally specified event-frame introduces a third hermeneutic strategy for participants in a ritual, namely extracting meaning from the ritual by reference to its relevance in relation to local event-frames.

6.3 Pragmatic Repertoires of Magical Rituals

It is an open important question whether it is possible to divide magical rituals into separate pragmatic repertories defined by 'purpose' or 'meaning.' In order to discuss this possibility, it is necessary to analyse two parameters. The first parameter concerns the 'orientation' of magical rituals to the event-frames in which they themselves form a part, and the relation of this ritual event-frame to other event-frames, whether prior or parallel to the ritual action. The question is whether a ritual shall be classified as *prospective* or *retrospective* (cf. Tambiah 1968: 189), i.e. whether the purpose of the ritual is to effect the emergence of a whole new state of affairs, or to recreate an old one that has been disrupted. The second parameter is the question of how this network of interrelated event-frames interacts with the basic meaning inherent in the image-schematic properties of the ritualised element. The question is whether a typology of the general purposes of magical rituals, such as *constructive*, *protective* and *destructive*, can be made by relating the network of event-frames in which the ritual is embedded to the image-schematic structures inherent in the ritualised actions.

6.3.1 Prospective and Retrospective Magic

The first parameter primarily concerns the focus of attention. Some magical rituals are *prospective* as they are aimed to produce a new state, wherefore the focus of participants in the ritual and the direction of the ritual action are towards representations of this future state. In this context, it does not matter whether it is a repeated or a once in a lifetime activity, e.g. whether it is for producing this year's crop or for winning the love of your life. Of importance is the emphasis placed on the future state of affair, that is, on the essentialist and image-schematic representations directly connecting the action to a desired future event-state, and on the altered prognostic procedure relating the present ritual action to the emergence of a new situation by authoritative cultural models. Very often, magical rituals aimed to produce a new event-state are performed in intimate relation to other activities aimed at the same goal. This mean that event-frames structuring magical rituals are brought into accordance with event-frames structuring practical activities, either at a general level, working towards the same goal, or, at a more specific level, in which magical actions are believed to help overcome particular obstacles hindering the unfolding of the overarching sequence of events.

In chapters 4 and 5, I analysed the Trobriand *Yowota* ritual focusing on the *Vatuvi*-spell. The *Yowota* is an inaugurative ritual performed every year in relation to the beginning of the agricultural cycle, whereas the *Vatuvi*-spell is used on several important occasions during the agricultural cycle. The magical rituals of the Trobrianders are intertwined with the practical activities during the whole cycle and this to such a large extent that it is the garden magician, the *Towosi*, that decides at what time specific actions are inaugurated:

> Magic appears side by side with work, not accidentally or sporadically as occasions arise or as whim dictates, but as an essential part of the whole scheme and in a way which does not permit an honest observer to dismiss it as a mere excrescence (Malinowski 1935a: 55)

In this way, Trobriand magic is not only embedded in its own event-frame, structuring 'a before and after' in relation to the instrumental ritual, but is also related to an overall sequential scheme that structures the agricultural calendar as a whole combining practical and ritual actions (see charts in Malinowski 1935a: 435-51). Magical rituals accompany all major activities in the garden, and the *Vatuvi*-spell is employed at the most important ones. The purpose of the physical activity of gardening is, of course, to produce crops, both for consumption and for symbolic purposes. The Trobrianders distinguish the physical aspects from the ritual aspects of gardening, and "the way of garden work" has another specialised purpose than "the way of magic", even though the more general purpose of both activities is to get a successful harvest (76-77). According to Malinowski, the general and abstracted aim of magical rituals is to control aspects of gardening that the gardener otherwise has no or limited control over. This is in accordance with the analysis made in the preceding chapters and with one of the general principle of manipulative magic. Manipulative magic is based on a conceptual mapping that facilitates the manipulation of an inaccessible domain through actions performed in a more accessible domain. The whole agricultural cycle is thus a conglomerate of both practical and ritualised actions aimed at the overall purpose of a successful harvest, a prospective goal structured by an event-frame. A basic hypothesis is that the representation of such an event-frame will always be intimately related to a *counterfactual event-frame* representing what happens in case the instrumental actions are not performed, i.e. if no garden work is done, or, of more interest in this context, if no magical rituals are performed.

The mere presence of Malinowski at the Trobriand Islands prompted questions concerning the garden magic used in his homeland, and the Trobrianders found it difficult to believe that anything would grow well without the assistance of garden magic (62-63). Counterfactual reasoning about the consequences of *not* performing the prescribed action is an integrated part in representations of magical ritual actions embedded in an event-frame. This is illustrated in figure 6.3:

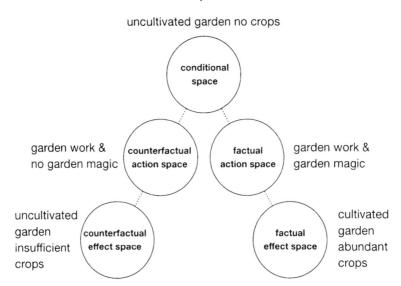

Figure 6.3: Network of factual and counterfactual event-frames

This kind of representation supplies a huge amount of inferential potential for the explanation of actual agricultural success or failure. An abundant crop is the result of skilled garden work and good magic, and a bad and insufficient harvest is the result of either unskilled garden work (not represented above) or insufficient or inadequate garden magic. It should be kept in mind that the dichotomous nature of the figure represents the ideal types active before and during the ritual and practical process of gardening, based on a combination of "if I do y, then x", and "if I do not y, then z"-type of reasoning. Malinowski gives a tragic example of this in relation to the *Vakavayla'u* ritual, the burning of the scrub cut down in the gardens:

> One of the resident magistrates, not aware of the necessity for magical burning, was tempted, in passing the cut and dried garden, to put a match to it. ... He lit the garden, and soon the night was ablaze with high-towering flames. In a few minutes he was surrounded by a crowd of natives, half despairing, half angry, who then explained to him for the first time their magical theory of gardening, besought him never to do anything of this sort again, and prophesied that the gardens would suffer. And indeed this was a year of drought—hence the beauty of the bonfire—so the prophecy did come true, and the white man for once contributed by his acts to the strengthening of native beliefs (Malinowski 1935a: 112).

The Trobrianders are well aware of the fertilising effect of the ashes resulting from the burning of the cut-down scrub (Malinowski 1935a: 110), but the importance ascribed to the magical procedure connected to the process should not be underestimated. The example illustrates the conditional character of the magical rites, leaving only the two alternatives presented in figure 6.3. But when the interrelated event-frames are used subsequently as a culturally approved model to explain different agricultural results, they are transformed into a graded structure and placed in a force-dynamic field with parameters of both practical labour and magic. Thus, a moderate harvest can be the result of moderately skilled labour and moderately strong magic, skilled labour and insufficient magic, or unskilled labour but strong magic, and so on. This transformation into a graded structure is a feature of the domain to which the event-frame is applied, and other domains will expose a clear either-or structure also in the subsequent judgement (either you win or you do not win the lottery).

The social structure of the Trobriand society and the symbolic significance of yams also play a role in the relation between agricultural results and magical actions. Even though a successful garden is connected with much pride, Malinowski explains that only chiefs, and those gardening for a chief, should have perfect gardens (standard plots), and that men of lesser rank risk serious consequences should their gardens equal or even surpass those of the chiefs (60). "Ill health or even death by sorcery rather than renown would then reward his [the commoner's] labours" (83, see also 176). Besides the direct relation between wealth and social status, there is the relationship between magic and political authority. Garden magic is owned by the politically ruling lineage and all ritual actions are performed first in the chief's garden by the magician himself, and only subsequently performed in a minor version in the other gardens, without the garden magician directly taking part. The chief's gardens, or standard plots, are, as the name reveals, the exemplary garden, and all other gardens should be less perfect copies of these plots. These aspects of land tenure and agricultural success can be analysed as a metonymic extension of magical efficacy structured by a CENTRE-PERIPHERY schema, according to which the standard plots get most magic, and the magical efficacy lessens as we approach the periphery of the garden plots. A commoner exposing a more successful garden than the standard plot not only exceeds the chief in possession of the primary symbol of status, but also indicates that either he is in possession of stronger magic than his superiors, or that he has used sorcery to diminish the success of all other gardens leaving his own in front. So, the event-frame facilitates inference from results to ascribed instrumental causes of the results.

As we have seen in the analysis in chapter 5, the *Yowota* ritual in general and the *Vatuvi*-spell in particular are not only embedded in a very general event-frame informing the cultural model of magic as a necessary instrument used in order to get a successful harvest. The elements, both actions and objects, linguistically referred to in the *Vatuvi*-spell point in two more specified directions. First, they point to the metaphors that, by referring to perceptual features of the gardens, outline the process the garden will undergo if all things work out well ("swelling", "rising" etc.). This is an example of metaphors used to establish iconic connections between the Conditional space and the Effect space, combined with identity connections such as "garden" referring to the one and same garden in all mental spaces. Second, they point to the actions linguistically referred to in the expelling or exercising of very specific elements believed to be a hindrance for the correct unfolding of this sequential process (pest and diseases). In this case, an alternative event-frame is evoked due to the reference to elements, pests and diseases, whose presence can prompt the replacement of a desired with an undesired event-frame. Therefore, this aspect of the spell has no 'procreative' element, but functions instead as a 'protection' against an unwanted temporal development, namely the destruction or diminishing of the crops due to pests and diseases. So, we find a representation according to which the positive progression of the garden towards abundant harvest under certain circumstances can be interrupted and replaced by a negative event-frame leading to an insufficient harvest. Besides their relation to the superordinate event-frame, magical actions are thus intimately related to subordinate event-frames that divide the overall frame, in this case the whole agricultural cycle, into smaller sequences (e.g. the growing of the branches of the yams). Each of these event-frames contain specialised actions aimed to help or facilitate the progress towards the overall goal, and each has specific magical actions associated to them, such as the "spider formula" believed to stimulate the growth of branches, using the similarity between yam's branches and the spiders' webs (MF 18, Malinowski 1935a: 148). Attached to all these interrelated event-frames are negative conditionals or counterfactual spaces outlining possible alternative unfoldings of events, if certain actions, both practical and ritual, are not performed. Thus, a magical ritual with a pre-specified goal, e.g. agricultural success, can be embedded as the instrumental cause in several interrelated event-frames at the same time. Further, rituals often contain conceptual means to evoke these different spaces in participants as a supplement to the obvious contextual reference based on the performance of the ritual in a specific situation. In prospective magic, the focus is on the creation of a new or transformed state of affairs in the Effect space, by ritual actions performed in the Action space, and on avoiding events, actions, or objects that might jeopardise the progress towards this desired goal. Metaphors and metonymies are used in the ritual in order to refer to and thereby evoke the desired state of affairs in the Effect space, but also to evoke possible alternative negative event-frames, if the correct actions are not performed.

In *retrospective* magic, the focus of the ritual action is on states of affairs preceding the ritual performance. There are two basic aspects of this type of magic. First, ritual actions are motivated by representations of perceptual features characterising the event-state preceding the ritual performance. Examples of this are cases of magic taking part in healing rituals, in which symptoms of the disease are treated through manipulative magic based on similarity relations to perceptible properties of the disease.

> At a certain time of their growth the stems of the creeper *araka* lose their leaves. These are replaced by a double row of bands, joined to the stalks, which

little by little dry, split, and fall in small pieces just as the extremities of the hands and feet disappear in *'la lèpre mutilante'*. This creeper is highly thought of as furnishing a treatment for this kind of leprosy (Evans-Pritchard 1937: 450).

The similarity based counterpart connections between the creeper and the disease are all quite obvious. But why is it that the creeper is used to *cure* and not *provoke* leprosy? One might as well expect that the peculiar perceptual features of the creeper would make it an excellent tool for a sorcerer wishing to impart leprosy on an enemy, just like the reference to the bush-hen's nest or the anthill will facilitate an abundant crop on the Trobriand Islands. A possible answer lies in the development of creeper itself. The losing of leaves and the double row of bands are part of the plant's growth-cycle, and like the plant survives its transformation, so will the person suffering from leprosy (Tambiah 1985: 74). This, however, cannot be an answer in itself, as other cases show that extensions of the simile are constrained by the motivation behind its use. The Azande do not intend the sun to stay in the sky forever, even though nobody bothers to remove the stone from the tree, and the Trobrianders do not intend their yams to be alive and hatch like chickens from a bush-hen's nest. The metaphorical mappings are constrained by another factor besides the internal structure in the blend described in chapter 4 and 5. This is the obvious constraint imposed by the fact that rituals, in which these magical actions take part, are embedded in motivated event-frames. The overall goal motivates not only the elements mapped but also the extent and the result of the mapping, in this case the removal and not infusion of the symptoms. The aim is to restore the person to his/her former health, and in order to do so one tries to remove the perceptual features that separate him/her from a person of normal health. In a way, the ritual seeks to ritually annul the undesirable aspects of the Conditional space, which in case it succeeds will leave the person cured.

Unfortunately, Evans-Pritchard does not describe the ritual context in which this medicine is used in the attempt to heal a person suffering from leprosy, but, elsewhere in his book on Zande witchcraft, oracles and magic, he mentions the diagnosis of leprosy and the event-frames attached to it. This points to the second basic aspect of retrospective magic. Evans-Pritchard describes the Zande idea of "the second spear", which is a metaphor for witchcraft believed to be the second, and most important cause responsible for an unfortunate event (Evans-Pritchard 1937: 74). He gives the example of a man dying of leprosy. The disease is believed to exist independently of any human or human-like agent, and is ascribed certain causal expectations (e.g. that the extremities of the body will fall off), as are other physical objects or events. This 'materialist' representation of the disease is the first causal event-frame applied in order to understand the situation. This is combined with two other lines of reasoning. The reason the man contracted the disease is ascribed to a breach of taboo against incestuous relations. He would not have contracted the disease had he not broken a basic social prohibition against incest. Finally, the reason he dies from the disease is believed to be witchcraft and must be revenged by his family. In case no witch had interfered, the man would have been sick from leprosy, but would not have died. In this case, no less than three event-frames relating causes to actions and results are active in determining what actually happened. Evans-Pritchard gives several other examples of representations of a plurality of causes and the "second spear" active in Zande causal thinking (74-78).

The example illustrates how several event-frames can be condensed in the classification of the event-states that form the basis of ritual action. This is important, as the event-frames believed to be responsible for this state influence not only what kind of ritual needs to be performed (healing a breach of social taboo, or revenging witchcraft), but also what the ritual actions consist in. Anthropologist Gilbert Lewis gives a lucid example of this plurality of causes from his study of illness among the Gnau of Papua New Guinea:

> In the village in the Sepik where I was working, a man had a sudden pain in his knee. A few hours after its onset, while he lay inside his house, a cricket jumped out of the thatch onto his painful leg. A few minutes earlier, a girl from the hamlet above had walked past. She was the 'grandchild' of a man who had died with a painful leg caused, it was said, by a certain spirit. The villager thought the 'shade' (spirit) of the dead man must have followed the girl, entered the cricket, jumped onto his knee, and alerted the spirit; his knee became more painful. He voiced his fears, his wife relayed them, and his kin discussed them. (In fact he had tried to catch the cricket to kill it but had failed.) (Lewis 1995: 560-61)

As Lewis explains, the contiguous relation perceived between the girl, the cricket and the sick man are related in a causal hypothesis explaining why the man is sick by reference to a malevolent spirit. Both weak causal links based on basic cognitive representations of contagious transfer of essence, and explicit cultural models of the spirits of the dead man interact in the construction of this event-frame. The consequences of this causal classification of the disease are that the girl is sent away and the relevant spirit is invoked. These actions, however, results in a change of explanatory frame:

> After an appeal to the spirit of the dead man, people lost interest in that particular explanation for the sick man's pain as matters became worse and other explanations were developed (Lewis 1995: 561).

This example enables the identification of three basic characteristics of the interaction between the diagnostic process and ritual action:

1. The ritual event-frame in retrospective magic presupposes one or several event-frames that are represented as leading to the state of affairs prompting the ritual action. Thus, we see the existence of much larger networks of causal strings relating event-frames to each other and forming mini-narratives of inter-

related events. A pertinent question in this respect is how far back people entertain representations of this network or narrative? This is pragmatically determined as the direction and extension of the network is socially negotiated at all intersections between event-frames, thereby deciding the *need* to evoke further event-frames relevant in order to determine the future course of actions (cf. Hilton 1995). In Lewis' example, the disease is first classified as caused by a malevolent ancestor spirit represented as transported to him by a series of contagious interactions. We therefore have two interrelated event-frames. The first explains how the spirit invaded the man, and the second explains the disease by reference to contact with a particular spirit. Both levels are used to act upon, as the girl is made to leave the village despite having very good reasons to stay (the prospect of marriage). She must therefore be represented as potentially still able to be a vehicle for the spirit by virtue of a genealogical link. Second, in order to heal the man, the spirit is directly appealed to. When none of these actions help, both interconnected event-frames are abandoned as an explanation, and there is no need to evoke further event-frames connected to the same narrative sequence. Another example of the pragmatic limitation of causal networks is the representation of the intimate connection between witchcraft and genealogy among the Azande. Evans-Pritchard describes how witchcraft is believed to be an essential substance that is inherited between father and son or mother and daughter. Once a man is classified as a witch, his whole male lineage should be represented as witches, but this does not happen as the Azande employ only the notion of witchcraft to explain concrete events (Evans-Pritchard 1937: 23-26). Again, the possible unfolding of a comprehensive network of interconnected event-frames are constrained by pragmatic factors motivating the degree of extension.

2. The second characteristic feature of the interaction between classification of event-states and ritual action is the abductive type of reasoning involved. As Lewis' example illustrates, once the ritual action intended to counter the disease fails, the whole diagnosis is rejected because the classification is put in doubt. If the malevolent spirit did not cause the disease, then the ritual containing an appeal to this spirit will, of course, not be judged as an effective remedy against the disease, and another causal scenario is sought out, which might lead to new types of ritual action, and so forth. This is an excellent example of abductive reasoning: an event-state, C (disease), is classified as it would follow deductively from a culturally specified cause, B (a spirit), working on a prior event-state, A (no disease). This results in the causally structured event-frame (EF1), in which B causes the change from A to C (a spirit causes disease from no disease). Acceptance of this classification leads to the representation of a new event-frame (EF2), in which a prescribed type of ritual action is the instrumental cause, B1, that by countering B should change the ritualised event-state C1 (ritualised disease) into the equally ritualised event-state A1 almost identical to the original event-state, A, (non-disease).[9] Thus, we have a causally organised event-frame involving ritual action, EF2, opposing the classificatory event-

frame, EF1 (magical action counters the forces of the spirit thereby healing the patient). This is represented in figure 6.4:

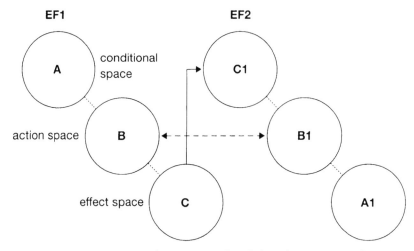

Figure 6.4: Dynamic interaction between ritual and classificatory event-frame

The interaction between the two event-frames illustrated in the model has two interesting implications. First, there is a force-dynamic interaction between the instrumental causes of the two event-frames (double arrow). The healing ritual must be stronger than the power of the spirit in order to heal the patient, either in direct force or in persuasive power. This feature is evident in the metaphors of 'fight', 'strength', and 'force' surrounding many magical rituals aimed to counter a specified opponent—and we have already seen some of the representations used to invest force in the ritual, such as implication of strong magical agency or diverse iconic features such as repetition and prosody. Second, representations of the second event-frame (EF2) containing the ritual action should be understood as a ritualised reaction to the cultural model containing the first event-frame (EF1). By these two implications, the inferential potential used in judging the ultimate result of a ritual action is further broadened. The first places the ritual action of EF2 in a force-dynamic relation to the instrumental cause of EF1, as specified by a cultural model. Failure to reach the desired result can be explained by claiming that the magic used in the ritual was too weak in the face of a mighty opponent. The second takes the success of the ritual to be determined by the correct classification that constitutes the Conditional space. In case of ritual failure, the classification of an event as an example of the 'preconditional' first event-frame, EF1, can be questioned. This entails that representations of the efficacy of the ritual performed need not be doubted (e.g. "the ritual is efficient against witchcraft, but this is not a case of witchcraft"). Instead the ritual is represented as performed on the wrong premises, that is, as addressing the wrong and not the real cause (that can be undefined).[10] This can lead to a further search for and social negotiation of possible explanations based on culturally approved models and concepts.

3. The process of choosing between alternative explanatory event-frames—leading to different types of reactions—is a general feature of explanations and is not restricted to magic or religion. Thus, if my car will not start, there are several possible explanations leading to different actions. The question is what distinguishes magic from other types of action based on causal explanations? We have already seen how the act of ritualisation radically transforms the ritual event-frame from non-ritual event-frames. Ritualisation points to the third characteristic of the interaction between ritual action and diagnosis of prior event-frames: the proclivity to employ event-frames based on intentionality and magical agency to explain physical events found in certain discursive and cultural contexts (e.g. the explanation of the Zande man's death of leprosy as caused by witchcraft). As we saw above, the classification of the initial event-state, or Conditional space of EF2 as the result of a preceding EF1 cannot be separated from the overall content of the event-frame containing the ritual action. That the two event-frames are represented mentally as temporally organised should not lead us to believe that the ritual action necessarily arises as an answer to a pre-existing explanatory event-frame, even when it is explicitly presented as such. In fact it may be the other way around. In the case of magical rituals, the more or less abstract representation of ritualised action (involving magical agency able to change a situation into another situation) is a prerequisite for the viability of explanatory event-frames involving similar magical agency, represented as causing the situation that the ritual acts upon. To paraphrase Humphrey and Laidlaw, ritualised actions *call* for an interpretation (1994: 194), and this interpretation can lead to the creation of event-frames explaining the presence of magical agency in the ritual by referring to the presence of magical agency in the event-frame that the ritual is seen as acting upon. In this perspective, a ritual countering the effects of witches on human beings would be a prerequisite for strong representations of witches actually harming people.

This can be understood from two perspectives. The first perspective is phylogenetic and leads to the hypothesis that it is ritualisation of actions that facilitates the creation of representations of magical agency in the course of human evolution. The second and more instrumental perspective is epigenetic and leads to the hypothesis that the presence of magical agency in rituals is a prerequisite for the acquisition of strong representations of explanatory event-frames, in which magical or superhuman agency functions as the intentional agent causing one state to change into another. The epigenetic hypothesis predicts that children growing up in a religious tradition that emphasises *symbolic* interpretations of ritual actions and de-emphasises the active role of magical agency and concrete ritual results will be less likely to employ event-frames involving magical or superhuman agency in order to explain or interpret real-world events outside a ritual context. Contrarily, children growing up in a religious tradition de-emphasising symbolic interpretations of ritual actions, and emphasising the active role of magical agency and the efficacious character of ritual actions, will be more likely to utilise event-frames involving magical agency to explain or interpret events outside the ritual context. This is despite the fact that *both* religious traditions in question will have an explicit mythology involving magical agency as the intentional agent(s) causing changes in the world. In short, *actions* involving magical agency facilitate the emergence of *explanations* involving magical agency. This hypothesis is in accordance with the results of experiments performed by the developmental psychologist, E. Subbotsky (1994), addressing the magical beliefs of pre-school children. Telling a narrative that involves magical agency changing the direction of time (magic water making things it touches as they were two years ago) was not sufficient to alter the verbalised belief of most children about time, e.g. that things cannot grow younger. But *participating* in an event involving magical water 'mysteriously' making an old stamp new made practically all the children accept that magic was involved, at least in this particular case. Further, some of the children explained their subsequent refusal to drink the magic water on the ground of the absence of another bottle of magic water able to make them older again (Subbotsky 1994: 103-8). These children made extensive inferences based on assumptions about the potential existence of magical agency countering the effects of the magical water. Thus, cultural representations of magical agency able to cause certain events are considerably strengthened by the existence of ritual actions represented as countering or using this agency actively in effecting the creation of a new event-state. In chapter 7, I shall examine further evidence of the importance of rituals involving magical agency in facilitating more general representations of event-frames and narratives involving strong magical agency as the intentional agent.

The human proclivity to represent certain event-states as the result of 'magical' actions by super-human agents is strengthened by a combination of two factors: (a) the embedding of ritualised magical action as the instrumental cause in event-frames; and (b) the proliferation of strong explanatory models involving magical or superhuman agency in cultural settings involving ritualised actions with active magical agency. The existence of ritual actions involving magical agency and aimed at securing and protecting specified outcomes, will thus enhance the relevance of explanatory models involving similar magical agencies. Cross-culturally, certain aspects of life—the course of life, fertility, transition to adult status etc.—are protected by magical agencies through ritualised actions. Special or extraordinary events—death in young age, having no children in a marriage, birth of twins etc.—are also explained as interventions of magical agencies. I believe these two contexts of evoking superhuman agents are causally connected. Strong explanatory models involving magical agencies are dependent on the existence of ritual event-frames containing magical agency either protecting the general course of events (e.g. an agricultural cycle, the life of a human being) or reacting to specific obstacles to this course.[11] The existence of a cultural model explaining an abundant harvest in terms of the performance of potent garden magic will almost automatically facilitate the emergence of models explaining why specific instances went wrong despite the correct performance of the magical rituals. Explanatory event-frames involving magical agency can thus be seen as mirroring the role played by magical agency in ritual event-frames. Once both ritual and explanatory event-frames involving magical agency are established, they will enter into a loop based on a mutual reinforcement of the epistemic value of the magical agency involved. The more rituals performed in order to protect or enhance a given activity by invoking magical agencies, the more will similar magical agencies be relevant to explain breach of expectations. Further, the more explanations of specific events are done by reference to the action of magical agencies, the more important will the rituals be in which other magical agencies counter potentially malevolent influences.

To summarise: the existence of ritualised actions aimed to produce specific event-states (prospective) or reacting towards undesirable event-states (retrospective) through the means of magical agency are a prerequisite for strong representations of magical or superhuman agency in explanatory event-frames. The classification of the initial event-state and of how this state came about is inherent in all types of action representations. This result in the construction of causal networks only limited by domain-specific causal expectation, pragmatic factors of relevance and motivation, and by pre-established conceptual connections. In ritual actions, both event-frames and related networks are transformed. Magical rituals invoke magical agency to ensure the desired result of the ritual action. This, in turn, prompts the occurrence of representations of magical agency as the instrumental cause at other levels in the causal network. In prospective magic, magical agency appears both in the counterfactual representation of consequences of *not* performing the ritual, and in representations of magical agency working against the desired result. In retrospective magic, magical agency appears at different slots in the complex network of interrelated event-frames prompting the performance of ritual action. This appearance is made highly relevant by the representation of magical agency responsible for ritual efficacy. Using gods, witches, spells and magical medicine as the explanation of particular states of affairs are made possible by the crucial role such magical agencies have in the performance of ritual actions.

6.3.2 Second Parameter: Image-schematic Structures

As argued above, magical rituals are focused in a specific direction depending on whether their goals are to create whole new event-states or to recreate disrupted prior event-states. This typology, however, does not tell us much about *how* the change or reconstruction is brought about, i.e. how the immediate purpose relates to representations of the basic aspects of the actions performed. Designating magical actions on the basis of their general purpose, e.g. as being procreative, productive, constructive, protective, punitive, destructive etc., has a long tradition in anthropological research (e.g. Evans-Pritchard 1937; Firth 1967). Usually these terms are used without much consideration of what prompts this classification. The question remains how such a general typology referring to the pragmatic purpose of the performance of magical rituals can be constructed? Is it possible to determine not only that magical rituals are embedded in event-frames as the instrumental cause, but also what type of instrument they have become? We have seen how difficult it is to extract the purpose or meaning of a given ritual solely by means of observation and knowledge of the intentional and causal relations between agents, actions and objects contained in the ritual. The ritualisation of ritual elements makes it difficult to relate the actions performed by the ritual agent to his or her intentions, thereby obstructing the extraction of a specific meaning or purpose of a given ritual (Humphrey & Laidlaw 1994). This difficulty is further reinforced by the tendency for the same rituals to be used in different contexts, adding to the causal distance between the event-states preceding and following a given ritual, and the ritualised actions functioning as instrumental cause. With this in mind, is it at all possible to construct a typology of magical actions in their pragmatic setting? Whereas the analysis of the direction of the ritual, discussed above, is intimately connected to its relation of other event-frames, we now turn to more basic structures constraining the relation between ritual actions and pragmatic settings.

Throughout this book, it has been argued that image-schematic structures play a significant role as a deep-level cognitive format facilitating the mapping between mental spaces. Image-schematic structures found in ritual action have yet another function in their direct relation to the pragmatic setting of the ritual. A useful way to approach the question of the relation between the experience of image-schematic structures and pragmatic setting is to explore whether there is a basic inventory of image-schemata which structures different pragmatic types of magical rituals. In what way do image-schemata constrain the pragmatic purpose ascribed magical actions? Can relations of image-schematic structures be systematised in order to give a general typology of ritual 'purpose'?

One of the most important and fundamental image-schematic structures in magical rituals (as well as in everyday cognition), and therefore a natural example, is the CONTAINER-schema (Johnson 1987: 21-23, 39-40). We have already encountered this several times as a basic schema active in both rituals of transformation and contagion and in simpler manipulative rituals aimed to exercise elements from a given space. The CONTAINER-schema is basic to organisation of elements in space, and fundamental in the spatial relation between essence and perceptible appearance, for instance found in sanctified bread of the Catholic Eucharist. In this, and in similar cases, the CONTAINER-schema is in a dynamic interaction with other schematic structures, most notably a TRAJECTORY-schema, that organise the relation of other elements to the CONTAINER. Containers contain something, and they have a border that can be transgressed. From an analytic point of view, the interaction between the CONTAINER and the TRAJECTORY-schema can be represented as a series of dynamic schemata:

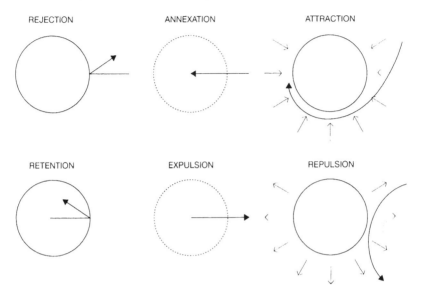

Figure 6.5: Interaction between CONTAINER- and TRAJECTORY-schemata

The three examples at the top of figure 6.5 all involve cases in which an element moves along a TRAJECTORY towards a bounded space, the result of which is governed by a force-dynamic relationship between the strength of the border and the strength of the movement along the TRAJECTORY. In the case of magic involving a REJECTION-schema, the border of the CONTAINER is relatively strengthened in order to prevent external influence to enter into the closed space. This is exemplified by the numerous cases of magical actions aimed to protect the body or a physical space against intrusion, for instance in the elaborate construction of a magical wall around the Trobriand gardens (Malinowski 1935a: 123-32). In the opposite case of magic involving an ANNEXATION-schema, the boundary surrounding the contained space is relatively weakened or even opened in order to receive and incorporate the external influence into the bounded space. This is the case in all instances of positive or negative contagion, for example in the Catholic communion involving the ingestion of sanctified bread in order to obtain the desired quality of Christ. Finally, there is the case of magic involving an ATTRACTION-schema in which the CONTAINER functions as an attractor to the TRAJECTOR of elements that will stay in close proximity of its boundary. This kind of schematism is exemplified in the Aguaruna hunting magic, in which magical stones, *yuka*, are ascribed a special essence that is believed to attract either game or persons of the opposite sex (Brown 1985: 86).

The three schemata at the bottom of figure 6.5 illustrate cases in which an element moves along a TRAJECTORY *away* from the CONTAINER. Again we find a force-dynamic relationship between the strength of the border and the strength of the movement. In the case of magic involving a RETENTION-schema, the boundary of the CONTAINER is relatively strengthened, not to keep out influence, but in order to retain elements already in it. Once again, the material collected by Malinowski provides an excellent example. The Trobrianders perform magical rituals aimed to keep the harvested yams inside the designated storehouses for as long as possible by using the metaphor of "anchoring" the storehouse containing the yams (MF 28, Malinowski 1935a: 221), thus preventing it from leaving a bounded area. In the opposite case of magical rituals involving an EXPULSION-schema, the relative strength is altered so the element can cross the boundary from the inside to the outside of the CONTAINER. This schema is active in cases of exorcism whether it is from body or some other space that is conceptualised as the CONTAINER, for instance in the *Vatuvi*-spell analysed in chapter 5 (other good Trobriand examples of exorcism see MF 7 and MF 31, Malinowski 1935a: 114, 236). The schema is also active in cases of ritual purification involving the excretion of an element from inside the CONTAINER. The final case is magic involving a REPULSION-schema, in which a CONTAINER functions as a repellent to an external TRAJECTORY. An example of this is talismans or spells warding of evil influences.

At this point, it is important to emphasise that the image-schematic structures are in themselves of neutral value, despite any value implied by the illustrations given above. In all schemata, the element approaching or departing the CONTAINER can be understood as either positive or negative. The relative value should be understood as a property ascribed in both the local pragmatic situation of the ritual and through the pre-established symbolic interpretations of the ritual elements, in this case to both the TRAJECTORY and CONTAINER. Another important issue is the question of ritual focus in relation to the force-dynamic interaction between CONTAINER and TRAJECTORY. The strength of both CONTAINER and TRAJECTORY can vary to allow for a change of state depending on the focus of both ritual and explanatory event-frames.

This short description should give an impression of the dynamic complexity resulting from the construction of more complex image-schemata by the conjunction of two basic image-schematic structures. The relation between CONTAINER and TRAJECTORY can account for a substantial amount of the inferential potential inherent in transformative magical actions involving contagious practices of essence flow (described in chapter 5.1). Furthermore, it can be found in the skeletal inferential structure inherent in many metaphorical expressions and actions, for instance in the exorcising of garden pests and diseases found in the *Vatuvi*-spell (5.2.2). The *Yowota* ritual, of which the *Vatuvi*-spell is a part, is an inaugural ritual performed prior to the planting of the garden. How does this relate to the basic image-schematic structure of EXPULSION found in the spell? Why exorcise something that is not there yet? The answer is that the exorcism is a pre-emptive strike against a possible future obstruction to the desired unfolding of the events, which entails that the superordinate event-frame, of which the ritual forms a part, is represented as one single coherent structure. The representation of this overarching event-frame (see figure 6.3) is present at all stages in the agricultural cycle—an observation supported by the fact that the *Vatuvi*-spell is used on different stages during the agricultural cycle, from planting to harvest. Thus, the event-frame can be understood as a narrative structure with an initial state followed by a sequence of actions resulting in a terminal state. Ritualisation severs the causal and intentional connection between results and the actions performed, entailing that a magical ritual influencing the superordinate event-frame can be performed at any specific time, as long as it is inside this event-frame. This is, of course, in stark contrast to representations guiding the execution of practical actions. The Trobrianders would never perform *practical* actions aimed to free a garden, not yet cultivated, from pests and diseases that are not even present.

Image-schematic structures found in magical rituals therefore form a basic semantic inventory of ritual action that delimits their pragmatic embedding. This limitation, however, is restricted by two factors: (a) ritualisation entails that image-schematic structures are related to an overarching event-frame organising the pragmatic context the ritual is a part of. Image-schematic structures need not be in compliance with the immediate context, but only with the overall purpose of the whole ritual sequence; (2) valuation of individual elements of the ritual can vary both as a result of different perspective and interest, and as a result of historical change. Representations of something entering in an ANNEXATION-schema cannot be changed, but the valuation of what enters can change radically through change of perspective or historical development.

Notes

1. This is, of course a scant and simplified account of both the symbolist and the intellectualist approaches. For a more detailed account, see chapter 2 of the present work. For a philosophical treatment of the relationship between symbolist and intellectualist accounts, sympathetic to the latter, see Skorupski 1976. For a defence of the symbolist approach, see Beattie 1964, 1967, 1970. For a defence of the intellectualist approach in the rationality debate, see Jarvie & Agassi 1967; Horton 1970; Agassi & Jarvie 1973. See Wilson 1970 for an anthology comprising both positions.

2. It should be noted that Humphrey and Laidlaw distinguish between liturgical rituals with a high frequency of ritualised actions forming part of stipulative rituals, and performative rituals with a lesser frequency of ritualised actions and a more important role for the ritual agent (Humphrey & Laidlaw 1994: 8-12). This resembles my distinction between different types of magical agency (chapter 4).

3. Drawing lots is an extreme case of the absence of ordinary agency. All kinds of procedures ensure that the logical agents of the actions cannot influence the result. The action is subsequently represented as being without agency altogether or as a result of the intervention of superhuman agency.

4. It is possible that individuals have several spaces organising related events preceding the ritual, as well as it is possible that there are representations of several possible effect spaces, depending on the performance of actions in the action space. The division of the event-frame into three distinct temporal spaces has, of course, affinity to the division of the ritual process into three distinct phases of "separation", "transition", and "absorption" (van Gennep 1909; Turner 1969). The focus here, however, is not so much on the actual ritual unfolding, but on the mental representations connected to the performance.

5. Humphrey and Laidlaw (1994: 14) referring to philosopher Carlos J. Moya (1990).

6. For an excellent treatment, see the volume edited by Sperber, Premack and Premack (1995).

7. This notion of a *weak* causal framework is inspired by ethologist Hans Kummer's (1995) distinction between weak causal representations based on associative learning and events organised by spatio-temporal contiguity, and *strong* causal representations based on domain-specific reasoning not limited by spatio-temporal contiguity.

8. This classification may itself be performed with the help of magical techniques such as divination and omens.

9. See Lewis (1975) for an excellent description of the ritualisation of persons believed to have serious illnesses.

10. This is two examples of the so-called "secondary elaborations" used to explain unsuccessful magical action (Evans-Pritchard 1937: 475-8; Cf. Horton 1967).

11. By 'strong' explanatory models, I mean models not only used to explain certain events but which also in a significant way influence decisions about the future course of action. In contrast, 'weak' explanatory models are of an almost proverbial nature and do not influence decisions about the future course of actions.

7
Ritual Purpose and the Relation Between Magic, Culture and Religion

Following the description of magical actions presented in the last four chapters, the question of how these different levels of description are related naturally arises. From a cognitive point of view, the question can be reformulated: what cognitive processes and constraints influence representations of magical ritual action, and what factors and parameters are present in participants' representations of ritual purpose? In order to address this question, a model follows that depicts the parameters present in an idealised participant's formation of representations of ritual purpose. Presenting and discussing the model will serve as a condensed summary of the most central hypothesis and arguments of this book. This will lead to a more general discussion of what these can tell us about the relation between magic and cultural systems, institutionalised ritual activity and religion, respectively.

7.1 Summary

The previous four chapters have focused on the cognitive foundation of magical actions: how conceptual blending is used in delegating magical agency; transfer of essence and transformation of schemata; and how magical rituals are embedded in networks of event-frames constrained by pragmatic parameters. I have also touched upon the role of idiosyncratic and culturally specified symbolic interpretations of magical ritual, a theme that will be elaborated upon below. In unison, this can be described as three interacting hermeneutic levels available to participants in forming representations of the purpose of ritual action.

Figure 7.1 illustrates the intricate relationship between the different factors and hermeneutic levels at stake in participants' representations of ritual meaning or purpose. Four main sources feed inferential potential to the formation of these representations. It is important to emphasise that all of them need not be evoked, but that different ritual interpretations will focus on different aspects. From the left, (a) and (b) cover the pragmatic embedding of ritual action in a Network of Event-Frames or Narrative Sequences and their Temporal Orientation. Four representational clusters contribute to the creation of the comprehensive narrative network.

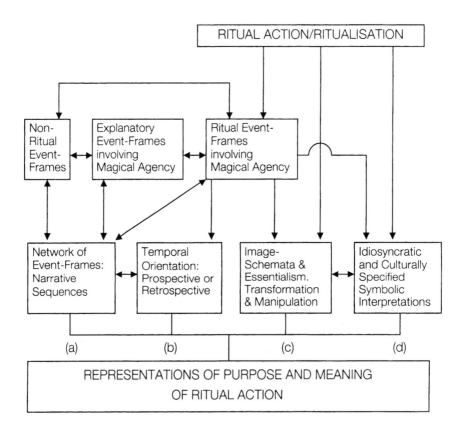

Figure 7.1: Schematic model of parameters involved in representations of ritual purpose and meaning.

First we have the Ritual Event-Frame itself, which is the most important structure delivering input to both other event-frames and to conceptual structures. As described in chapter 6, the special character of ritual action sets it apart from ordinary instrumental action in several aspects. By means of ritualisation of agents, actions or objects, the intentions of the agent are severed from the actual actions performed. Rituals are more or less stipulated actions, which imply that agents only have intentions in relation to the whole ritual sequence, leaving its parts intentionally underdetermined. This in turn facilitates representations of Magical Agency responsible for the constitution of the ritual action and/or responsible for its instrumental efficacy. Ritual event-frames transform not only the relation between intentions and actions, but also the causal relation between the actions performed and both their conditions and effect. Ordinary domain-specific expectations are severed, giving rise to two hermeneutic strategies: Image-Schematic and Essentialist interpretations, on the one hand, and Idiosyncratic and Culturally Specified Symbolic Interpretations on the other. As these function as independent input to representations of ritual purpose and meaning they will be treated separately below.

The Ritual Event-Frame is in a dynamic relationship with three other types of representations (represented by double arrows). First, Ritual Event-Frames interact with Explanatory Event-Frames involving Magical Agency. These are often described as underlying explanations of a certain state of affairs that give rise to prescribed ritual actions. But it might be the other way around. Ritualisation and ritual actions give rise to representations of magical agency, which in turn can be used to apply agency to happenings in the world. If magical agency is active in ritual actions, why should it not be active in other types of happenings? Irrespective of their internal causal relation, ritual action and local explanations are intimately connected as the diagnosis of a state of affair leading to ritual action involves other event-frames. These, however, need not involve magical agency. The second type of representation is exactly such Non-Ritual Event-Frames organising the practical instrumental work to which many magical rituals are intertwined. Together, ritual, explanatory and non-ritual event-frames form a comprehensive network or narrative sequence. The ritual's temporal relation to the other event-frames is organised by the third type of representations structuring whether the ritual has a Prospective or a Retrospective Orientation. Prospective rituals that aim at producing a new state of affair, give rise to both a factual event-frame structuring expectations to the ritual's result and a counterfactual event-frame structuring expectations of what will happen if the ritual is *not* performed. Retrospective rituals aim to restore a disrupted state of affairs. They evoke past actions as explanatory event-frames legitimising the ritual performance and place it in a force-dynamic relationship to the agency believed to be responsible for the disruption. Thus, the Prospective and Retrospective orientations both give a direct clue to the overall purpose of the ritual action (b) and organise the temporal relations between the ritual event-frame and other event-frames in the larger narrative network.

Together (a) and (b) constitute a *pragmatic* level, where representations of ritual purpose and meaning are constructed by emphasising the ritual's embedding in specific situations organised by explanatory and non-ritual event-frames. The pragmatic level constitutes one of three hermeneutic strategies participants can utilise in the construction of ritual meaning and purpose. But the meaning and purpose of ritual action is found not only in its pragmatic embedding—ritual actions have a fundamental semantic inventory extracted through very basic cognitive operation. This basic semantic inventory is in a dynamic relation to more or less conventionalised symbolic interpretations, whether idiosyncratic or culturally approved. In figure 7.1, (c) and (d) represent these two additional hermeneutic strategies. The Ritual Event-Frame facilitates a search for weak causal relations (based on similarity and spatio-temporal contiguity) between Condition, Action and Effect and the employment of culturally available or idiosyncratically invented Symbolic Interpretations.

This leads to the role of conceptual blending in magical rituals. A basic premise of this book is that ritual in general, and magical rituals in particular are constructed through conceptual blending, giving rise to representations of magical agency and facilitating representations of transfer and manipulation. Image-Schemata and Psychological Essentialism are both fundamental cognitive mechanisms used in basic-level categorisation—both play a significant role in the conceptual blending constitutive to magical rituals. In the construction of a ritual space found in the *genetic* blend, psychological essentialism and image-schemata facilitate the projection of magical agency into the ritual blend—a prerequisite for representations of ritual efficacy. Without the projection of magical agency into the blend, the ritual will not be represented as having any instrumental efficacy, and the genetic blend is, therefore, a fundamental cognitive operation in representations of magical actions.

Other factors, however, are more important in representations of the meaning and purpose of specific ritual actions, i.e. of the particular actions performed in the ritual sequence. These actions can be analytically divided into two types, transformative and manipulative magical actions, a division based on two different types of pragmatic goals utilising two different types of conceptual blends. In transformative magic, the goal is to transform the essence or qualities of some element by means of forward contagion. When the essence of an element is transformed, it gives rise to a discrepancy between the perceptual and essential features of an element, as when the bread of the Eucharist is ascribed the essence of Christ. Based on this observation the first principle of transformative magic is proposed: *the greater ontological discrepancy between an element's physical appearance and its ascribed essence, the stronger attention on the possessor of magical agency responsible for this discrepancy.* Thus, a transformation of the intuitively grasped relation between perceptual characteristics and inner essence will provoke a search for the responsible agency, and the greater the discrepancy the more power it will be ascribed. In cases where the essence is not changed but a 'quality' is added, we find representations of 'essence' flow between elements belonging to different mental spaces, as when the essence of the sanctified bread is transferred to the recipient during Communion. Recognition of the schematic properties of this essential transfer is expressed in a second principle of transformative magic: *(a) the deeper a penetration into the receiving bodily container, (b) the more open/fragile the yielding container, and (c) the more powerful the transmitted essence, the more efficacious the contagious transfer.* Thus, we have a force-dynamic interaction between a CONTAINER and a TRAJECTORY crossing its boundary.

In manipulative magic, the aim is not to change the essence of some element, but rather to change its schematic properties, i.e. the causal and structural relations between elements in a particular domain. This is achieved by manipulating a blend between elements projected from two mental spaces, as when the Trobriand gardens are 'cleansed' of pest and diseases even before the garden is planted. In constructing the necessary counterpart connections between the two mental spaces, both metonymic links based on notions of backward contagion, and similarity are utilised. What is referred to as metonymic or indexical links and metaphorical or iconic links connect otherwise distinct mental spaces. Several principles governing manipulative magic are proposed in chapter 5, outlining how schematic properties can be transferred between conceptual domains. The most important in this context is the final principle stating that *conceptual blending in magical rituals will map image-schemata belonging to a manipulative domain onto a less manipulative domain thereby enabling the agent to interact with this domain.* The means of manipulation will, of course, constrain representations of ritual purpose but, as we have seen, several methods are often combined, leaving only common schematic properties behind.

Together, transformative and manipulative magic aims to change an existing state of affairs by means of ritual actions involving a strong emphasis on representations of essence and image-schemata. This points to the overall hypothesis defended in this book, namely that *by means of ritualisation, culturally specified symbolic meaning and domain-specific causal relations of ritual elements are de-emphasised or even violated in order to forward their inherent essentialist and schematic properties.* These essential and schematic properties are used to create counterpart connections between conceptual spaces, but are also transferred in order to transform or manipulate one domain by means of another. It is exactly this focus on essential and schematic properties that facilitate that the essence of Christ can be transferred to members of the communion and that the Azande can align the stone to the sun in order to check its progress. The hypothesis also entails that epistemic judgements as to the possibility and truths of these ritual actions are secondary symbolic elaborations dependent upon cultural conventions and discursive genres, whereas the iconic and indexical connections employed in magical rituals are directly perceived because of their reliance on fundamental cognitive procedures of both domain-specific and domain-general categorisation.

As image-schematic structures and psychological essentialism are basic cognitive operations used in individuals' ongoing and direct interaction with the surrounding world, they constitute a *phenomenological* level that, like the pragmatic level, supplies a hermeneutic strategy for interpreting ritual actions. In utilising this strategy, participants emphasise not how ritual event-frames are related to other event-frames, but, rather, the basic meaning experienced in the actions performed. As discussed above, experiences that violate causal expectation will provoke a search, not only for phenomenologically grounded basic meaning structures but also for available symbolic interpretations. Forming the third hermeneutic strategy available for ritual participants, magical actions provoke the construction and employment of Idiosyncratic and Culturally Specified Symbolic Interpretations. In order to address this complex interaction the remaining part of this chapter will analyse the relation between magical ritual action on the one hand, and cultural conceptual systems, institutionalised religious ritual, and religion on the other.

7.2 Magic and Cultural Conceptual Systems

If magical rituals involve ritualisation resulting in de-emphasising symbolic meaning, how should we describe the relation between magic and cultural conceptual systems? Earlier in this book, I emphasised that magic should not be construed as a 'system' comparable to, for example, a system of religious rules and dogmas or a linguistic system. Magical actions and procedures might be systematically explored and developed, as we saw in the example utilising the ESSENCE-LINK between a dog and the sword used to stab it (see chapter 5), but that is a secondary symbolic elaboration of a primary indexical relation based on a representation of essence. Magic is not a kind of systematic science, even though it can develop in that direction, as, for instance, in the European Renaissance. Still, magical actions and representations are often deeply embedded in cultural systems and function as a 'conservative' force that supports already existing explanatory event-frames and systematised theologies. This conservative aspect of magical action—confirming existing structures of meaning—is balanced by an inherent 'exoticism' investing magical efficacy outside established ritual structures or in elements segregated from their position in a religious system. Magic is not a kind of religious system, even though it is intimately connected to pre-existing religious systems. It is more correct to understand it as a conglomerate of more basic representations of magical agency, manipulation and transfer leading to representations of ritual efficacy.

The question remains what ramifications this has for the relation between magical action and the conceptual system emerging in the interaction between culture and cognition. Cultural models are abundant in magical rituals, and this might seem to contradict the claim that symbolic features are de-emphasised in magical rituals. But the contradiction is only apparent. Magical rituals naturally employ a substantial amount of established configurations of meaning, as for instance in the conventional metaphoric mappings between the domain of gardening and the domain of sailing among the Trobrianders. If domains are connected regularly in a given culture, these connections are utilised in magical rituals for obvious reasons. The mappings do not seem strange to the participants, they can be utilised in several perceptual modalities and they are expanded into several specific counterpart connections. This can be equated with the role of conventional metaphors in conceptual blending of mental spaces found in linguistic discourse. Whereas conceptual blends are constructed in a specific pragmatic and discursive situation, conventional metaphors are part of the structure defining a cultural conceptual system. Conventional metaphors and established configurations of meaning thus function as 'weighted' clusters in a symbolic system likely to appear if a domain taking part in such a cluster is addressed. Magical rituals are, therefore, intimately related to entrenched conceptual structures where certain connections are more likely than others. Certain counterpart connections and blends are simply biased in the conceptual system.

Conceptual systems also contain a substantial number of prescriptive and explanatory models relating events to causes. These are culturally reified explanatory event-frames that, by virtue of their relations to other types of event-frames (including ritual) and their abundant display in public and private discourse, are likely to be employed in specific situations. Among the Azande, 'serious disease' is related to 'witches' as a cultural default model. Such models play an important role in magical rituals by directing attention in a specific direction and by inducing certain modes of reaction. As we have seen, prescriptive and explanatory models are important in the construction of networks of event-frames.

At another level, basic schematic structures organising several cultural models are also found in magical rituals. This is what Shore refers to as the "foundational schemata" pervasive in a conceptual system and structuring several cultural models (Shore 1996: 45). An example of such foundational schemata is the system of image-schemata structuring cosmology, the construction of houses, the construction of altars and the performance of rituals among the Maya Indians of Yucatán (Hanks 1990). These basic schemata organise several domains by a spatial organisation that constitutes a skeletal cosmology that is also present in magical rituals. When the Trobrianders exorcise pests and diseases out of the garden, the direction is towards the northwest—the same direction in which other objects are exorcised, where the spirits of the dead go and where babies come from (Malinowski 1935b: 264). This is an example of a directional image-schema of wider cultural diffusion appropriated in a magical ritual. As was the case with the relation between the narrative description and the practical experience of 'magical water' in Subbotsky's psychological test (Subbotsky 1994), the use of a particular schema in magical actions revitalises it as an experiential structure of the individuals participating in the ritual. Conceptual structures are connected to personal experience by being embedded in concrete ritual action. Northwest is not just 'the place babies come from' or a symbolic destination for all unwanted entities used in narrative discourse, but a physical location in a specific direction seen from the garden and the perspective of the people participating. The direction can be blocked, and pests and diseases need a vehicle of transportation in order to move—all basic inferential aspects of movement in a specific direction. Thus, the symbolic meaning of 'northwest', defined by its position in a conventional web of other concepts, is de-emphasised in favour of a concrete direction represented by iconic and indexical features. This gives a wider significance to the notion of the genetic blend used to create a ritual space. By means of the ritual blend, representations of sacred agent, objects and actions are directly related to or even identified with counterparts of the concrete profane world, thus enabling a partial fusion of the world as lived and the world as imagined, to paraphrase Clifford Geertz (1993).

The Eucharist can exemplify the complex interaction between symbolic interpretation based on the position in a symbolic system, and the directly experienced indexical and iconic features. Broadly speaking, the Reformation was, among other things, an attempt to purge Christian rituals of magical efficacy in favour of a symbolic interpretation emphasising 'faith'. Luther writes in *The Pagan Servitude of the Church*:

> In every sacrament, the merely outward sign is incomparably less important than the thing symbolized... It almost seems to me that ... long ago, we had lost the content of the sacrament while contenting for the outer sign; and that while striving for what is of minor importance, we are hostile to the things of greatest value and alone worth while (Luther 1953: 220).

In most Protestant interpretations, the outer signs—the bread and wine of the Eucharist—are radically disjoined from their directly perceived meaning and they become mere symbols related to the signified by a *conventional* association of bread and wine with the body and blood of Christ. This is in contrast to the more basic meaning inherent in actual actions performed in the ritual, in which the essence of Christ is transferred into the bread and wine, which is thereafter consumed by the believers in order to acquire the essence as a temporary quality (chapter 5.1). When bread and wine are interpreted symbolically, all the inferential potential inherent in the actions based on CONTAINER-schemata and representations of ESSENCE are ignored and the direct meaning, associated with eating the bread, disappears. If the action is merely symbolic, nothing *really* happens when you eat the bread and the ritual only functions as a symbolic sign embedded in a referential network of other symbols. Thereby, representations of the purpose of the ritual is produced by further, possibly verbalised, symbolic interpretations of why the ritual is performed, what its effect is etc. In that case, the ritual ceases to be magical as its meaning and purpose is defined solely by being embedded in specifying symbolic network. One could say that it is 'weighed down' by a substantial amount of symbolic meaning that overrides the direct experience of infusion and transfer of a desirable essence.

Thus there is a direct negative correlation between the degree of symbolic meaning present in a ritual and representations of ritual efficacy, which entails that the less amount of symbolic meaning, the more efficacious the ritual can be. This basic correlation explains the tendency to import foreign and opaque symbolic material ascribed magical efficacy and to decrease the symbolic meaning associated with known materials by extreme iteration, strange linguistic procedures, new (ritual) context and all the other means of de-symbolising described in previous chapters. The purpose of all these operations is to strengthen representations of ritual efficacy by directing the attention of ritual participants to iconic and indexical properties of the elements used. This has intriguing sociological perspectives that will be touched upon below, but it also affects the symbolic and conceptual system of which it is a part. First, it facilitates novel interpretations of already known symbolic material. When sanctified water can be used to heal the sick and protect homes, and holy bread is used to protect against theft, it is not due to established symbolic interpretations, but rather because both are directly represented as containing powerful magical agency obtained through a former ritual (Thomas 1991: 32, 51). Sanctified bread or water is thus utilised as the instrumental cause in an unauthorised ritual event-frame. The development towards symbolic interpretations of rituals, however, is spontaneous as ritual actions in general prompt subsequent interpretations (Humphrey & Laidlaw 1994). Magical rituals provoke the construction of new symbolic interpretations that are either minor transformations of already established symbolic models or more idiosyncratic interpretations that might solidify and spread to other people and thereby constitute a genuinely new explanatory frame. The condemnation of illicit ritual practices as 'demonic' is also part of such appropriation of ritual actions to established symbolic systems thereby both grounding and altering the system itself.

Second, the exoticism of magical ritual also facilitates import of novel symbolic material into conceptual systems. This will, of course, provoke novel interpretations, as these elements must be integrated into already existing, symbolic systems. For instance, Egyptian hieroglyphs played an important role as a 'magical' alphabet with occult powers in Renaissance Europe. This role was diminished substantially as the hieroglyphs were deciphered and their everyday and profane linguistic function was revealed. The search for the exotic did not abate but moved on to India and Tibet and, more recently, pre-literate people are ascribed secret knowledge and magical abilities.[1] This search for magical agency, outside one's own culture, is not a Western phenomenon, even though it has reached an unprecedented level due to colonialism and globalisation. Evans-Pritchard describes how the Azande understand the substantial amount of foreign medicine circulating in the Zande exchange system of magical medicines as dangerous and particularly efficacious (1937: 416-8), and how the neighbouring tribes are "a constant source of new and powerful medicine" (1929: 637). This illustrates a general tendency of ascribing strong, morally dubious magical powers to neighbouring people and their rituals. In the actual performance of magical rituals such 'foreign' practices can be appropriated as particular strong magical agencies.

A further entailment of the negative correlation between symbolic meaning and magical agency lies in the fact that new magical practices spread and gradually become integrated into the cultural conceptual system through further symbolic elaboration. As a result, magical agency is diminished due to a larger emphasis on the symbolic interpretations developing gradually. This, in turn, results in either a search for new magical agency outside the conceptual system or in the revitalisation of already existing elements by rejection or demarcation of symbolical explanations and active de-emphasis of symbolic properties (cf. Evans-Pritchard 1929: 636). The tedium effect, described by Whitehouse (2001) as an inevitable result of often-repeated ritual actions, can be analysed as a result of the continuous process of symbolic interpretation removing the action from the concrete lived-in world, rather than the mere frequency of its reproduction (Sørensen 2005).

Thus, we have a dynamic system with two basic attractors. The first attractor is the ascription of magical agency, which seems to work best outside or beneath established symbolic interpretations and explanatory frames. The less known and more mysterious the ritual elements are, the more powerful and efficacious. The second attractor is the human proclivity to explain actions by creating cultural models and symbolic structures thereby embedding the actions in larger conceptual networks. Magical rituals are the objects of elaborate symbolic interpretations aimed to integrate them in wider networks of pre-configured structures of meaning and cultural theories. This seems to diminish the magical agency ascribed, at least if the symbolic interpretation invades the *ritual* domain. This qualification points to the many possible ways these opposing forces can be integrated: (a) in the construction of complex religious and magical concepts, combining intuitive and counterintuitive properties, that are recalcitrant to exact symbolic interpretation (Boyer 1994); (b) in the embedding of magical agencies in a special ritual frame emphasising iconic and indexical interpretations of ritual action and leaving symbolic interpretations outside; (c) in the active de-symbolisation of elements used in rituals through diverse performative operations that strengthen representations of magical efficacy; and (d) in limiting access to symbolic knowledge of ritual elements, by means of esotericism or discourses of secrecy.

This dynamic aspect of magical ritual entails that magic plays both a conservative and an innovative role in the development of cultural systems. It is conservative in the emphasis placed on tradition, whether based on the legitimate authority of the ritual agent, on the iconic reproduction of ritual actions or on the conventionally ascribed essential qualities of objects. All these things are generally prescribed by tradition. But by focusing on the ritual efficacy generated by basic cognitive mechanisms of categorisation and by de-emphasising symbolic relations, magical rituals are an innovative cultural factor for the following reasons: (a) by importing new ritual elements and practices believed to be efficacious; (b) by prompting new symbolic interpretations of both new and pre-existing conceptual elements; and (c) by pointing to essential and image-schematic properties of symbolic elements. Magical agency is infused in the gap created by the removal of intentions and casual expectations directly related to the concrete actions performed in the ritual, on one hand, and the lack of extensive symbolic interpretations constraining these in a symbolic straitjacket on the other. Thereby, more basic cognitive principles are evoked that, besides the ascribed efficacy, may prompt a re-evaluation of the ritual elements in terms of (new) secondary symbolic interpretations.

7.3 Magic and Institutionalised Ritual

If magic is not a cultural system comparable to religion and science, but rather a method of innovation, of motivated contact to the sacred domain, and of utilising already established means of contact in order to achieve socially or individually specified purposes, how does magic relate to institutionalised religious rituals? Based on the observations above it can be asserted confidently that magic is situated in a complex relationship to institutionalised ritual practices, in particular religious ritual practice. Magic is not in contrast to religion and neither is all religion magical. Rather, magic plays a substantial role in the creation of new religions and religious rituals, in the formation of constitutional rules in rituals controlling access to magical agency, and as a hermeneutic strategy available to participants in institutionalised ritual actions.

Magic is an innovative force in the emergence of new religions and ritual structures because of two factors. First, as a result of the reinterpretation of existing, symbolic and causal structures facilitated by ritualisation, new symbolic interpretations can arise and these may crystallise into new symbolic systems backed by social institutions. More important in this context, the possible ascription of magical agency to individual agents facilitates the emergence of not only new interpretations of existing rituals, but of whole new ritual structures. As argued in chapter 4, agent-based magical agency can take several forms based on different types of role-value connections. Some agents contain magical agency due to traditional ascription based on formal procedures, others due to perceptual or iconic features, and yet others due to representations of essential connections linking the present agent to an element in the sacred space. Of importance, at this point, is primarily the last two types, and in particular the relatively rare cases in which the ascription of magical agency is both purely agent-based, and *not* instituted by formal or symbolic ascription, whether through initiation or genealogy.

If an agent is connected to the sacred space by means of an identity or an essence-based counterpart relation (e.g. to a god or a spirit), the rest of the ritual procedure need not be prescribed or formalised in order to establish this link, nor do they need to function as indices of a symbolic or formal connection. In such cases, the agent is entitled to define the very premises of ritual interaction with the sacred space, as he or she is the sole connection to it. At this point the distinction between regulatory and constitutive rules argued by philosopher John Searle can be helpful (Searle 1969: 33-42). According to Searle, regulatory rules direct behaviour that exists independently of the rules. Rules of etiquette directing how one eats regulate only behaviour associated with eating but do not constitute the behaviour itself (I can break the rules and still eat). Constitutive rules, on the other hand, cannot be violated or ignored as they define behaviour in a specific context. One cannot play chess and ignore or violate the rules of chess. Several writers (e.g. Tambiah 1979; Humphrey & Laidlaw 1994) have noticed the role of constitutive rules in religious rituals. It is obvious that most religious rituals are based on constitutive rules that cannot be broken if one is to perform that particular ritual—we have seen several examples of this in the preceding chapters. Trobriand spells must be correctly pronounced by the correct magician and an ordained priest must perform the Eucharist, otherwise the rituals have not been performed. What should be noted is the fact that constitutive rules seem to be especially important in the parts of the rituals responsible for infusing magical agency into the ritual. As magical agency is a necessary condition for the efficacy of ritual actions, this comes as no surprise. In some cases, however, constitutive rules have not been defined as magical agency is ascribed a person for reasons other than formal, rule-based ones, i.e. the rules guiding ascription of magical agency have yet to be defined. In situations where a person is represented as directly connected to the sacred space and thus as a permanent holder of magical agency, he or she can perform ritual actions in novel ways and the actions are still judged as efficacious by participants. Such 'unbound' ritual actions are only constrained by the mappings and counterpart connections needed in order to achieve the desired result. This situation is probably an ideal case never empirically found, and the freedom of ritual forms only a matter of degree. Our magical *bricoleur* is constrained by the history of the concepts and actions he or she has at their disposal (Lévi-Strauss 1966), and it is extremely difficult to become recognised as a bearer of magical agency without complying to certain culture-specific expectations as to behaviour and essential relations. These considerations aside, personally contained magical agency is important as it enables the creation of new constitutive rules that will define ritual actions and formalise the magical agency contained by that particular person. Agent-based magical agency facilitates the construction of new rituals organising future ascription of magical agency.

This can shed light on what happens in the institutionalisation of new magical rituals. People might look for sources of magical agency outside established channels for various reasons—for instance if established rituals have been purged of magical agency or changing political circumstances have taken away traditional sources of legitimacy. New forms of magical rituals are created in two ways: (1) as a radical transformation of existing rituals or as appropriation of foreign ritual practices to a new ritual context; (2) as an agent-based ascription of agency facilitating the construction of new constitutive rules. This is obviously the case in the numerous examples of magical healing and wonders ascribed founders of most religions that function as indices of the essential link between the agent and a sacred domain. Counter-intuitive properties and events thus play a pivotal role as indices of this essential link for all new religious movements focusing on the special abilities of a single individual.

But what happens when the person responsible for the essential link disappears? One obvious possibility is that the ritual structure vanishes or is consumed by another ritual structure and that participants either return to established rituals structures or seek another person represented as containing magical agency. This is probably the most common development throughout history. In other cases, however, we see a *metonymic diffusion* of the links to the sacred domain when the initial agent is gone. The initial agent is sanctified and placed in the sacred domain, and real or pseudo-genealogical lines of descent from the originator can therefore constitute an essential link to the sacred space by means of which magical agency is infused to the ritual. In the same way, objects once in contact with the agent retain magical agency due to a metonymic link to the original container of magical agency, specific places and times become reservoirs of magical agency, and most importantly, ritual actions are formalised into exact iconic reproductions of the actions once performed by the now sanctified agent. All these things are an expression of the same tendency, namely the institutionalisation of magical agency by formalising metonymic genealogy, classifying certain objects, places and times as containers of magical agency, and by ritualising actions into prescriptive formulas. This process, however, is by no means harmonious. Differences in opinion and struggles over who can define access to magical agency are almost inevitable, in particular because control of access to magical agency is tightly connected to political power. The result is probably always a compromise, combining several of the means to retain magical agency and, on an institutional level, the danger of schisms based on disagreement on access to magical agency is imminent.

This hypothesis has several entailments. First, new magical rituals will originate in personalised or agent-based magical agency legitimising the construction of constitutive rules of ritual action. Second, the rejection of established ritual structures distinguishing agent-based and non-formal magical agency is replaced by *ritualisation* of ritual elements as a means to infuse magical agency into the ritual. So, from being based on the special character of a particular person forming a link to the sacred space, magical agency becomes based on the ritualisation of actions, objects and agents. Third, ritualisation entails that ritual elements will become subject to symbolic interpretations as ritualised actions *call* for such interpretations (Humphrey & Laidlaw 1994). Thus, a circle is formed in which strong emphasis on symbolic interpretations provoke a search for magical agency elsewhere which, if it is not already ritualised, will be based on a special agent. When this agent disappears, actions aimed to invest magical agency are ritualised, and finally ritualisation provokes new symbolic interpretation. This is modelled in figure 7.2 below. The first loop represents the ritual use and revitalisation of already existing or imported symbolic material. Ritualisation is a general heading chosen for the process of de-symbolisation and emphasis on iconic and indexical properties. The second loop has another entity, Agent-based Magical Agency, in which magical agency is present, not due to ritualisation, but due to an ascribed direct relation between an agent and the sacred space. This relation, in turn, is ritualised once the agent is gone and access to magical agency is defined by constitutive rules and achieved through de-symbolisation. This, in turn, provokes a process of interpretation leading to crystallisation of interpretative symbolic frames.

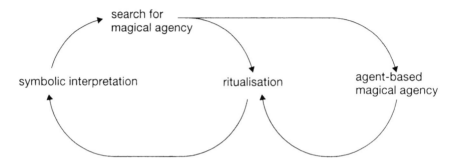

Figure 7.2: Loop between symbolic interpretation, ritualisation and agent-based magical agency

Some readers may have noticed a resemblance to Max Weber's theory of charisma and its rationalisation into symbolic structures (Weber 1976). In his elaborate sociology of religion, Weber argues that magic is intimately related to a naturalistic or pre-animistic stage in the development of human society closely associated to primitive and rural societies. The magician is a charismatic person who, motivated by mundane and practical concerns, ritually manipulates the world through analogies. Later on, these procedures undergo the universal process of rationalisation according to which they are embedded in mythological structures and explained by reference to rational relations between symbols (Weber 1976: 245ff; Morris 1987: 68-79). There are obvious similarities between Weber's account of rationalisation and this account of symbolisation of originally non-symbolic ritual.[2] This process, however, cannot be explained by reference to social structure alone, and in particular, not by reference to a general trajectory of social evolution. The process by which new ritual structures emerge or old ones are revitalised and infused with magical agency, is continuous, as are the processes by which these non-symbolic structures are symbolised and related to explanatory frameworks and thus lose some if not all of the magical agency.

Another basic difference is that I hold that all religious rituals in principle can be used magically, i.e. used to change some state of affairs by means of essence-flow and transfer of image-schematic properties. Figure 10.1 describes three inputs to the construction of ritual purpose. From the viewpoint of the individual participant they can be seen as three interacting hermeneutic strategies available to ritual participants. The first strategy is *phenomenological* ([c] in the figure) and based on participants' direct experience of agents, actions and objects in the ritual organised by representations of essence and image-schematic structuring. Of course, conceptual structures play a role on this level, for instance in designating magical agency to certain culturally defined entities, but the basic interpretative methods are based on cognitive mechanisms used in basic-level categorisation. The second strategy is *pragmatic* ([a] and [b] in the figure). At this level, participants interpret rituals on the basis of their position in interrelated event-frames. Thus, ritual actions are represented as the instrumental cause in a ritual event-frame, which in a complex manner relates to other event-frames. Again, conceptual structures plays a role in the cultural models relating causes to effects by default and certain events to culturally prescribed actions. The basic mechanisms at work, however, are a permutation of a basic action representation schema (Lawson & McCauley 1990), the image-schematic and force-dynamic representations of the structure and the relative force of actions performed. Finally, the third hermeneutic level available to participants is semiotic or symbolic (d). Participants will usually have access to a reservoir of more or less authorised symbolic interpretations of the ritual action performed. Even though such symbolic interpretations might involve a substantial creative element, as they can be constructed 'on the fly' as spontaneous interpretations of a ritual action, the degree of idiosyncrasy is limited and interpretations will be more or less in accordance with available interpretational and explanatory frames. Symbolic interpretations can also be systematised, as in theological discourse, but these are usually far from the interpretational frames available to ordinary participants and are relatively slow in transforming from expert into cultural models.

All three levels are present in all rituals, but in magical rituals the symbolic level is strongly de-emphasised. In rituals traditionally classified as magical, such as private healing or exorcism, we find esoteric language, magical objects etc., as these explicitly address the two first hermeneutic levels and downplay the third. The same strategy, however, can be employed in interpreting most kinds of religious rituals. Religious rituals contain magical or superhuman agency represented as essences, they contain image-schematic properties either ensuring the correct diffusion of essence or directing the manipulation of schemata, and most have the magical component of changing some state of affairs into another. By emphasising representations of essence, image-schematic properties, and by the instrumental position of the ritual in a large event-frame, participants can understand rituals as containing magical efficacy.

Based on these observations it can be argued that most religious rituals have magical transformation or manipulation as their point of origin, and that symbolic interpretation is a secondary *historical* development as well as a secondary mental process. This point needs clarification. Not everybody who participates in religious rituals 'believes' in magic or utilises the magical potential inherent in the ritual. The question of 'belief' is extremely complex both linguistically and philosophically (see Needham 1972). Perhaps it is not a question of belief in the first place, but a combination of suspension of disbelief effected by the ritualised context and of basic mental representations evoked by the ritual actions performed. When we enjoy the work of a good stage magician, we are constantly fooled by our senses into 'believing' something that we do not 'really believe.' We are simply following the cultural consensus that this kind of performance is illusionary. In contrast, most religious and magical rituals are embedded in a context emphasising the genuineness of the actions, which are thus surrounded by a positive epistemic evaluation. They are not only claimed to be true. Men and women of relatively high social ranking state that the soil of the garden is a pregnant woman or that bread and wine is the flesh and blood of Christ. A strict symbolic interpretation of such statements would obviously render them untrue, or call for extreme scholastic manoeuvres, but these actions are not primarily evaluated on the grounds of their compatibility with a symbolic system, but experienced and represented as doing something, as having an *effect*. Interpreted as a special kind of action embedded as the instrumental cause in an event-fame, religious rituals can be represented as magical, even if this representation is in opposition to established theological interpretations.

To summarise, new ritual structures emerge through the appearance of non-formalised, agent-based magical agency that, due to the direct relation to the sacred space, facilitates the creation of new constitutive rules. When the special agent is gone, the new structure returns to the conventional mode of acquiring magical agency, subsumed under the concept of ritualisation. The process of metonymic diffusion explains the relation between the ritualised elements and the original agent. Magical and religious rituals alike are interpreted by participants with the help of three hermeneutic strategies: the first two are emphasised in magical rituals and in cases where religious rituals are employed as magical instruments, and the third is used in relating ritual action to pre-established symbolic systems. Thus, magic is a creative force in generating new ritual structures and a force in revitalising already existing structures.

7.4 Magic and Religion

Now we approach the intricate and controversial question of the relationship between magic and religion. Magic and religion cannot be understood as two equal systems in a state of competition and mutual exclusion. Instead, magic is deeply embedded in most religious rituals and magic is one of two major forces active in the creation of new religious institutions.[3] Definitions of religion are numerous and cannot be dealt with in this context. It suffices to say that religion is a much broader and more encompassing concept than magic, and that religion covers a much broader spectrum of human behaviour, institutions, history and conceptual structure than magic does. Of primary concern is the relation between magic and the ritual aspects of institutionalised religion, and how this relation influences wider aspects of religions as systems of belief.

At this point it is instructive to return to Lévy-Bruhl's theory of participation discussed in chapter 2.4. Lévy-Bruhl's evolutionary description of how participation is objectified into ideological structures can be restated as a synchronic description of the relation between primarily emotionally felt and unconscious participation between elements in the world, and crystallisation of these into explicit ideological structures. This sheds light on the relation between magic, as the manipulation of participatory relations, and religion as a symbolic and increasingly rationalised system of belief. The notion of participation can be expanded into covering the two interrelated processes used in creating counterpart connections between conceptual spaces: iconic relations of similarity and indexical relations of essential link or identity. Participation is pre-conceptual, that is, it is a fundamental feature in conceptual structures that cannot be explained by reference to the concepts themselves or the system they form when combined. (Lévy-Bruhl 1975: 36-38). Participatory connections are spontaneously felt and perceived, and they are emotionally valued even when somewhat constrained by pre-figurations in cultural conceptual systems. It is only through hard reflexive work that concepts can be relatively independent of participatory features.

This spontaneous emergence of participatory connections or, in the terminology of this book, creation of new conceptual mappings, can be utilised in magical actions if just a few people acknowledge their existence and if magical agency is represented as infused into the ritual by the mechanisms described above. The only thing needed to create a new magical ritual is *(a) agreement between a few people on the existence of certain counterpart connections, (b) the infusion of magical agency and (c) its embedding as the instrumental cause in an event-frame.* This 'chaotic' tendency producing countless new magical rituals is counterbalanced by the structuring force of conceptual connections already crystallised into ideological structures, such as religions. Because of these ideological structures, many people share representations of conceptual connections. Magical agency is centralised and formalised and ritual practice, based on the participatory connections, is directly related to other structures of belief and to other institutions. But if the emphasis on symbolic interpretations is too strong and all but obliterate the basis of the mapping—leading to a growing 'abstraction' of the relation—this will prompt a search for new and active connections in another context. Viable religious institutions must find a balance between the symbolising tendency, facilitating the construction of common institutions and the embedding of ritual practice in a conceptual structure, and the power inherent in the spontaneously felt participation found in the conceptual blend. If this balance is achieved, they can enter into a relation of mutual reinforcement, as described in the treatment of ritual and explanatory event-frames. From this perspective, the development of religious institutions can be seen as a conflict between the centripetal forces active in crystallising common symbolic interpretations and institutionalising magical agency, and the centrifugal force of spontaneously felt participation and emergence of unauthorised and non-institutionalised magical agency.[4]

These observations shed a new light on the, often noted, general hostility of established and institutionalised religions towards so-called magical practices. Actually, there are good reasons why magic turned out to be a polemical term directed against other religions and particularly against other religious practices. Magical actions performed outside the established and authorised religious rituals *are* a threat to established religions on two grounds. First, magical practices are in direct competition to established religious rituals concerning ritual efficacy and the strength of, access to and type of magical agency. Magic comes to designate non-controlled and potentially anti-social ritual efficacy. Agent-based magical agency represented independent of established constitutive rules are seen as particular dangerous as it facilitates the establishment of new constitutive rules created in relation to contemporary conceptual structure. Because of its independence of established constitutive rules and institutional structure, it can incorporate more recent social and conceptual development and thus form a more up to date relation between ritual and conceptual structures. This is of potential sociological importance as, in most societies, authority enabling the construction of constitutive rules is intimately related to structures of secular power and consequently to political force.

Second, proponents of established religions recognise the emotional and cognitive power of non-institutionalised magical action. They are 'subversive' and 'evil' as they promise results through magical agency either not directly related to established systems of beliefs, or performed in unauthorised ritual contexts. Further, by addressing the phenomenological and pragmatic hermeneutic levels in relation to a specific goal, they often entail a high emotional intensity. Even though eternal life and salvation or other more distant religious goals can be invested with emotional value, more direct embeddings of ritual structures in event-frames concerning life and death, harvest or starvation, or physical or psychological wellbeing will most likely contain higher emotional intensity. Magical actions can therefore either provoke a revitalisation of well-known magical agency in alternative ritual contexts or present altogether alternative types of magical agency. In both cases, magical actions pose a threat to the established ritual structure and system of belief by presenting an alternative ritual context and/or alternative magical agency.

The general hostility of established religion to unauthorised magical actions points to a potential conflict at three levels. (a) By means of ritualisation and a focus on ritual efficacy, magical actions are excellent methods to generate and mobilise social forces (i.e. the intentions of a group of people) that can be focused in almost any direction depending on the event-frames to which the ritual is related. Fundamental to this is the conflict between types and access to magical agency. (b) Ritualised actions lead to symbolic interpretation that will potentially crystallise into competing systems of belief. (c) Ritualised actions will sooner or later be institutionalised in order to control access to magical agency. This possibly leads to competing social institutions.

The conflict between established ritual actions related to elaborated systems of belief, on the one hand, and the more chaotic and spontaneous emergence of participatory connections and alternative types of magical agency on the other, can results in several types of interaction. From a logical point of view, there are three general types of reactions provoked in established religion by unauthorised magical action. *Appropriation*, in which alternative magical rituals are incorporated into the established ritual structure and interpreted in relation to the existing system of belief. *Rejection*, in which the established religion rejects and combats unauthorised magical actions with a wide range of instruments. And *segregation*, in which the alternative ritual practice is either ignored or delegated a special social position at the margin of society, among certain social groups, or as fulfilling certain ritual functions not addressed in the established ritual structure. This third possibility could be called a state of truce between two ritual structures, members of the established structure accepting the presence of the unauthorised ritual structure as long as it does not develop competing social institutions and systems of belief. The existence of one or more ritual structures parallel to established and authorised religious ritual, with people making use of both, is probably more the rule than the exception and the relative strength might shift due to socio-political circumstances (cf. Firth 1967, Humphrey & Laidlaw 1994: 230-2).

Whereas the established religious system in general, and its ritual actions in particular, can remain relatively unchanged in this state of truce, this is not so in cases of appropriation or rejection. It is obvious that appropriation or assimilation entails a change in the ritual structures through the introduction of new elements that are ritualised in order to infuse magical agency. Such new practices provoke symbolic activity in order to interpret these new elements into the existing system of belief, which changes the system to some degree. It is less obvious that also active rejections of unauthorised magical actions will prompt re-evaluation, reflection and, possibly, change in established ritual structure. This is so because it is the unauthorised ritual, with its strong focus on ritual efficacy and access to magical agency that sets the agenda and defines the battleground. Established religion can claim that the alleged magical agency is fraudulent and that no ritual procedure can effect the postulated change of state. Such a rejection of the efficacy of an unauthorised ritual, however, will also influence judgements concerning the extent of ritual efficacy of authorised magical rituals as it entails more general considerations and epistemic judgements of ritual efficacy as such. Rejection of some types of ritual efficacy might backfire into a general rejection of all types of ritual efficacy. Besides, it is a relatively weak argument as it addresses the symbolic level of interpretation by appealing to a judgement of belief, which probably will not deter people strongly wishing a change of state—e.g. getting well instead of sick—into trying alternative methods if current mythology acclaims their efficacy. This is the case in the strong surge into alternative medicine in the West despite the active resistance of both established religion and medicine. Magical rituals address a concrete level of practical results, and if it works, e.g. if I get well, who cares whether it ought to work according to a system of belief?

An alternative mode of rejection entails the recognition of the efficacy of the unauthorised ritual, but a simultaneous demonisation of the action by reference to a more comprehensive event-frame, such as social morality or religious salvation. Here a literary example is illustrative. The magical instruments and mechanisms acquired by Doctor Faust from Mephistopheles are efficacious but immoral and paid for with the unacceptable price of the soul. The instrumental efficacy of unauthorised magic in relation to a specific event-frame is in this case judged as a hindrance for the correct unfolding of an overlying event-frame—the salvation of the soul. The influence on established religion due to this reaction is of a double nature. First, it often enhances a dualistic understanding of the world as filled with evil forces, witches, demons, evil spirits etc. that must be fought. The construction or revitalisation of ritual means to do so follows naturally. Second, it entails a stronger emphasis on the schemata involved in the overlaying event-frame and, thereby, a focus on ritual means to protect the unfolding of the desired schemata. The rejection of allegedly immoral magical rituals prompts a focus on how to further the desired event-frame, how to protect it from undesirable influences and how to fight such influences if they have appeared. This will all lead to re-evaluation and further emphasis on the ritual and magical dimension of established religion. Finally, established religion can reject unauthorised magical rituals by claiming that the established ritual structure contains greater efficacy through access to stronger magical agency. This is a struggle between the relative power of magical agency and, therefore, established religion needs to emphasise the efficacious elements in its own ritual. This can be done by means of ritualisation and de-emphasis on symbolic interpretation in order to turn the ritual into the instrumental cause in particular contexts.

These considerations lead to the final summary of the relation between established religion and unauthorised magical action. Magic in general can be seen as an innovative force in three ways. First, magical rituals can effect the emergence of new religious systems through the process of ritualisation leading to symbolic interpretation. This is strongest in cases of non-formalised, agent-based magical agency involving the construction of brand new constitutive rules of ritual action, but it can also be found in possible reinterpretations of known symbolic elements. Through their employment in magical rituals, known symbols are stripped of conventional relations to other symbols, a process, which facilitates transformation of meaning. Second, magic is focused on ritual efficacy and is therefore open for import of foreign ritual elements and structures believed to enhance this efficacy. This tendency is strengthened by the de-symbolising aspects of magical actions in which iconic and indexical properties of objects are utilised at the expense of symbolic relations, thus facilitating import of efficacious elements and structures independent of their symbolic embedding. In this respect, magic can be described as a 'syncretistic engine' that brings about exchange of ritual elements and structures between religious traditions and ethnic groups. The de-symbolising aspect of magical actions enhances this, as 'exotic' signs seem to be ascribed extraordinary power. Finally, magic is indirectly innovative by effecting a reaction in established religions against competition from unauthorised magical rituals. Thus, non-institutionalised ritual actions indirectly affect the form and structure of established and institutionalised religious rituals, at least in cases where these are confronted.

Instead of understanding magic and religion as two equal systems opposing each other, I propose a more dynamic explanation. Magic is a general mode of ritual behaviour that, when appearing outside established, authorised and institutionalised religious rituals, prompts the creation of either new systems of beliefs and religious institutions, or provoke a re-evaluation, reflection and possibly change of already established ritual structures. Utilising very basic cognitive processes, magic is a permanent force in the historical development of institutionalised religion. It constantly challenges established religions' abstract and context-distant symbolic interpretations by directing attention to concrete, context-near and goal-directed understandings of ritual action. Due to the very structure of our cognitive system, the disenchantment of the world proposed by Weber is always followed by a re-enchantment, creating new ways of infusing our everyday world with magical agency.

Notes

1. The Theosophical Society is an excellent example of this search for the exotic. Its founder, Madame Blavatsky, first found the ancient wisdom in ancient Egypt (*Isis Unveiled* from 1877). Later, India and Tibet became the home of the 'Masters' (*The Secret Doctrine* from 1888). The Theosophical Society also exposes another basic feature of the quest for the exotic, namely the notion of esoteric, secret doctrines underlying all public expressions (Sørensen 2000).

2. See Sørensen (2005) for a discussion of the relation between ascription of ritual efficacy, Weber's notion of charismatic authority and Harvey Whitehouse's theory of Modes of Religiosity.

3. The other major force is millenarism that facilitates the construction of strong institutions by establishing exclusive access to salvation before the end of the world. This cannot be treated any further in this context.

4. This has affinity with Malley's description of religion as a complex dynamic system according to which such things as metaphor and analogy press the system toward chaotic structure, whereas such things as ritual press it towards a frozen order (Malley 1995, 1997). Contrary to Malley, I argue that ritualisation in itself contains the contrasting influence of both order and chaos.

References

Agassi, J. & I. C. Jarvie. 1973. "Magic and Rationality Again." *British Journal of Sociology* 24: 236-45.
Ahern, E. M. 1979. "The Problem of Efficacy: Strong and Weak Illocutionary Acts." *Man* 14: 1-17.
———. 1982. "Rules in Oracles and Games." *Man* 17: 302-12.
Alverson, H. 1991. "Metaphor and Experience: Looking Over the Notion of Image Schema." In *Beyond Metaphor: The Theory of Tropes in Anthropology*, edited by J. W. Fernandez. Stanford: Stanford University Press.
Andreesco-Miereanu, I. 1987. "Magic: Magic in Eastern Europe." In *Encyclopedia of Religion*, edited by M. Eliade. New York: Macmillian and Free Press.
Anttonen, V. 1992. "Interpreting Ethnic Categories Denoting 'Sacred' in Finnish and an Ob-Ugrian Context." *Temenos* 28: 53-80.
———. 2002. "Identifying the Generative Mechanisms of Religion: The Issue of Origin Revisited." In *Current Approaches in the Cognitive Science of Religion*, edited by I. Pyysiäinen & V. Anttonen. London: Continuum.
Atran, S. 1995. "Causal constraint on categories and categorial constraints on biological reasoning across culture." In *Causal Cognition: A multidisciplinary debate*, edited by D. Sperber, D. Premack & A.J. Premack. Oxford: Clarendon.
———. 1996 "Modes of thinking about living kinds; Science, symbolism, and common sense." In *Modes of Thought: Explorations in Culture and Cognition*, edited by D. R. Olson & N. Torrance. Cambridge: Cambridge University Press.
Austin, J. L. 1962. *How To Do Things With Words*. Oxford: Oxford University Press.
Avis, J. & P. L. Harris. 1991. "Belief-desire reasoning among Baka children." *Child Development* 62: 460-67.
Baillargeon, R. 1994. "Physical reasoning in young infants: Seeking explanations for impossible events." *British Journal of Developmental Psychology* 12: 9-33.

References

Baillargeon, R.,Kotovsky, L. & Needham, A. 1995."The acquisition of physical knowledge in infancy." In *Causal Cognition: A multidisciplinary debate*, edited by D. Sperber, D. Premack & A.J. Premack. Oxford: Clarendon.

Baal, J. van & Beek, W. E .A. van. 1985. *Symbols for Communication: An Introduction to the Anthropological Study of Religion*, Assen, Van Gorcum.

Barret, J. & F. Keil. 1996. "Conceptualizing a Nonnatural Entity: Anthropomorphism in God Concepts." *Cognitive Psychology* 31 (3): 219-247.

Beattie, J. 1964. *Other Cultures*. London, Cohen & West.

———. 1967. "Divination in Bunyoro, Uganda, in J. Middleton: *Magic, Witchcraft, and Curing*. Austin: University of Texas Press.

———. 1970. "Reason and Ritual", in *Rationality*, edited by B. Wilson. Oxford: Blackwell Publications.

Belier, W. W. 1995. "Religion and magic: Durkheim and the *Année sociologique* group." *Method and Theory in the Study of Religion* 7, no. 2: 163-84.

Bell, C. 1992. *Ritual Theory, Ritual Practice*. Oxford: Oxford University Press.

Berlin, B. & P. Kay. 1969. *Basic Color Terms: Their Universality and Evolution*. Berkeley: University of California Press.

Betz, H. D. 1987. "Magic: Magic in Greco-Roman Antiquity." In *Encyclopedia of Religion*, edited by M. Eliade. New York: Macmillian and Free Press.

———. 1991 "Magic and Mystery in the Greek magical Papyri." In *Magika Hiera: Ancient Greek Magic and Religion*, edited by C. A. Faraone & D. Obbink. New York: Oxford University Press.

Bilde, P. 1999. "Ny vin på nye flasker? Grundlæggelsen af kristendommen som en ny religion i hellenistisk-romersk tid." In *Nye religioner i hellenistisk tid og idag*, edited by P. Bilde & M. Rothstein Aarhus: Aarhus University Press.

Blavatsky, H. P. 1877. *Isis Unveiled: A masterkey to the mysteries of ancient and modern science and theology*. New York.

———. 1987 (1888). *The Secret Doctrine* (3 vol.). Adyar: Theosophical Publishing House.

Boyer, P. 1990. *Tradition as Truth and Communication: A cognitive description of traditional discourse*, Cambridge, Cambridge University Press.

———. 1992. "Causal Thinking and Its Anthropological Misrepresentation." *Philosophy of the Social Sciences* 22 no.2: 187-213.

———. 1993. "Pseudo-natural kinds." In *Cognitive Aspects of Religious Symbolism*, edited by P. Boyer. Cambridge: Cambridge University Press.

———. 1994. *The Naturalness of Religious Ideas: A Cognitive Theory of Religion*. California: University of California Press.

———. 1995. "Causal understandings in cultural representations: cognitive constraints on inferences from cultural input." In *Causal Cognition: A multidisciplinary debate*, edited by D. Sperber, D. Premack & A.J. Premack. Oxford: Clarendon.

———. 1996. "Religion as an impure object: a note on cognitive order in religious representations in response to Brian Malley." *Method & Theories in the Study of Religion* 8(2): 201-14.

———. 2001. *Religion Explained: The Human Instincts that Fashions Gods, Spirits and Ancestors*. London: Vintage.

Brandt, P. A. 2000. "Causation and Narration", paper given at the winter symposium: *Structures of Causal Meaning*. Centre for Semiotics, University of Aarhus.

Brier, B. 1980. *Ancient Egyptian Magic*. New York: William Morrow and Company, Inc.

Brown, M. 1985 *Tsewas' Gift: Magic and meaning in an Amazon society*. Washington D.C: Smithsonian Institution Press.

Brugman, C. 1988. *The Story of Over: Polysemy, Semantics, and the Structure of the Lexicon*. New York: Garland Publ.

Bruner, J. 1990 *Acts of Meaning*. London: Harvard University Press.

Budge, E. A .W. 1961. *Amulets and Talismans*. New York: University Books.

Butler, E. M. 1993 (1948) *The Myth of the Magus*. Cambridge: Cambridge University Press.

Cannon, W. B. 1942. "'Voodoo' death." *American Anthropologist* 44 (2): 169-81.

Carey, S. 1995. "On the origin of causal understanding." In *Causal Cognition: A multidisciplinary debate*, edited by D. Sperber, D. Premack & A.J. Premack. Oxford: Clarendon.

———. 1996. "Cognitive domains as modes of thought." In *Modes of Thought: Explorations in Culture and Cognition*, edited by D. R. Olson & N. Torrance. Cambridge: Cambridge University Press.

Carey, S. & E. Spelke 1994. "Domain-specific knowledge and conceptual change." In *Mapping the Mind: Domain Specificity in Cognition and Culture*, edited by L. A. Hirschfeld & S. A. Gelman. Cambridge: Cambridge University Press.

Chandler, M. J. & Lalonde, C. E. 1994. "Surprising, magical and miraculous turns of events: Children's reaction to violations of their early theories of mind and matter." *British Journal of Developmental Psychology* 12: 83-95

Cherry, J. L. 1992. *Animism in Thought and Language*. Unpublished Ph.D. dissertation. University of California, Berkeley

Cosmides, L. & Tooby, J. 1994. "Origins of domain specificity: The evolution of functional organisation." In *Mapping the Mind: Domain Specificity in Cognition and Culture*, edited by L. A. Hirschfeld & S. A. Gelman. Cambridge: Cambridge University Press.

Culianu, I. P. 1987. "Magic: Magic in Medieval and Renaissance Europe." In *Encyclopedia of Religion*, edited by M. Eliade. New York: Macmillian and Free Press.

Cunningham, G. 1999. *Religion and Magic: Approaches and Theories*. Edinburgh: Edinburgh University Press.

Damasio, A. 2000. *The Feeling of What Happens: Body, Emotion and the Making of Consciousness*. London: Vintage.

D'Andrade, R. 1987. "A folk model of the mind." In *Cultural Models of Language and Thought*, edited by D. Holland & N. Quinn. Cambridge: Cambridge University Press.

———. 1995. *The Development of Cognitive Anthropology*. Cambridge: Cambridge University Press.

Deacon, T. 1997. *The Symbolic Species: The co-evolution of language and the human brain*. London: Penguin Books.

Douglas, M. 1995 (1966)*Purity and Danger. An analysis of the concepts of pollution and taboo*. London and New York: Routledge.

Durkheim, E. 1965 (1915). *The Elementary Forms of the Religious Life*. New York: The Free Press.

Durkheim, E. & M. Mauss. 1969. *Primitive Classification*. Chicago: University of Chicago Press.

Elksnis, A. & M. Szachara. 1996. "Children's magical beliefs: A report on recent studies in developmental psychology." *Method and Theory in the Study of Religion* 8, no. 2: 191-200.

Evans-Pritchard, E. E. 1929. "The Morphology and Function of Magic." *American Anthropologist* 3: 619-41, reprinted in B. P. Levack (1992): *Anthropological studies of witchcraft, magic and demonology*, London, Garland Publ.

———. 1937. *Witchcraft, Oracles and Magic among the Azande*. Oxford: Clarendon Press.

———. 1971. *Theories of Primitive Religion*. Oxford: Clarendon Press.

Fadh, T. 1987. "Magic: Magic in Islam." In *Encyclopedia of Religion*, edited by M. Eliade. New York: Macmillian and Free Press.

Faraone, C. A. 1991. "The Agonistic Context of Early Greek Binding Spells." In *Magika Hiera: Ancient Greek Magic and Religion*, edited by C. A. Faraone & D. Obbink. New York: Oxford University Press.

Faraone, C. A. & D. Obbink (eds.). 1991. *Magica Hiera: Ancient Greek Magic and Religion*. Oxford: Oxford University Press.

Fauconnier, G. 1994. *Mental Spaces: Aspects of Meaning Construction in Natural Language*. Cambridge: Cambridge University Press.

———. 1997. *Mappings in Thought and Language*. Cambridge: Cambridge University Press.

Fauconnier G. & M. Turner. 1996. "Blending as a Central Process of Grammar." In *Conceptual Structure, Discourse, and Language*, edited by A. E. Goldborg. Stanford: Center for the Study of Language and Information.

———. 1998. "Conceptual Integration Networks." *Cognitive Science*, 22 (2): 133-87.

———. 2002. *The Way We Think: Conceptual Blending and the Mind's Hidden Complexities*. New York: Basic Books

Fillmore, C. 1982. "Frame Semantics." In *Linguistics in the Morning Calm*, edited by The Linguistic Society of Korea. Seoul: Hanshin Publ. Co.

Finnegan, R. 1969. "How To Do Things With Words: Performative Utterances Among the Limba of Sierra Leone." *Man* 4: 537-52.

Firth, R. 1967. "The sociology of 'magic'." In *Tikopia Ritual and Belief*, edited by R. Firth. Boston: Beacon Press.

———. 1997. "An Anthropologist's Reflection on Symbolic Usage." In *Magic, Witchcraft, and Religion: An Anthropological Study of the Supernatural* (fourth ed.), edited by A. C. Lehmann & J. E. Myers. Mountain View, CA: Mayfield Publishing Company.

Frankfurter, D. 1995. "Narrating Power: The Theory and Practice of the Magical *Historiola* in Ritual Spells." In *Ancient Magic and Ritual Power*, edited by M. Meyer & P. Mirecki. Leiden: E. J. Brill

Frazer, J. G. 1911. *The Golden Bough: A Study in Magic and Religion (Third Edition). Part I: The Magic Art and the Evolution of Kings.* Vol. 1. London: MacMillan and Co. Ltd.

Freud, Sigmund. 1995a. "Obsessive Actions and Religious Practice." In *The Standard Edition of the Complete Psychological Works of Sigmund Freud*, vol. IX. Translated from the German under the general editorship of James Strachey. London: Hogarth Press.

———. 1995b. "Totem and Taboo." In *The Standard Edition of the Complete Psychological Works of Sigmund Freud*, vol. XIII. Translated from the German under the general editorship of James Strachey. London: Hogarth Press.

Gächter, O. & A. Quack. 1989. "Symbole, Magie und Religion." *Anthropos* 84: 521-529.

Gallie, W.B. 1956. "Essentially Contested Concepts." *Proceedings of the Philosophical Society* 51.

Gardner, D. S. 1983. "Performativity and Ritual: The Mianmin Case." *Man* 18: 346-60.

Geertz, C. 1993 (1973). "Religion As a Cultural System." In *The Interpretation of Cultures*. London: Fontana Press.

Geertz, H. 1975. "An Anthropology of Religion and Magic, I." *Journal of Interdisciplinary History* 6, no. 1: 71-89, reprinted in *Anthropological studies of witchcraft, magic and demonology*, edited by B. P. Levack (1992). London: Garland Publ.

Gelman, R., F. Durgin & L. Kaufman. 1995. "Distinguishing between animates and inanimates: not by motion alone." In *Causal Cognition: A multidisciplinary debate*, edited by D. Sperber, D. Premack & A.J. Premack. Oxford: Clarendon.

Gelman, S., J. Doley & G. Gottfried. 1994. "Essentialist beliefs in children: The acquisition of concepts and theories." In *Mapping the Mind: Domain Specificity in Cognition and Culture*, edited by L. A. Hirschfeld & S. A. Gelman. Cambridge: Cambridge University Press.

Gennep, A. van. 1909. *Les Rites de Passage. Études systématique des Rites.* Paris: Émile Nourry.

Gentner, D. 1983. "Structure-mapping: A theoretical framework for analogy." *Cognitive Science* 7: 155-70.

Gibbs, R. W. Jr. 1994. *The Poetics of the Mind: Figurative Thought, Language, and Understanding.* Cambridge: Cambridge University Press.

Glucklich, A. 1997. *The End of Magic.* Oxford: Oxford University Press.

Gopnik, A. & H. M. Wellman. 1994. "The theory theory." In *Mapping the Mind: Domain Specificity in Cognition and Culture*, edited by L. A. Hirschfeld & S. A. Gelman. Cambridge: Cambridge University Press.

Goudge, T. A. 1973. "Evolutionism." In *Dictionary of the History of Ideas: Studies of Selected Pivotal Ideas* vol. 11, edited by P. P. Wiener. New York: Charles Scribner's Sons.

Goudriaan, T. 1987. "Magic: Magic in South Asia." In *Encyclopedia of Religion*, edited by M. Eliade. New York: Macmillian and Free Press.

Grady, J. E. 1997. *Foundations of Meaning: Primary Metaphors and Primary Scenes.* Ph.D. dissertation. Dept. of Linguistics, University of California, Berkeley.

Grady, J., T. Oakley & S. Coulson. 1999. "Conceptual Blending and Metaphor." In *Metaphor in Cognitive Linguistics*, edited by R. Gibbs. Amsterdam & Philadelphia: John Benjamins.

Graf, F. 1995. "Excluding the Charming: The Development of the Greek Concept of Magic." In *Ancient Magic and Ritual Power*, edited by M. Meyer & P. Mirecki. Leiden: E. J. Brill

Greene, T. M. 1997. "Language, Signs and Magic," In *Envisioning Magic: A Princeton Seminar and Symposium*, edited by P. Schäfer & H. Kippenberg. Leiden: Brill

Greimas, A. J. 1966. *Sémantique Structurale.* Paris: Larousse.

Greimas, A. J. & J. Courtés. 1988. *Semiotik: Sprogteoretisk Ordbog.* Århus: Aarhus Universitetsforlag, translation of (1979) *Semiotique. Dictionnaire raisonné de la theorie du langue.* Paris: Hachette

Hammond, D. 1970. "Magic: A Problem in Semantics." *American Anthropologist* 72: 1349-56

Hanegraaff, W. J. 1998. "The Emergence of the Academic Study of Magic: The Occult Philosophy in Tylor and Frazer." In *Religion in the Making: The Emergence of the Sciences of Religion*, edited by A. L. Molendijk & P. Pels. Leiden: Brill.

Hanks, W. 1984. "Santification, Structure, and Experience in a Yucatec Ritual Event." *Journal of American Folklore,* 97 (384): 131-166.

———. 1990. *Referential Practice: Language and Lived Space among the Maya.* London: University of Chicago Press.

Harris, P. L. 1994. "Unexpected, impossible and magical events: Children's reactions to causal violations." *British Journal of Developmental Psychology* 12: 1-7.

Harris, P. L., E. Brown, C. Marriot, S. Whittall & S. Harmer. 1991. "Monsters, ghosts, and witches: Testing the limits of the fantasy-reality distinction in young children." *British Journal of Developmental Psychology* 9: 105-123.

Harper, D. 1987. "Magic: Magic in East Asia." In *Encyclopedia of Religion*, edited by M. Eliade. New York: Macmillian and Free Press.

Hesse, M. 1966. *Models and Analogies in Science*. Notre Dame: Notre Dame University Press.

Hill, D. R. 1987. "Magic: Magic in Primitive Societies." In *Encyclopedia of Religion*, edited by M. Eliade. New York: Macmillian and Free Press.

Hilton, D. J. 1995. "Logic and language in causal explanation." In *Causal Cognition: A multidisciplinary debate*, edited by D. Sperber, D. Premack & A. J. Premack. Oxford: Clarendon.

Hirschfeld, L. A. 1988. "On acquiring social categories: cognitive development and anthropological wisdom" *Man* 23: 611-38.

———. "Is the acquisition of social categories based on domain-specific competence or knowledge transfer?" In *Mapping the Mind: Domain Specificity in Cognition and Culture*, edited by L. A. Hirschfeld & S. A. Gelman. Cambridge: Cambridge University Press.

———. 1995. "Anthropology, psychology, and the meaning of social causality." In *Causal Cognition: A multidisciplinary debate*, edited by D. Sperber, D. Premack & A. J. Premack. Oxford: Clarendon.

Hirschfeld, L. A. & S. A. Gelman. 1994. "Toward a topography of mind: An introduction to domain specificity." In *Mapping the Mind: Domain Specificity in Cognition and Culture*, edited by L. A. Hirschfeld & S. A. Gelman. Cambridge: Cambridge University Press.

Holyoak, K. J. & P. Thagard. 1996. *Mental Leaps: Analogy in Creative Thought*. Cambridge: MIT Press.

Horton, R. 1970. "African traditional thought and Western science." In *Rationality*, edited by B. Wilson. Oxford: Blackwell Publications.

Humphrey, C. & J. Laidlaw. 1994. *The Archetypal Actions of Ritual: A Theory of Ritual Illustrated by the Jain Rite of Worship*. Oxford. Clarendon Press.

Hutchins, E. 1980. *Culture and Inference: A Trobriand Case Study*. Cambridge: Harvard University Press.

———. 1994. *Cognition in the Wild*. Cambridge, MIT Press.

Jackendoff, R. 1992. "Is There a Faculty of Social Cognition." In *Languages of the Mind*, edited by R. Jackendoff. London: MIT Press.

Jackendoff, R. & B. Landau. 1992. "Spatial Language and Spatial Cognition." In *Languages of the Mind*, edited by R. Jackendoff. London, MIT Press.

Jakobson, R. & M. Halle. 1956. *Fundamentals of Language*. The Hague: Mouton.

Jarvie, I. C. & J. Agassi. 1967. "The Problem of the Rationality of Magic." *British Journal of Sociology* 18: 55-74.

Jensen, J. S. 1993. "Is a phenomenology of religion possible? On the ideas of a human and social science of religion." *Method and Theory in the Study of Religion* 5 (2): 109-135.

Johnson, C. N. & P. L. Harris 1994. "Magic: Special but not excluded." *British Journal of Developmental Psychology* 12: 35-51.

Johnson, M. 1987. *The Body in the Mind: The Bodily Basis of Meaning, Imagination, and Reason*. London: University of Chicago Press.

———. 1993. *Moral Imagination: Implications of Cognitive Science for Ethics*. London: University of Chicago Press.

Karmiloff-Smith, A. 1995 (1992). *Beyond Modularity: A Developmental Perspective on Cognitive Science*. London: MIT Press.

Keesing, R. M. 1984. "Rethinking Mana." *Journal of Anthropological Research*, 40: 137-56.

———. 1987. "Models, "folk" and "cultural": paradigms regained?" In *Cultural Models of Language and Thought*, edited by D. Holland & N. Quinn Cambridge, Cambridge University Press.

———. 1993. "'Earth' and 'path' as complex categories: semantics and symbolism in Kwaio culture." In *Cognitive Aspects of Religious Symbolism*, edited by P. Boyer. Cambridge: Cambridge University Press

Keil, F. C. 1987. "Conceptual development and category structure." In *Concepts and conceptual development: Ecological and intellectual factors in categorisation*, edited by U. Neisser. Cambridge: Cambridge University Press.

———. 1994 "The birth and nurturance of concepts by domains: The origin of concepts of living kinds", in *Mapping the Mind: Domain Specificity in Cognition and Culture*, edited by L. A. Hirschfeld & S. A. Gelman. Cambridge: Cambridge University Press.

———. 1995 "The growth of causal understanding of natural kinds" in *Causal Cognition: A multidisciplinary debate*, edited by D. Sperber, D. Premack & A. J. Premack. Oxford: Clarendon.

Kippenberg, H. G. 1998. "Survivals: Conceiving of Religious History in an Age of Development." In *Religion in the Making: The Emergence of the Sciences of Religion*, edited by A. L. Molendijk & P. Pels. Leiden: Brill

Kirkland, J. 1994. "Talking Fire out of Burns: A Magico-Religious healing Tradition", In *Herbal and Magical Medicine: Traditional Healing Today*, edited by J. Kirkland, H. F. Mathews, C. W. Sullivan III & K. Baldwin. Durham: Duke University Press

Klausen, B. 1999. *Religion og Kognition*. Århus: Aarhus Universitetsforlag

Kreitzer, A. 1997. "Multiple levels of schematization: a study in the conceptualisation of space." *Cognitive Linguistics* 8(4): 291-325.

Kummer, H. 1995. "Causal knowledge in animals." In *Causal Cognition: A Multidisciplinary Debate*, edited by D. Sperber, D. Premack & A. J. Premack. Oxford, Clarendon Press.

Lakoff, G. 1987. *Women, Fire, and Dangerous Things: What Categories Reveal about the Mind*. Londo: University of Chicago Press.

---. 1993 "The Contemporary Theory of Metaphor." In *Metaphor and Thought*, edited by A. Ortony. Cambridge: Cambridge University Press.

Lakoff, G. & Johnson, M. 1980. *Metaphors We Live By*. London: University of Chicago Press.

Lawson, E. T. & R. N. McCauley. 1990. *Rethinking Religion: Connecting Cognition and Culture*. Cambridge: Cambridge University Press.

Leach, E. 1976. *Culture and Communication*. Cambridge: Cambridge University Press.

Lehmann, A. 1920. *Overtro og Trolddom*, (2 vol.). København: J. Frimodts Forlag

Leslie, A. M. 1994. "ToMM, ToBy, and Agency: Core architecture and domain specificity." In *Mapping the Mind: Domain Specificity in Cognition and Culture*, edited by L. A. Hirschfeld & S. A. Gelman. Cambridge: Cambridge University Press.

---. 1995 "A theory of agency." In *Causal Cognition: A multidisciplinary debate*, edited by D. Sperber, D. Premack & A. J. Premack. Oxford: Clarendon.

Lévi-Strauss, C. 1966. *The Savage Mind*. Chicago: University of Chicago Press.

---. 1987. *Introduction to the Works of Marcel Mauss*, London, Routledge & Kegan Paul.

---. 1993a (1963). "The Sorcerer and His Magic." In *Structural Anthropology 1*. London, Penguin Books.

---. 1993b (1963). "The Effectiveness of Symbols." In *Structural Anthropology 1*. London: Penguin Books.

Lévy-Bruhl, L. 1910. *Les fonction mentales dans les sociétés inférieures* Paris: Alcan.

---. 1949. *Les carnets de Lévy-Bruhl*. Paris: Presses Universitaires de France.

---. 1975. *The Notebooks on Primitive Mentality*. Oxford: Basil Blackwell.

---. 1978. *Primitive Mentality*. New York: AMS.

---. 1985. *How Natives Think*. Princeton: Princeton University Press.

Lewis, G. 1975. *Knowledge of Illness in a Sepik Society*. London: The Athlone Press, University of London.

---. 1986. "The look of magic." *Man* 21: 414-37.

---. 1995. "The articulation of circumstance and causal understandings." In *Causal Cognition: A Multidisciplinary Debate*, edited by D. Sperber, D. Premack & A. J. Premack. Oxford: Clarendon Press.

Littleton, C. S. 1985. "Lucien Lévy-Bruhl and the Concept of Cognitive Relativity." Introduction to L. Lévy-Bruhl: *How Natives Think*. Princeton: Princeton University Press.

Lloyd, G. E. R. 1990. *Demystifying Mentalities*. Cambridge: Cambridge University Press.

---. 1993 [1979]. *Magic, Reason and Experience: Studies in the origins and development of Greek science*. Cambridge: Cambridge University Press.

Luther, Martin. 1953. *Reformation Writings of Martin Luther. 1. vol: The Basis of the Protestant Reformation*, edited by B. L. Woolf. New York: Philosophical Library.

Malinowski, B. 1935a. *The Coral Gardens and their Magic.* London: George Allen & Unwin Ltd. Vol. 1.

———. 1935b. *The Coral Gardens and their Magic.* London: George Allen & Unwin Ltd. Vol. 2.

———. 1992 (1948). *Magic, Science and Religion and Other Essays.* Illinois: Waveland Press Inc.

Malley, B. 1995. "Explaining order in religious systems." *Method & Theories in the Study of Religion* 7(1): 5-22.

———. 1997. "Causal holism in the evolution of religious ideas. A reply to Pascal Boyer." *Method & Theories in the Study of Religion* 9(4): 389-99.

Mandler, J. 1992."How to build a baby II: Conceptual primitives." *Psychological Review* 99: 587-604.

Marett, R. R. 1930. "Magic." In *Encyclopedia of Religion and Ethics*, edited by J. Hastings. T. & T. Clark.

———. (1979) *The Threshold of Religion.* New York: AMS Press.

Mauss, M. 1972. *A General Theory of Magic.* London; Routledge & Kegan Paul.

Mauss, M. & H. Hubert. 1950 (1902-3). "Esquisse d'une théorie générale de la magie." In M. Mauss: *Sociologie et Anthropologie*, Paris, Presses Universitaires de France.

McCarthy, J. C. 1956. *Problems in Theology I: The Sacraments.* Dublin: Browne and Nolan Limited.

McCauley, R. N. 1987. "The role of theories in a theory of concepts." In *Concepts and conceptual development: Ecological and intellectual factors in categorisation*, edited by U. Neisser. Cambridge: Cambridge University Press.

McCauley, R. & Lawson, E. T. 2002. *Bringing Ritual to Mind: Psychological Foundations of Cultural Forms.* Cambridge: Cambridge University Press.

Medin, D. L. & A. Ortony. 1989. "Psychological essentialism." In *Similarity and analogical reasoning*, edited by S. Vosniadou & A. Ortony. Cambridge: Cambridge University Press.

Merkel, I. & A. G. Debus (eds.). 1988. *Hermeticism and the Renaissance.* London: Associate University Presses.

Meyer, M. & P. Mirecki. 1995. "Introduction." In *Ancient Magic and Ritual Power*, edited by M. Meyer & P. Mirecki. Leiden: E. J. Brill.

Meyer, M. & R. Smith. 1994. *Ancient Christian Magic; Coptic Texts of Ritual Power.* San Francisco: Harper.

Middleton, J. 1987. "Magic: Theories of Magic." In *Encyclopedia of Religion*, edited by M. Eliade. New York: Macmillian and Free Press.

Mithen, S. 1996. *The Prehistory of the Mind: A Search for the Origins of Art, Religion and Science.* London: Thames & Hudson Ldt.

Morris, B. 1987. *Anthropological Studies of Religion: An Introductory Text.* Cambridge: Cambridge University Press.

Morris, M. W., R. E. Nisbett & K. Peng. 1995. "Causal attribution across domains and culture." In *Causal Cognition: A Multidisciplinary Debate*, edited by D. Sperber, D. Premack & A. J. Premack. Oxford: Clarendon Press.

Moya, C. J. 1990. *The Philosophy of Action.* Oxford: Polity Press.

Needham, R. 1972. *Belief, Language, and Experience.* Oxford: Basil Blackwell.

Nemeroff, C. J. 1995. "Magical Thinking About Illness Virulence: Conceptions of Germs From "Safe" Versus "Dangerous" Others." *Health Psychology* 14(2): 147-151.

Nemeroff, C. J. & P. Rozin. 1989. "'You Are What You Eat'. Applying the Demand-Free 'Impressions' Techniques to an Unacknowledged Belief." *Ethnos* 17 (1): 50-69.

———. 2000. "The Making of the Magical Mind: The Nature and Function of Sympathetic Magical Thinking." In *Imagining the Impossible: Magical, Scientific, and Religious Thinking in Children*, edited by K. S. Rosengren, C. N. Johnson and P. L. Harris. Cambridge: Cambridge University Press.

O'Keefe, D. 1982. *Stolen Lightning: A Social Theory of Magic.* Oxford: Martin Robertson.

Ormsby-Lennon, H. 1988. "Rosicrucian Linguistics: Twilight of a Renaissance Tradition." In *Hermeticism and the Renaissance*, edited by I. Merkel & A. G. Debus. London: Associated University Presses.

Peel, J. D. Y. 1969. "Understanding Alien Belief-Systems" *British Journal of Sociology* 20: 69-84.

Peirce, C. S. 1931-35. *Collected Papers I-IV*, edited by C. Hartstone & P. Weiss. Cambridge, MA: Belknap.

Penner, H. H. 1989. "Rationality, Ritual, and Science." In *Religion, Science, and Magic*, edited by J. Neusner. Oxford: Oxford University Press.

Phillips III, C. R. 1991. Nullum Crimen sine Lege: Socioreligious Sanctions on Magic. In *Magika Hiera: Ancient Greek Magic and Religion*, edited by C. A. Faraone & D. Obbink. New York: Oxford University Press.

Pocock, D. F. 1972. "Foreword." In Marcel Mauss: *A General Theory of Magic.* London: Routledge & Kegan Paul.

Propp, V. 1968 [1928]. *Morphology of the Folktale.* Austin: Texas University Press.

Quinn, N. & D. Holland. 1987. "Culture and Cognition." In *Cultural Models of Language and Thought*, edited by D. Holland & N. Quinn. Cambridge: Cambridge University Press.

Rappaport, R. A. 1999. *Ritual and Religion in the Making of Humanity.* Cambridge: Cambridge University Press.

Ray, B. 1973. "'Performative Utterances" in African Rituals." *History of Religions* 13: 16-35.

Remus, H. 1999. "'Magic', Method, Madness." *Method and Theory in the Study of Religion* 11(3): 258-98.

Ricks, S. D. 1995. "The Magician as Outsider in the Hebrew Bible and the New Testament." In *Ancient Magic and Ritual Power*, edited by M. Meyer & P. Mirecki. Leiden: E. J. Brill

Ritner, R. K. 1995. "The Religious, Social, and Legal Parameters of Traditional Egyptian Magic." In *Ancient Magic and Ritual Power*, edited by M. Meyer & P. Mirecki. Leiden: E. J. Brill

Rosch, E. 1977. "Human Categorisation. In *Advances in Cross-cultural Psychology* (vol. 1), edited by N. Warren. London: Academic Press.

Rosengren, K. S, C. W. Kalish, A. K. Hickling & S. A. Gelman. 1994. "Exploring the relation between preschool children's magical beliefs and causal thinking." *British Journal of Developmental Psychology* 12: 69-82.

Rozin, P. & C. Nemeroff. 1990. "The laws of sympathetic magic: a psychological analysis of similarity and contagion." In *Cultural Psychology: Essays on Comparative Human Development*, edited by J. W. Stigler, R. A. Shweder & G. Herdt. Cambridge: Cambridge University Press.

Rozin, P., M. Markwith & C. Nemeroff. 1992. "Magical Contagion Beliefs and Fear of AIDS." *Journal of Applied Social Psychology* 22 (14): 1081-92.

Rozin, P., C. Nemeroff, M. Horowitz, B. Gordon & W. Voet. 1995. "The borders of the self: Contamination sensitivity and potency of the mouth, other apertures and body parts." *Journal of research in Personality* 29: 318-340.

Saler, B. 1997. "Lévy-Bruhl, Participation, and Rationality." In *Rationality and the Study of Religion*, edited by J. S. Jensen & L. H. Martin. Aarhus: Aarhus University Press.

Schank, R. C & R. Abelson. 1977. *Scripts, Plans, Goals and Understanding: An Inquiry into Human Knowledge Structures*. Hillsdale: Lawrence Erlbaum Associates.

Searle, J. R. 1969. *Speech Acts: An Essay in the Philosophy of Language*. Cambridge: Cambridge University Press.

Segal, A. F. 1981. "Hellenistic Magic: Some Questions of Definition." In *Studies in Gnosticism and Hellenistic Religions*, edited by R. van den Broek & M. J. Vermaseren. Leiden: E. J. Brill.

Senft, G. 1985. "Weyeis Wettermagie. Eine ethnolinguistische Untersuchung von fünf magischen Formeln eines Wettermagiers af den Trobriand Inseln." *Zeitschrift für Ethnologie* 110: 67-90.

———. 1987. "Rituelle Kommunikation auf den Trobriand Inseln." *Zeitschrift für Literaturwissenschaft und Linguistik* 65: 105-130.

———. 1997. "Magic, missionaries and religion: Some observations from the Trobriand Islands." In *Cultural Dynamics of Religious Change in Oceania*, edited by T. Otto & A. Borsboom. Leiden: KITLV Press.

Shelley, C. & P. Thagard. 1996 "Mythology and analogy." In *Modes of Thought: Explorations in Culture and Cognition*, edited by D. R. Olson & N. Torrance. Cambridge: Cambridge University Press.

Shore, B. 1996. *Culture in Mind: Cognition, Culture, and the Problem of Meaning*. Oxford: Oxford University Press.

Shweder, R. A. 1977. "Likeness and Likelihood in Everyday Thought: Magical Thinking in Judgements about Personality." *Current Anthropology* 18 (4): 637-58.

———. 1984. "Anthropology's romantic rebellion against the enlightenment, or there is more to thinking than reason and experience." In *Culture theory: Essays on Mind, Self, and Emotion*, edited by R. A. Shweder & R. A. Levine: Cambridge: Cambridge University Press.

———. 1986. "Divergent Rationalities." In *Metatheory in Social Science: Pluralisms and subjectivities*, edited by D. W. Fiske & R. A. Shweder. Chicago: University of Chicago Press.

Skorupski, J. 1976. *Symbol and Theory: A Philosophical Study of Theories of Religion in Social Anthropology.* Cambridge: Cambridge University Press.

Smith, J. Z. 1987. *To Take Place: Toward Theory in Ritual.* Chicago: University of Chicago Press.

———. 1990. *Drudgery Divine: On the comparison of Early Christianities and the Religions of Late Antiquities.* Chicago: University of Chicago Press.

———. 1995. "Trading Places." In *Ancient Magic and Ritual Power*, edited by M. Meyer & P. Mirecki. Leiden: E. J. Brill.

Soergel P. M. 1997. "Miracle, Magic, and Disenchantment in Early Modern Germany." In *Envisioning Magic: A Princeton Seminar and Symposium*, edited by P. Schäfer & H. Kippenberg. Leiden: Brill.

Spelke, E. S., A. Phillips & A. L. Woodward. 1995. "Infant's knowledge of object motion and human action." In *Causal Cognition: A Multidisciplinary Debate*, edited by D. Sperber, D. Premack & A. J. Premack. Oxford: Clarendon Press.

Sperber, D. 1975. *Rethinking Symbolism.* Cambridge: Cambridge University Press.

———. 1986. "Is Symbolic Thought Prerational?" In *Symbols as Sense*, edited by M. L. Foster & S. H. Brandes. New York: Academic Press.

———. 1994. "The modularity of thought and the epidemiology of representations." In *Mapping the Mind: Domain Specificity in Cognition and Culture*, edited by L. A. Hirschfeld & S. A. Gelman. Cambridge: Cambridge University Press.

———. 1996. *Explaining Culture: A Naturalistic Approach.* Oxford: Blackwell Publishers.

———. 2001. "Mental Modularity and Cultural Diversity." In *The Debated Mind: Evolutionary Psychology Versus Ethnography*, edited by H. Whitehouse. Oxford: Berg.

Sperber, D., D. Premack & A. J. Premack. 1995. *Causal Cognition: A Multidisciplinary Debate.* Oxford: Clarendon Press.

Stjernfelt, F. 1989. "Ægishiálmr – den islandske 1600-tals magi mellem tegn og blik." *Religionsvidenskabeligt Tidsskrift* 15: 23-56.

Subbotsky, E.V. 1985. "Preschool Children's Perception of Unusual Phenomena." *Soviet Psychology* 23: 91-114.

———. 1994. "Early rationality and magical thinking in preschoolers: Space and time." *British Journal of Developmental Psychology* 12: 97-108.
Swartz, M. D. 1995. "Magical Piety in Ancient and Medieval Judaism." In *Ancient Magic and Ritual Power*, edited by M. Meyer & P. Mirecki. Leiden: E. J. Brill.
Sweetser, E. 1987. "The definition of *lie*; an examination of the folk models underlying semantic prototype." In *Cultural Models of Language and Thought*, edited by D. Holland & N. Quinn. Cambridge: Cambridge University Press.
———. 1995. *From etymology to pragmatics: Metaphorical and cultural aspects of semantic structure*. Cambridge: Cambridge University Press.
Sweetser, E. & Fauconnier, G. 1996. "Cognitive Links and Domains: Basic Aspects of Mental Space Theory." In *Spaces, Worlds, and Grammar*, edited by G. Fauconnier & E. Sweetser. London: University of Chicago Press.
Sørensen, J. 2000. "Theosophy: Metaphors of the Subject." *Temenos. Nordic Journal of Comparative Religion* 35-36: 225-248.
———. 2002. "'The Morphology and Function of Magic' Revisited." In *Current Approaches in the Cognitive Science of Religion*, edited by I. Pyysiäinen & V. Anttonen. London: Continuum.
———. 2004. "Religion, Evolution, and an Immunology of Cultural Systems." *Evolution and Cognition* 10: 61-73.
———. 2005. "Charisma, Tradition and Ritual: A Cognitive Approach to Magical Agency." In *Mind and Religion: Psychological Foundations of Religiosity*, edited by H. Whitehouse & R. N. McCauley. Walnut Creek, CA: AltaMira Press.
———. 2005. "Acts that work—or how gibberish becomes efficacious actions." *RSSI Reserches Sémiotiques/Semiotic Inquiry* 25 (1-2)
Talmy, L. 2000. *Toward a Cognitive Semantics*. Cambridge, MA: MIT Press.
Tambiah, S. J. 1968. "The magical power of words." *Man* 3: 175-208.
———. 1979. "A Performative Approach to Ritual." *Proceedings of the British Academy* vol. LXV: 113-69.
———. 1985. "Form and Meaning of Magical Acts." In *Culture, Thought, and Social Action: An Anthropological Perspective*. Cambridge: Harvard University Press.
———. 1990. *Magic, Science, Religion, and the Scope of Rationality*. Cambridge: Cambridge University Press.
———. 1996. "Relations of analogy and identity: Towards multiple orientations to the world." In *Modes of Thought: Explorations in Culture and Cognition*, edited by D. R. Olson & N. Torrance. Cambridge: Cambridge University Press.
Thomas, K. 1975. "An Anthropology of Religion and Magic, II." *Journal of Interdisciplinary History* 6 (1): 71-89. Reprinted in *Anthropological studies of witchcraft, magic and demonology*, edited by B. P. Levack (1992): London, Garland Publ.

———. 1991 [1971]. *Religion and the Decline of Magic*. London: Penguin Books.
Tolaas, J. 1991. "Notes on the origins on some spatialization metaphors." *Metaphor and Symbolic Activity* 6: 203-18.
Tomasello, M. 1999. *The Cultural Origins of Human Cognition*. Cambridge, MA: Harvard University Press.
Turner, M. 1996. *The Literary Mind*. New York: Oxford University Press.
———. 2001. *Cognitive Dimensions of Social Science*. Oxford: Oxford University Press.
Turner, V. W. 1969. *The Ritual Process: Structure and Anti-Structure*, Itchaca: Cornell University Press.
Tylor, E. B. 1865. *Researches into the Early History of Mankind*. London: John Murray. Reprinted in *The Collected Works of Edward Burnett Tylor* vol. II. London: Routledge & Thoemmes Press.
———. 1866. "Religion of the Savages." *Fortnightly Review* 6. Reprinted in *The Collected Works of Edward Burnett Tylor* vol. VI. London: Routledge & Thoemmes Press.
———. 1871. *Primitive Culture: Researches into the Development of Mythology, Philosophy, Religion, Art, and Custom* (2 vol.). London: John Murray. Reprinted in *The Collected Works of Edward Burnett Tylor* vol. III-IV. London: Routledge & Thoemmes Press.
———. 1881. *Anthropology: An Introduction to the Study of Man and Civilisation*. London MacMillan & Co. Reprinted in *The Collected Works of Edward Burnett Tylor* vol. V. London: Routledge & Thoemmes Press.
———. 1883 "Magic." In *The Encyclopedia Britannica* ninth edition, vol. 15. Reprinted in *The Collected Works of Edward Burnett Tylor* vol. VII. London: Routledge & Thoemmes Press.
Versnel, H. S. 1991. "Some reflections on the relationship magic-religion." *Numen* 38: 177-197.
Vetter, G. B. 1958. *Magic and Religion: Their Psychological Nature, Origin, and Function*. New York: Philosophical Library.
Vishnu Purana. Translated by H. H. Wilson. Indische Studien.
Watt, H. 1912. "Eucharist." In *Encyclopædia of Religion and Ethics*, edited by J. Hastings. Edinburgh, T. & T. Clark.
Weber, M. 1976. *Wirtschaft und Geseelschaft*. Mohr: Tübingen.
Whitehouse, H. 2000. *Modes of Religiosity: A Cognitive Theory of Religious Transmission*. Walnut Creek, CA.: AltaMira Press.
Wiebe, D. 1987. "The Prelogical Mentality Revisited." *Religion* 17: 29-61.
Winch, P. 1970. "Understanding Primitive Society." In *Rationality*, edited by B. R. Wilson. Oxford: Blackwell Publication.
Wilson, B. R. (ed.) 1970. *Rationality*. Oxford: Blackwell Publication.
———. 1973. *Magic and the Millennium: A Sociological Study of Religious Movements of Protest among Tribal and Third-World Peoples*. London: Heinemann.

Wooley, J. D. & K. E. Phelps. 1994. "Young children's practical reasoning about imagination." *British Journal of Developmental Psychology* 12: 53-67.

Yates, F. A. 1964. *Giordano Bruno and the Hermetic Tradition*. London: Routledge and Kegan Paul.

———. 1972. *The Rosicrucian Enlightenment*. London: Routledge and Kegan Paul.

Zusne, L. & W. H. Jones. 1989. *Anomalistic Psychology: A Study on Magical Thinking* (2nd ed.). Hillsdale: LEA.

Østergård, S. 2000. "Mental Causation." Paper given at the winter symposium: *Structures of Causal Meaning*. Centre for Semiotics, University of Aarhus.

Index

abduction, 38, 48, 67, 151, 161
Abelson, Robert P., 49, 204
action:
  goal-directed, 13, 36;
  instrumental, 15, 22, 65, 69, 103, 143, 148, 155, 172;
  magical, 3, 6, 9-11, 13-14, 17-19, 24-29, 31-33, 38, 40-41, 45, 56, 59-60, 65, 76-77, 80, 87, 95-97, 101, 106-107, 116, 125, 128, 130, 132-133, 136-137, 141-142, 154, 157-159, 162, 164-168, 170-171, 174, 176-177, 187-190;
  practical, 14, 18, 20, 22-23, 26, 143, 169;
  ritual, 1-2, 5-6, 13-14, 16-23, 26-27, 50, 53, 64-65, 67-68, 72, 74, 76, 85, 87, 92, 97-100, 106, 110-112, 121, 133, 136, 141-145, 147-148, 150-155, 157-158, 160-166, 169, 171-175, 177, 179-183, 185-186, 189-191
action representation schema, 64, 72, 104, 185
Agassi, Joseph, 12, 169, 193, 199
agency:
  action-based, 67-69, 80;
  agent-based, 65, 69, 71, 80, 85, 183;
  object-based, 69-72;
  ritual, 68-69, 72, 78, 85
agent:
  ritual, 67, 85, 90-91, 97-98, 100, 104, 129, 142, 147, 166, 169, 180;
  superhuman, 6, 19, 90, 100, 164
Aguaruna, 70, 84, 167
amulet, 1, 72, 93
analogical reasoning, 11, 202
analogy, 11, 51, 54, 184, 191, 198, 204, 206
anthropomorphism, 76
Armenian Church, 1
artefact, 44, 47, 72, 73
association, 11, 26, 57, 95, 178;
  of ideas, 11, 95
associative psychology, 11
Austin, John L., 19-20, 22, 68, 193, 194, 203
Azande, 5, 17, 71, 77-78, 81-84, 91, 93, 97, 113, 120-122, 129, 131, 138, 159, 161, 163, 175, 177, 179, 196;
  agriculture, 81;
  magic, 77, 81-82, 84;
  magical medicine, 71, 82;
  myths, 82;
  oracles, 17, 81, 159;
  spell, 82, 91, 121;
  witchcraft, 81, 131, 159

baptism, 104-105, 109
Beattie, John, 12, 14, 22, 169, 194
behaviour, 2, 14-15, 17-19, 23, 27-29, 33, 35, 38, 46-47, 67, 81, 93, 107, 120, 122, 128, 143, 181, 186;
expressive, 2;
magical, 2, 14, 32;
ritual, 9, 29, 191
belief, 2, 10-11, 13-14, 17, 18-19, 21, 23-25, 27, 29, 31, 36, 38, 56, 67, 71, 74, 81, 83, 85, 93, 95-96, 106-107, 112-114, 122, 131, 134, 136, 138, 143, 149-150, 156, 164, 185-189, 191, 197;
counter-intuitive, 63, 152;
epistemic judgement of, 106, 122, 175, 189
belief-desire reasoning, 36, 38, 50, 57, 76, 150
beliefs:
explicit, 18;
implicit, 90;
intuitive, 38, 71
blend, 5, 53-56, 61, 64-65, 74-77, 87-88, 91-92, 111, 121, 124, 126-127, 129, 159, 174-175, 178, 187;
genetic blend, 75-76, 79, 83, 86-88, 174, 178;
linguistic blend, 88, 92, 117;
schematic blend, 117
blending, 38, 52-55, 63, 91-93, 111, 119, 128, 133, 174. *See also* conceptual blending
Boyer, Pascal, 3, 7, 13, 38, 47, 60-61, 63, 66, 70-71, 92, 100, 102, 107, 135, 142, 144, 149, 151-152, 180, 194, 200, 202
Brandt, Per Aage, 7, 148, 195
Brown, Michael F., 70-71, 167, 195, 199

categories, 2-4, 17, 25-26, 32, 35, 37-41, 44, 56-57, 60-61, 67, 70, 73, 76, 134-136, 151, 193, 200;
social, 37, 66, 199
categorisation, 4, 31-33, 35-40, 42-45, 49-51, 56, 58, 60-62, 64, 67, 70, 97, 99, 102, 135, 137, 146, 149, 175, 180, 200, 202;
basic level, 33, 36, 39-40, 43, 50, 55, 58, 61, 64, 84, 108, 130, 133, 136, 146, 174, 185
Catholic, 96
Catholic Church, 10, 85
Catholic Eucharist, 65, 77, 85, 98, 101, 103, 166, 174, 178, 182, 207
Catholic Mass, 5, 141
Catholic Sacraments, 10
causal assumptions, 35, 43, 49, 56, 60, 108, 149, 151, 159, 165, 176
causality, 22, 35, 43, 50, 57, 71, 112, 143, 150, 199;
instrumental, 68, 87, 142, 147, 152-153, 157-158, 161-162, 164-166, 179, 185-187, 190;
intentional, 36;
strong, 38, 151, 170;
teleological, 36;
weak, 151, 160, 170, 174
causal relation, 14, 45, 48, 50, 57, 68-69, 72, 85, 96, 112, 115, 131, 148-149, 166, 173, 175
causal structure, 50, 72, 181
causal underdetermination, 50, 151-152
causal unfolding, 113, 128, 141, 143, 149
causation, 85, 96, 112
cognitive flexibility, 39
completion, 53
composition, 53
concepts, 2, 4, 9, 10, 16, 17, 18, 22, 25-26, 28, 35, 37-40, 45, 48, 50-51, 62-64, 92, 100, 102, 105,

108, 125, 135-137, 139, 146, 152, 163, 177, 180, 182, 186-187, 196, 197, 200, 202;
colloquial, 2;
explanatory, 2;
poly-synthetic, 26
conceptual blending, 5, 33, 41, 52-53, 55, 60, 63, 77, 92, 96-98, 131-133, 141, 148, 171, 174-175, 177;
as heuristic method, 54
conceptual model, 47, 54, 76, 101, 105
conceptual structure, 15, 31, 33, 37, 45, 47, 51, 62, 64, 70, 100, 106, 115, 121, 172, 177, 185-188
contagion, 5, 11, 16, 31, 45, 56, 95-96, 102-104, 106-107, 109, 112, 114-115, 117, 134, 166-167, 204;
backward, 96, 103, 111-112, 115, 128-129, 134, 175;
forward, 96, 103, 106, 109, 112, 115, 129, 134, 174
contamination, 96
contiguity, 11, 22, 103, 107, 123, 170, 174
Coptic papyrus, 1
counterpart connection, 55, 57-59, 61, 66, 69, 73, 76, 86, 96, 100, 105-106, 111-115, 118, 121, 126, 128-131, 133-134, 136, 159, 175-176, 182, 187
cultural conceptual system, 6, 26, 58, 64, 105, 176-177, 179, 187
cultural model, 14, 18, 33, 42, 45-51, 64, 93, 108, 110, 118, 120, 127-128, 136, 146, 149, 151-154, 157, 160, 162, 164, 177, 180, 185
cultural system, 32, 64, 105, 111, 136, 144, 171, 176, 180-181;
immunology of, 137

deduction, 47
deductive model, 47
denotative fallacy, 21
de-symbolisation, 120, 137-138, 180, 183, 190
diagnosis, 44, 110, 141, 147-150, 152, 159, 160-161, 163, 173
divination, 113, 170
domain, 5, 19, 33-39, 42-43, 45-46, 48-55, 57-58, 60, 63-64, 71, 74, 76-77, 84, 96, 100, 102-103, 107-108, 111, 116, 118-119, 121-122, 124-127, 129, 131-133, 136, 146, 155, 157, 175-177, 180, 183, 195, 199-201, 203;
animate, 35;
biological, 37, 44;
cognitive, 33-34, 43, 55, 102;
conceptual, 33, 42, 44-45, 48, 50-52, 54-55, 58, 61, 63, 92, 100, 102, 122, 128, 131, 133, 135-136, 175;
epistemic, 34, 42;
functional, 34;
mental, 36, 42;
ontological, 34-36, 39, 43-45, 49-51, 60, 101-102;
perceptual, 34, 41;
physical, 35, 42, 44;
profane, 63-65, 70, 76-77, 84, 97;
psychological, 36, 42;
sacred, 15, 63-64, 66-67, 70, 72, 74-77, 90, 92, 99, 146, 181-183;
social, 37, 42, 44, 124;
source, 52, 128;
structured, 132;
target, 52, 57, 97, 128, 131;
unstructured, 133
domain-general, 4, 39, 43-45, 51, 55, 58, 60-61, 175
domain-specificity, 4, 33-34, 36-39, 43-45, 50-51, 56, 60-62, 70,

76, 107, 135, 149, 151, 165, 170, 173, 175, 195, 199, 201
Durkheim, Emile, 15, 25, 194, 196

Egyptian hieroglyphs, 72, 179
elaboration, 54, 176, 179
emic/etic, 16
emotion, 19, 24-26, 28, 31-32
emotionalist approach, 19, 24, 28, 31
empiricist philosophy, 10-11, 20
enlightenment, 10, 205
esotericism, 180
essence, 2, 32, 35-37, 44, 48, 50, 56-57, 60, 66-67, 69-71, 73, 80, 83-84, 95-110, 114, 117, 128-130, 133-136, 141, 160, 166-168, 171, 174-176, 178, 185;
 ascription of, 35, 56, 58, 72, 102, 105, 108, 135
essence change, 102, 106-107
essence link, 103, 114, 128-129
essence retention, 102, 107
essentialism, 37, 43-44, 56, 69, 73, 84, 130, 202;
 psychological, 36-37, 43-44, 50, 55-56, 59, 61, 67, 70, 73, 76, 80, 87, 97, 102, 107, 150, 174-175
Eucharist, 65, 98, 101, 103, 174, 178, 182, 207. *See also* Catholic Eucharist
Evans-Pritchard, Edward E., 17, 19, 71, 74, 77-78, 81-82, 84, 90-91, 93, 113, 116, 120, 153, 159, 161, 166, 170, 179-180, 196
event-frame, 45, 49, 113, 141-142, 147-149, 151-155, 157, 159-166, 169-175, 177, 185, 187-188, 190;
 counterfactual, 155-156, 173;
 explanatory, 163, 165, 168, 173, 176-177, 187;
 factual, 173;
 motivated, 159;
 ritual, 146, 154, 160, 163-164, 173, 175, 179, 185
evolution, 11-12, 15, 25, 27, 55, 95, 96, 107, 187
exorcism, 1, 4, 21, 124-126, 168-169, 185
exoticism, 176, 179
explanation, 3, 6, 10-16, 18-19, 23-25, 27-29, 31-33, 54, 61, 70-71, 77, 89, 96, 100-101, 110, 114, 132, 138, 144-145, 152, 156, 160-161, 163-165, 173, 180, 191, 193, 199;
 religious, 12;
 scientific, 1;
 sociological, 15

family-resemblance, 32
Fauconnier, Gilles, 7, 38, 52-55, 59, 93, 111, 148, 196, 206
Fillmore, Charles, 49, 197
Firth, Raymond, 85, 166, 189, 197
force-dynamics, 42-44, 50, 57-59, 61, 73, 76, 109, 118, 121, 123, 125, 131, 149, 157, 162, 167-168, 173, 175, 185
frame semantics, 49
Frazer, James G., 10-11, 13, 16, 24-27, 33, 95-96, 113, 115, 123, 132, 134, 197-198
Freud, Sigmund, 26-28, 197

Geertz, Clifford, 178, 197
genealogical lines, 66

Hanks, William, 62, 74, 177, 198
hermeneutic strategies, 28, 142, 152-153, 173, 175, 181, 184, 186
hermeneutic strategy:
 phenomenological, 175, 184, 188;
 pragmatic, 54, 185, 188;
 symbolic, 185

Hirschfeld, Lawrence A., 35, 37, 195, 197-201, 205
Holland, Dorothy, 46, 196, 200, 203, 206
Holy Communion, 100, 103-106, 109-110, 167, 175
Horton, Robin, 12, 169-170, 199
Hubert, Henri, 15-16, 29, 115, 202
Hume, David, 11
Humphrey, Caroline, 29, 68, 138-139, 142, 144-148, 153, 163, 166, 169-170, 179, 182-183, 189, 199

icon, 48, 59, 66, 70-71, 80, 96, 130, 146;
as defined by Peirce, 59
iconography, 71
Idealised Cognitive Models, 29, 45
identity connector, 66-67, 76, 80, 84-85
image-schema, 39-44, 49-50, 55-56, 58-61, 67, 69, 70, 72-73, 76, 84, 100, 118-119, 122, 125-126, 131-133, 136, 166, 168, 174-175, 177
imitation, 95
inanimate objects, 35
index, 44, 48, 50, 56, 58-61, 66, 68-70, 72-74, 80, 89-92, 96, 101, 106, 114-115, 130, 133, 137, 146, 150-152, 175-176, 178-180, 183, 187, 190;
as defined by Peirce, 57
induction, 39, 48;
problem of, 34, 39, 44
inference, 4, 25, 37-38, 41, 71, 107, 119, 151, 157, 164, 194
intellectualist approach, 10, 12, 15, 18, 24, 26, 29, 95, 143-145, 169
interpretation, 7, 14-15, 33, 42, 44, 48, 55-56, 58, 60, 68-70, 72-74, 100-101, 105, 118, 122, 128, 134, 136-137, 141, 143-146, 152, 163-164, 173, 178-181, 183, 185-187, 189;
idiosyncratic, 109, 137, 153, 171, 174, 179;
illicit, 152;
orthodox, 137, 152;
symbolic, 5-6, 15, 68, 100-101, 114, 134, 136-137, 145-147, 152-153, 163, 168, 171, 174, 176, 178-181, 183-185, 187-188, 190-191
iteration, 68, 90, 124, 178

Jarvie, Ian C., 12, 169, 193, 199
Johnson, Mark, 39-41, 51, 57, 108, 115, 132, 138, 145, 166, 200-201, 203

Karmiloff-Smith, Annette, 34, 39, 62, 200
Keil, Frank, 35-36, 62, 194, 200

Laidlaw, James, 29, 68, 138-139, 142, 144-148, 153, 163, 166, 169-170, 179, 182-183, 189, 199
Lakoff, George, 7, 29, 39-40, 45, 49, 51, 57, 115, 132, 134-135, 145, 200-201
language, 2, 5, 9, 17-21, 29, 34, 39, 42, 47, 50-51, 62, 68, 70, 72, 81, 87-92, 111, 138, 141, 145, 185, 196, 199;
archaic, 68, 89-91;
magical, 21, 88-91;
nonsense, 5, 89-90;
ritual, 21, 68, 89-90;
sacred, 19-20, 23, 88-92;
social aspects of, 87, 90;
ungrammatical, 90
Law of Contact, 11
Law of Similarity, 11
Lawson, E. Thomas, 7, 29, 38, 63-65, 70, 97-98, 104, 148, 185, 201-202

Leslie, Alan M., 35-36, 112, 150, 201
Lévi-Strauss, Claude, 92, 128, 182, 201
Lévy-Bruhl, Lucien, 22, 25-26, 28-29, 187, 201, 204
Lewis, Gilbert, 160-161
location, 74, 177
Locke, John, 11
Luther, Martin, 178, 202

magic:
  as action, 13, 17;
  as antisocial, 16, 23;
  as expression, 14-15, 18, 143;
  as innovative force, 6, 180-181, 190;
  as persuasion, 23;
  as polemical concept, 9, 16;
  as substitute activity, 20, 28;
  as syncretistic engine, 191;
  concept of, 2, 4, 16, 17;
  contagious, 95, 134;
  definitions of, 15-17, 32;
  homeopathic, 95, 134;
  imitative, 96;
  sympathetic, 11, 95, 204;
  typology of, 76, 134, 142, 166
magical agency, 5-6, 17, 65, 67-68, 71-74, 76-77, 80-85, 87, 89-92, 97-98, 101-102, 104, 107, 109, 111, 128-129, 131, 141, 146-147, 150, 153, 162-165, 169, 171, 173-174, 176, 179-191;
  and political power, 78, 85, 183;
  personally contained, 182
magical beliefs, 164, 196, 204;
  children's, 164, 196, 204
magical dolls, 116
magical object, 70-71, 73, 83-84, 185
magical rituals, 5-6, 15-19, 21-24, 26-28, 31, 33, 38, 53-55, 57, 61, 63-65, 67-68, 70-72, 74, 76-77, 80, 83, 87-91, 97, 106, 111-112, 116, 119, 125, 128, 130-133, 136, 141-142, 146-148, 153-155, 162-163, 165-166, 168-169, 171, 173-177, 179-180, 182-183, 185-187, 189-190;
  constructive, 154, 166;
  destructive, 154, 166;
  protective, 123, 154, 166
magical stones, 70-71, 84, 167
magical word, 21, 29
magic and religion, 2-3, 9-10, 12-20, 25, 60, 181, 186, 188, 190-191
magic and science, 9, 12
magician, 11, 67, 78, 80-81, 84, 88-89, 91, 97, 108, 116, 119, 123-124, 130-131, 154, 157, 182, 184, 186
Malinowski, Bronislaw, 17, 19-21, 26, 28-29, 46, 77-81, 90, 116-118, 123, 125, 127-129, 132, 138, 141, 154-158, 167-168, 177, 202
Malley, Brian, 61, 191, 195, 202
mana, 4, 15, 25
Manipulative Magical Action, 96, 111-112, 122, 131, 133;
  principles of, 128
mapping, 39, 41, 44, 46-48, 51-52, 54, 57-58, 61, 65, 71, 76, 79, 84, 111, 116-121, 124-127, 130-133, 136-137, 153, 155, 159, 166, 176, 182, 187
Marett, Robert R., 24-27, 202
materia medica, 116-117, 130, 138
Mauss, Marcel, 15-16, 29, 115, 196, 201-203
McCauley, Robert N., 7, 29, 38, 44, 63-65, 70, 97-98, 104, 148, 185, 201-202, 206
meaning, 4, 9, 17, 19-21, 23, 29, 33, 37, 47-48, 50-53, 57-58, 62, 68, 84-87, 90-92, 120, 137, 145-

146, 152-153, 166, 171-176, 178, 180, 190, 195, 199;
non-propositional, 145;
propositional, 146
Medin, Douglas, 35-36, 44, 56, 202
mentality, 28-29;
pre-logical, 25;
primitive, 20, 22, 25
mental spaces, 52-53, 56, 58, 96, 102, 106, 111, 115, 117, 122, 133, 148, 158, 166, 174-175, 177
metaphor, 21-23, 31, 39, 51-52, 54-55, 57-59, 64, 96, 111, 115, 117, 119, 128-129, 132, 134, 136, 138, 148, 157, 159, 162, 168, 177, 191, 207
metaphors:
conventional, 50, 53, 57-58, 117, 136, 176;
primary, 58-59
metonymic diffusion, 183, 186
metonymy, 21, 23, 31, 55-56, 64, 73, 96, 115-117, 128, 134, 148
Mill, John S., 11
millenarism, 191
model, 3-4, 6, 46-49, 53, 58, 63, 69-70, 74, 80, 88, 92, 98, 103-105, 119, 127, 136, 138, 149, 151, 157, 162, 171-172, 177, 196;
explanatory, 6, 164, 170, 177;
prescriptive, 148
modes of thought, 21-22, 195
monarch's touch, the, 85
motor representations, 25, 27, 29, 39, 43, 67
myth, 27-28, 63, 72, 79, 82, 84, 89, 90, 101, 118, 152, 184

narrative, 49, 63-64, 66-67, 100-101, 110, 161, 164, 169, 172-173, 177
Nemeroff, Carol, 56, 95-96, 106-107, 125, 135, 203-204

obsessive compulsory disorder, 27-28
O'Keefe, Daniel, 32
omnipotence of thought, 27
oracles, 17, 81, 159
Ortony, Andrew, 35-36, 44, 56, 201-202
Østergaard, Svend, 7, 148

participation, 25, 105, 187
law of, 26
Peirce, Charles S., 44, 48, 56, 59, 62, 203
performative approach, 20
Piaget, Jean, 108
Pocock, David F., 29, 203
post-colonialism, 4
postmodernism, 4
pragmatic approach, 19, 23, 26, 31
pragmatic context, 6, 19-21, 23, 89, 92, 141, 169
pragmatic level, 173, 175
primitivism, 2, 4, 112
prognosis, 110, 141, 148-149, 151-152, 154
propositions, 10, 17, 37, 40, 78, 153
prosody, 68, 80, 89-90, 162
pseudo-genealogical lines, 66, 86, 183
psychic unity, 10

Quinn, Naomi, 46, 196, 200, 203, 206

rationalisation, 184
Rationalist approach, 31
rationality, 13, 25, 112, 169, 206;
strong, 13;
weak, 13
rationality debate, 169
redundancy, 22-23, 90, 123-124
Reformation, 9, 178, 202
relativism, 4

relics, 1, 69, 111
religion, 2-3, 6, 9-10, 12-13, 15-16, 18-20, 25, 27, 29, 33, 38, 54, 59-61, 63, 89, 101, 106, 163, 171, 176, 181-182, 184, 186-191, 194, 200, 204;
  new, 6, 91, 181
religiosity:
  doctrinal mode, 110;
  imagistic mode, 110
religious categories, 63, 66
religious concept, 31, 38, 63-64, 100, 135
religious institutions, 4, 186-187, 191
religious system, 61, 176, 189-190, 202
representation:
  cognitive, 46, 71, 131, 142, 160;
  collective, 25-26;
  diachronic, 50;
  epidemiology of, 137, 205;
  social, 15
ritual:
  context, 20, 25, 90, 159, 163, 182, 188;
  efficacy, 6, 17, 23, 31, 64, 66-69, 71, 73, 76, 80, 86, 97, 101, 110, 147, 165, 174, 176, 178, 180, 188-191;
  as expressive, 14-15, 18;
  institutionalised, 6, 71, 171, 181;
  as instrumental, 155;
  intention, 29, 144-145;
  interpretation of, 172;
  language, 21, 68, 89-90;
  as meaningless, 145;
  procedural character of, 68, 73;
  prospective, 6, 154-155, 158, 165;
  purpose of, 100, 115, 139, 143, 171-173, 175, 184;
  retrospective, 6, 154, 158-160, 165

ritualisation, 20, 65, 136, 138-139, 142, 144-147, 163, 166, 169-170, 172, 175-176, 181, 183-184, 186, 188, 190-191
ritual practice, 9, 16, 27, 81, 179, 181-182, 187, 189;
  appropriation of, 47, 97, 145, 179, 182, 189;
  rejection of, 145, 183, 189-190;
  segregation of, 189
Robertson Smith, William, 27
role-value connection, 59-61, 66-67, 73, 80-81, 87, 181;
  essential criteria of, 38, 60, 73;
  formal criteria of, 59;
  functional criteria of, 59
Rosch, Eleanor, 40, 204
Rozin, Paul, 56, 95-96, 106-107, 109, 125, 135, 203-204
rules, 20, 127, 176, 181, 184, 188;
  constitutive, 181-183, 186, 188, 190;
  regulatory, 181

Schank, Roger, 49, 204
schema:
  episodic, 115;
  foundational, 177;
  narrative, 110
scripts, 49, 72
Searle, John, 19, 181, 204
semantics, 29, 145, 200;
  cognitive, 4, 29, 38
Shore, Bradd, 46-47, 105, 177, 204
Shweder, Richard E., 10, 29, 204-205
signs, 31, 44, 48, 55-56, 58, 61-62, 66, 69, 72-73, 87, 89, 102, 115, 137, 146-147, 178, 191;
  iconic, 44, 48, 50, 57-61, 66-70, 72-73, 80-81, 85, 87, 89, 92-93, 96, 100-101, 106, 111, 114, 125, 127, 129-130, 133-134, 137, 146-147, 150-152,

157, 162, 175, 178-181, 183, 187, 190;
indexical, 44, 48, 50, 56, 59-61, 66, 68-70, 72-74, 80, 89-90, 92, 96, 101, 106, 114-115, 130, 133, 137, 146, 150-152, 175-176, 178-180, 183, 187, 190;
symbolic, 57, 69, 72, 178
similarity, 2, 5, 11, 16, 31, 44, 48, 57-60, 68-69, 71-73, 80, 95-96, 100, 106, 111, 115, 121, 123, 127, 129-130, 133-135, 158-159, 174-175, 187, 204;
backward, 96;
forward, 96
Skorupski, John, 29, 95, 112, 169, 205
Smith, Jonathan Z., 9, 74
social determinism, 14, 18, 25;
opaque, 18;
transparent, 14, 87
social sciences, 9-10
society, 2, 12, 15-17, 20, 23-25, 27, 47, 78, 157, 184, 189, 195
space:
action, 148-149, 151, 170;
blended, 52-54, 60-61, 63-65, 75-76, 91-92, 99;
conditional, 148-149, 151, 159, 162-163;
effect, 148-149, 151, 170;
generic, 53, 55, 58, 60-61, 67, 69-70, 72-74, 76, 80, 84, 87-88, 100, 109, 113-114, 121, 126;
input, 53-56, 60-61, 63, 67, 75, 80, 88, 91
speech-act, 24, 68, 73, 80, 87, 89, 93
Spelke, Elisabeth S., 35, 195, 205
spell, 21, 25, 77, 80-82, 84-85, 89, 101, 116-117, 119, 123, 125, 127-128, 130, 158, 168

Sperber, Dan, 29, 35, 38, 62, 137, 144, 170, 193-195, 197, 199-201, 203, 205
structure, 3, 15-16, 33, 35, 38-41, 43, 46, 48-51, 53-54, 58, 61, 64, 68, 77, 84-85, 90, 92, 105, 107, 111, 116, 118, 121, 128, 130, 143, 144-145, 148, 150, 157, 159, 168, 172, 177, 183-186, 188-191, 200, 206;
conceptual, 15, 31, 33, 37, 45, 47, 51, 62, 64, 70, 100, 106, 115, 121, 172, 177, 185-188;
emergent, 52-55, 61, 64
Subbotsky, Eugene, 109, 138, 164, 177, 205
Sweetser, Eve, 7, 42, 53, 93, 138, 206
symbol, 14, 17, 23-24, 29, 47-48, 51, 57, 59, 62, 66, 73, 92, 112, 130, 134, 144-145, 157, 178, 184, 190;
expressive, 15
symbolic interpretation, 5-6, 15, 68, 100-101, 114, 134, 136-137, 145-147, 152, 163, 168, 171, 174, 176, 178-181, 183-185, 187-188, 190-191
symbolic meaning, 17, 28, 68, 73, 90, 92, 120, 146, 175-179
symbolic relation, 16, 73, 92, 101, 112, 129, 180, 190
symbolic systems, 16-18, 24, 26, 28, 59, 73, 144-145, 147, 177-179, 181, 186
Symbolist approach, 31, 143-145, 169

talisman, 72, 93
Talmy, Leonard, 7, 42, 49, 150, 206
Tambiah, Stanley J., 20-23, 29, 68, 89-90, 116-118, 122, 130, 154, 159, 182, 206

theory, 3, 5, 9, 12-13, 15, 19, 21, 24-25, 27, 29, 32, 36-40, 42, 46-48, 52, 63, 77, 90, 92-93, 95-96, 110, 113-114, 137, 150, 156, 184, 187, 191, 198, 201-202, 205;
explanatory, 3, 12, 32
Theory of Mind (ToM), 36
Theosophical Society, the, 191, 194
Thomas, Keith, 10, 20, 85, 100, 113-114, 153, 179, 206
Tikopia, 85, 197
topology networks:
one-sided, 53, 125;
shared, 111
Transformative Magical Action, 96-98, 102, 107, 133-134
translation, 17, 29, 198
transmission, 23, 38, 47, 63, 90-91, 102, 110, 137, 152
Trobriander, 46, 48, 77-82, 84-85, 90, 97, 116-119, 122, 124, 126, 128-129, 132-133, 136, 143, 147, 154-157, 159, 167-169, 175-177, 182, 199, 204;
agriculture, 78;
culture hero, 79-80;
magic, 77, 79, 81, 116, 129, 155;
myths, 79;
spells, 117, 119, 147, 182
Turner, Mark, 7, 38, 52-54, 61, 93, 111, 170, 196, 207
Tylor, Edward B., 10-11, 25, 27, 198, 207

vatuvi spell, 80

weapon-salve, 113-114
Weber, Max, 184, 191, 207
Whitehouse, Harvey, 7, 110, 180, 191, 205-207
windowing of attention, 42, 49, 150
witchcraft, 17, 81, 93, 102, 113, 131, 138, 159-163, 196-197, 206;
allegations of, 82

Printed in Poland
by Amazon Fulfillment
Poland Sp. z o.o., Wrocław